THE OPERATORS

Books by Frank Gibney

THE OPERATORS

THE SECRET WORLD (with Peter Deriabin)

THE FROZEN REVOLUTION

FIVE GENTLEMEN OF JAPAN

THE
OPERATORS

by Frank Gibney

Harper & Brothers   Publishers   New York

For Tiger, Margot and Bear

CONTENTS

ACKNOWLEDGMENTS

The origin of this book was one article, "The Crooks in White Collars," which appeared in the October 14, 1957, issue of *Life*, the sixth in a *Life* series on crime in America. Although both form and contents have naturally widened, I have retained much of the material of that article; I thank the editors of *Life* not only for their co-operation but for their assignment in the first place.

I have tried to credit quoted authorities and borrowed opinions wherever possible in the text. Among the many experts and interested bystanders who concern themselves with the problems of fraud in this country, I should like to thank for their particular co-operation: Chief Inspector David H. Stephens and Inspector Thompson Berdeen of the Post Office Department; Mr. Sam Stowe and Mrs. Lois Burns of the Federal Trade Commission; the Washington information officers of the Internal Revenue Service; Mr. Paul Windels, Jr., and others in both the Washington and New York offices of the Securities and Exchange Commission; Miss Maye A. Russ and others of the National Better Business Bureau; Mr. Charles Stickle and his staff at the New York State Attorney General's office; New York County District Attorney Frank Hogan and members of his staff, notably Assistant District Attorneys Jerome Kidder and Joseph Stone; former Assistant Attorney General Warren Olney and others at the Department of Justice; the office of the District Attorney, County of Los Angeles; the office of the U.S. Attorney, Southern District of New York; Mr. N. Morgan Woods, Jr., of the Association of Casualty and Surety Companies; and Messrs. Herbert Robinson, Norman Jaspan, J. J. Seidman, C.P.A., and—for his invaluable help with the original *Life* article—Raymond Price, all of New York City. It must of course be presumed, however, that any bobbled balls in the following pages bounced off my glove, not theirs.

I should like to add my gratitude to two Harper & Brothers editors, Mr. Evan Thomas, without whose help and advice this book would have remained only a vague idea, and Mr. John Appleton, whose excellent editing and editorial suggestions made the finished product far better than it would have been. It was a happy personal discovery to find publishers who take an interest in writing. Mr. Allan Forsyth, who worked with me throughout the book's preparation, deserves particular praise for his fine reporting and research assistance.

Finally, to my wife, who not only helped write the book but watched the gathering source materials crowd us out of two successive apartments, my great thanks.

F. B. G.

New York
March, 1960

THE OPERATORS

I

WHAT'S AN OPERATOR?

*. . . and there came on that foul image of fraud,
came on and landed his head and chest, but did
not draw his tail on to the bank. His face was the
face of a just man, so gracious was its outward
aspect, and all the rest was a serpent's trunk; he
had two paws, hairy to the armpits, and the back
and breast and both the flanks were painted with
knots and circlets—Tartars or Turks never made
stuffs with more colours in ground and em-
broidery . . .*

The Inferno, Canto XVII*

The morning of another good business day dawned bright
and clear. The reputable executive had two Alka-Seltzer tablets
and a cheerful breakfast and sent his children off to school with
fatherly counsel. His wife was slightly troubled about the maid's
Social Security payments, which were long past due; he suggested that she forget about them, since the maid was leaving
soon anyway. Then he climbed into his Thunderbird and drove
downtown.

Traffic was heavy and he was forced to leave the car in a No
Parking zone across from the office. He locked it carefully and

* Translation by John D. Sinclair.

1

on his way down the street ran into the veteran cop on the beat, who thanked him for a recent Christmas gift, the usual four bottles of good blended whiskey. Once in the office, he took care of the mail and some routine desk chores and settled at least one small but irritating personnel problem: when one of his middle-rank salesmen asked for a raise, he turned him down, but suggested with the broadest of winks that the man had carte blanche to go heavy on his expense account until the matter of raises came up formally late in the fall. Then he took an hour out with his personal income-tax consultant, who had just found a happy device for altering repair and depreciation costs on some rental property, for a handsome tax "profit." Before their conference was quite over, he handled an urgent long-distance call from his lawyer and unofficial investment counselor, who had found a good insolvent manufacturing company which was ripe for a nice tax-loss merger.

A few minutes before one, the reputable businessman walked over to his club, where he habitually lunched and played squash on the company expense account. There he entertained two visiting college classmates at a lavish meal; he insisted on signing the check. Back in the office, he had time to detail one of his assistants to "take care of" the building inspector with jurisdiction over their new plant site, thus getting as much red tape as possible out of the way. In the meantime his secretary had drafted several routine letters for him to sign. Among them was a note to an executive of a smaller firm with whom he had just signed a contract, thanking him for the gift of a new-model TV set.

At a brief conference later in the afternoon he congratulated his firm's controller on a bookkeeping device that was handily padding a few of the firm's more controversial accounts. Then he went into a half-hour huddle with the account executive from the ad agency about some trouble they had lately run into with the Federal Trade Commission on the subject of misleading commercials. (He advised the advertising man to keep up the same pitch until after the fall sales drive, FTC or no FTC.) In a crucial twenty-minute session, he won the consent of the firm's board chairman to the week's Big Deal, a sleight-of-hand exchange of shares with another company which ultimately promised a really large tax saving and some big stock profits, after several platoons of lawyers had worked out the corporate footwork. This done, he felt free to leave for home. Before he turned out the light in his office, he had his secretary wrap up one of the new company desk sets, which seemed just the thing for his study.

The reputable executive, as anyone could gather from this selective but by no means improbable account of his daily rounds, is what most of his society—viewing his actions dispassionately—would call an "Operator." He is also, by legal definition, a criminal. His business day, if he were successfully prosecuted, could conceivably result in a total of $31,500 in fines and no less than 33 years' imprisonment. Specific offenses would include:

> Penalty for willful nonpayment of employer's Social Security contributions: $10,000 fine and/or five years in jail.
>
> Penalty for attempting to influence a police officer with a gift: $5,000 fine and/or 10 years in jail.
>
> Penalty for filing a fraudulent income-tax return: $10,000 fine and/or five years in jail.
>
> Penalty for misusing an expense account, under Section 665 of the N. Y. State Penal Law: $500 fine and/or one year in jail.
>
> Penalty for bribing a public officer: $5,000 fine and/or 10 years in jail.

Penalty for secretly accepting a gift in return for corporate loans: $500 fine and/or one year in jail.

Penalty for appropriating company property to one's personal use: $500 fine and/or one year in jail.*

Yet no one would be more surprised than the businessman to be told this. About the criminal shading of some of his activities he would be blissfully ignorant. But even where his chicanery was done knowingly, his first reaction—if he were a typical Operator—would be one of surprised indignation that he, of all people, should be singled out for "persecution." After all, the reputable-looking Operator would protest, "Isn't everybody doing it?"

This book is about how everybody *is* doing it, a brief and necessarily undetailed survey of the vast and burgeoning volume of dishonest dealing in the United States today. The subject matter is not restricted to what criminologists, after the late Professor Ernest Sutherland, now call "white-collar crime," *i.e.*, "a crime committed by a person of respectability and high social status in the course of his occupation." It includes the current activities, often awesomely mechanized, of the swindlers, con men, grifters and embezzlers—the compulsive type of professional thief of whom O. Henry once wrote, in *The Gentle Grafter:* "Whenever he saw someone else with a dollar in his hand, he took it as a personal grudge, if he couldn't take it." But the obviously criminal act, the acknowledged illegality, is only a small part of the Operators' total activities. We must include also the wide area of legal but immoral sharp practices in business, labor and politics, often severely damaging to society but generally subtle enough to keep just beyond effective range of society's formidable but fixed legal gun positions.

* All these penalties noted are for violations of either federal or state laws. Only one state, New York, has been used for the sake of uniformity.

The very definition of "operator" must be made arbitrary and harshly comprehensive. For the Operator thrives on moral, not to say legal sleight-of-hand—it is no accident that modern slang use of the word derives originally from the eighteenth-century English slang for skilled pickpocket. Often the Operator is considered a pillar of the community. He may be, and in recent criminal cases has turned out to be, a Chicago architect, a prosperous automobile dealer in Denver, a member of Congress from Massachusetts, a physician in Omaha, a respected lawyer in Philadelphia or a veteran Internal Revenue Service agent in New York.

The Operator may be a bigtime juggler of corporations or a smalltime accountant skillfully barbering a friend's income tax. He may be a salesman padding his expense account to meet the payments on his car. He may take bribes or give them, whether the bribing involves a political scandal or a simple shift of business from one wholesaler to another. He may be a partner in a crooked accident-insurance racket, or a prosperous store owner with a weakness for faked markdowns. Or, all too likely, he may be just a decent, God-fearing American who had to put his finger in the till one day and never found the strength to pull it out.

Many of these people become Operators without realizing it. The boundaries are slippery between what is obviously right and obviously wrong and we are rich in our mirages of private morality and pressing self-justification. But no one can *remain* an Operator for long without resorting to some form of knowing, culpable deceit.

The Operator has always been present on the American scene. Inevitably, successful fraud increased and multiplied along with the expansion of the national economy. But in the early days of the Republic it was necessarily a penny-ante operation. The Operator was likely to be a gambler, a fast-

talking peddler or a sharp wit attracted by the opportunities
for crookedness in the field of trading and finance. "Is there no
way," the New York *Sun* apostrophized in January 1837, "to
reach the knaves who have flooded this city with checks made
out in the form of bills on banks in which they have not a dollar
deposited?" Later nineteenth-century economic progress
brought the Operator into the big time. By the 1890's, the
old-time "Robber Barons" had become Operators in the grand
manner. During a meeting of 17 railroad presidents at J. P.
Morgan's house in New York City, one of their number, A. B.
Stickney, delivered himself of the memorable observation: "I
have the utmost respect for you gentlemen individually, but
as railroad presidents I wouldn't trust you with my watch out
of my sight."

But it was left to our own era to take the ancient art of the
Operator and turn it into a broad-gauge way of life in which all
Americans—regardless of race, color, creed or economic status
—could participate. Never in our history has the practice of
fraud been so dignified by constant use and acceptance.

Here are a few indications of the Operators' recent activities, measured in terms of cold cash. Last year, by conservative estimate, some five billion dollars, roughly one per cent
of the total U. S. national product, changed hands under in-
numerable desks, counters or expensive restaurant tables in
kick-backs, pay-offs or bribes. The country's employers lost
more than half a billion to embezzling employees, from pilfer-
ing shop workers to absconding assistant secretary-treasur-
ers. More of the public's money evaporated through retail
chiseling. A half billion went down the drain in home-repair
frauds alone. Officials of the Securities and Exchange Commission do not even attempt to measure the high cost of stocks
worth slightly more than the paper they are printed on, aside
from putting it in the "hundreds of millions." In a six-month

period of 1957, six fly-by-night security outfits could make themselves an illicit profit of $4.5 millions. A big-timer like Alexander Guterma, on the other hand, was convicted of fraud by the U. S. government in 1960, after methodically bilking several companies and their stockholders in nine busy years of entrenched business swindling.

Officers of the Bureau of Internal Revenue could display a record harvest of $1,684,465,000 in additional taxes, penalties and interest on the 1958 returns of U. S. taxpayers and squeeze out an extra $1,012,000,000 from delinquent accounts. In the course of its enforcement activity the Bureau conducted more than 25,000 separate investigations, the majority of them for tax fraud.

The aggregate of rubber checks bounced a third higher than last year and almost 100 per cent higher than in 1952. The yearly loss to banks and individuals is now figured at well over a half-billion. The Post Office Department, with a record number of arrests in 1958, reported an increase of 29 per cent in mail-order and other fraud within its province between 1950 and 1958—2½ times the population increase, incidentally. Their cost was pegged at a "conservative" $100,000,000.

The aberrations of "regular" businesses are no more comforting. Although the 63 new antitrust actions brought by the Department of Justice—a 17-year high—in 1959 were sometimes as much a matter of legal interpretation as criminal corporate behavior, there was no mistaking the out-and-out crime of Operators who diverted to their own use money collected in employees' withholding and Social Security taxes: the delinquent accounts now amount to over $300 million. The Federal Trade Commission records an alarming rise in the total of consent orders and civil and criminal actions against companies in every industry, for various misrepresentations of their products. The number of actions for deceptive practices in 1959 stood at 267—twice the number instituted in 1956. And the FTC, with a staff of only 738 investigators and jurisdiction only in clearly interstate cases, is quick to admit that its cases are but a tiny percentage of the total. For 1960, the FTC has before it the additional and Herculean chore of combing the fraud out of the matted locks of the television and radio industry.

The foregoing drainage from the national pocketbook is in the record. Conspicuously not recorded are the amounts lost to stockholders and investors through issues juggled and corporations either grossly swollen or grotesquely contracted for the benefit of their exploiters. There is no count, either, of the money lost to the U. S. government in the acquisitions of insolvent companies by going concerns, as a device to obviate the paying of taxes. Of at least equal enormity is the robber baron's tax levied on the entire economy by the crookedness of bad union leadership.

Such records of the Operator's take are formidable; but they are only secondary to the real problem he poses to this country today. A habit of fraud is growing upon us. For the Operator can thrive only where he is tolerated, not to say invited. (It is the oldest maxim of the con man that "you can't cheat an honest man.") The disturbing thing about so much of the fraud in the United States is the eagerness of the suckers who succumb to it, their urge to make the fast buck faster, their alacrity at condoning sharp practices which earlier generations of Americans would at least have recognized as morally wrong—even if they helped clip the coupons.

Americans have always held a sneaking sympathy for the sharper, the gay rogue, the lad who cheats in examinations and never gets caught, the seasoned traveler who makes a work of art out of each customs declaration, the car owner—it would have to be a very skillful car owner these days—who manages to slip something over on a dealer in a trade-in. When the yegg in loud pin-stripes changes to a gray flannel suit, his transition is hailed as the American dream in action. The well-publicized entrepreneur Frank Costello was a case in point. There was never any doubt about the illicit nature of his activities. Yet he gained free access to the offices—and the parties—of some of the more respected citizens of New York, Los Angeles and other key business centers. Long after his activities had been exposed, he remained an object of public curiosity rather than public revulsion—a legitimate target for aspiring autograph hounds.

District Attorney Frank Hogan of New York County hammers away at such public indifference to criminals wearing cuff links. "We appear," he said, "to have developed a public morality which condemns—rather than praises—any private citizen who seeks to enforce the laws that we—as members of a free society—have called into being. . . . We make a sort of game of it, between law-enforcement officials and criminals, and sit complacently by, quite ready to applaud a brilliant stroke on either side."

This tendency to glorify the sharper has always been present in American literature and, as romance grows thinner and plots for our other native art form, the Western, exhaust themselves, it has become stronger. In some recent fictional works, notably Ayn Rand's *Atlas Shrugged,* the Operator in business comes through as a well-pressed Tamerlane, with a corps of busy appraisers, bookkeepers and assistant vice-presidents. As sophisticated a writer as John Marquand, who began his dissections of the national character with George Apley's stiff-necked birdwatchers, switched with the years to plot mergers with ruthless old diamonds in the rough like Willis Wayde, a fit contender in any business-fiction league.

Other nations have their own images of this sort: the ruthless intellectual tearing up his library card to sway the masses to his will, the literary giant who proves that society is as corrupt as he is, the mustachioed general storming the palace, the man from the county family sewing up elections as effortlessly as he knots his old school tie. And if the American zeal to perform prodigies with money and property is less soaring than the urge to master men's souls, or lead their bodies on the battlefield, it is not so dangerous.

Yet the urge to gain business success, and to cut corners in so doing, can in time produce a most unmoral tolerance for fraud. As early as 1832, Mrs. Trollope, that notoriously sharp-tongued English critic of American mores, could write (after failing in business in Cincinnati) her inflamed description of the dollar: "This sordid object forever before their eyes, must inevitably produce a sordid tone of mind and worse still, it produces a seared and blunted conscience on all questions of probity."

Almost 140 years and countless dollars later we find that the age of unparalleled abundance, of leisure, high investment profit and vast material expectations is leaving us with a sadly blunted conscience indeed.

It is no small part of the trouble that we have become, as a society, scandalously overprotected. A web of rules, regulations, safeguards, administrations and group thought winds its strands ever more tightly through a nation which still asserts itself to be just a bunch of good, individualistic, rugged free-enterprisers. This overprotection not only lets our guard down against chiseling; but it also encourages its own kind of revolt. The man who chuckles over a friend's tax dodge is displaying the same envy of direct action that leads him to sit night after night in a half-dark room watching TV private eyes gun down the opposition.

Then there is the urge to abundance. Each year more than $11 billion are spent in the United States on various forms of advertising. A tremendous amount of educated talent is devoted to convincing Americans that life cannot be bearable without the higher-quality dog food, the more "influential" magazine, the extra car—even more recently, the extra house. (We shall get into the question of the fraudulent or nearly fraudulent advertising claim in later chapters.) Stress on sheer acquisition naturally makes people greedy, and greed is the beginning of a cheat.

The Genial American Society of 1960 has come a long way from its watchful beginnings in the midst of what the Puritans (before they started to make money) liked to call "this evil, sinful world." The Genial Society takes abundance for granted. Its members are paradoxically careless of the possessions they seek so avidly, once they get them—they are so used to planned obsolescence. Yet while lacking the vigilance of the miser, they retain all of the miser's acquisitiveness.

The Genial Society frowns on indignation, except as directed against convicted murderers, native Communists or idealized instances of "graft and corruption"—and even in these rare cases where group anger is permitted, the members of the group seldom do much about the objects themselves. Toleration is its highest social good. Harsh words are anathema. In 1959 the U.S. Weather Bureau had to change the name of its new Discomfort Index of heat and humidity, due to public protest. And by "toleration" I mean a social philosophy that bears little relation to charity or respect for one's fellow man. We dislike surprises. We are pathetically afraid of "looking bad."

We are gullible, and have a near-fatal fascination for showmanship and show. We may or may not be dedicated to a search for visible symbols of power and prestige, but we look that way. It is a tribute to our aptitude for self-deception that the modern American, one of the most face-conscious national figures in history—at least as far as his private life is concerned—can still pretend to smile patronizingly at what he regards as the Oriental "sensitivity to face."

In a memorable questionnaire of representative car owners

in the 1950's about their preferences in a new model, almost all the people questioned listed as their prime criteria items like "fuel economy," "safety" or "engine performance." Since these qualities were somewhat at variance with the splayed fins and pointed windshields which everyone was then demanding in his car, a shrewd poll-taker asked another question: "What would your next-door neighbor prize in a car?" The answers came back quickly and almost uniformly: "style," "power and pickup," "chrome," etc.—all the qualities that people were actually buying. The "next-door neighbor's" criteria were obviously what each person wanted for himself. It would not have been good form to say so.

As a keynote example of the Genial Society's vulnerability, we might take the brief financial orbiting of Mr. Earl Belle of Pittsburgh. Mr. Belle is at the moment a resident of Rio de Janeiro, capital of one of the few countries which do not have an extradition treaty with the United States. For a few exciting years, he was regarded back home as a boy wonder in the finest tradition.

Belle graduated from the University of Pittsburgh in 1956 and burst upon the world with his degree, a small family benefice and a few contacts among Pittsburgh people with heavy cash balances remaining from their World War II profits. In two years he had control of the First National Bank of nearby Saltsburg, and a good reputation in the town for bringing new industry into it. Working with one Edward Talenfeld and his sons Murray and Barton, he used the bank's assets to buy up the happily named firm of Cornucopia Gold Mines. This he converted into a holding company with interests—mostly on option—in several reasonably functioning concerns.

Belle exuded coolness and confidence. At the very moment the SEC was oiling up its machinery to investigate his unorthodox stock buying and selling procedures, he had set about raising money for his ventures from several widely separated but equally unsuspecting banks. He borrowed $150,000 from the Manufacturers Bank in Edgewater, N.J.; $200,000 from the McKeesport, Pa., Peoples Union Bank; and a total of $475,000 from the Security National Bank of Huntington, N.Y. These and other activities were subsequently part of a monumental thirty-eight-count indictment.

With a flair for the *beau geste,* Belle affected a valet-companion, raccoon coats, gaily colored vests, a $5,000 Mercedes and a superbly convincing line of chatter. He got a fine press. Barely six months before his final exposure, he was interviewed by Mike Wallace, the New York TV interlocutor, in his column in the New York *Post.* Wallace cited him as an outstanding American, "a vigorous, tough-minded 26-year-old," who had "pyramided his profits into a $10-million industrial empire." Answered Belle, in a rare burst of frankness: "A dollar is round and you figure it rolled to you so easy, it can roll away. But if you claw your way up, nobody can take anything from you, because they didn't give you anything." (He was finally given his fraud and conspiracy indictment by a federal grand jury in Pittsburgh in 1960.)

An embarrassing number of publicists and financial authorities were charmed by the boyish ruthlessness of such statements, and hooked accordingly. Yet through the period of his greatest fame, he was already listed on the bulletins of the Better Business Bureau as suspect, since the SEC had early in the game undertaken action against his holding company. Any thorough reportorial investigation would have confirmed the existence of gaping loopholes in his financial log pile. But none thought of doing such a thing. He *looked* so successful.

The Operator by definition lives in a floating world* of big

---

* The term "floating world" is the direct translation of *Ukiyo,* the Japanese term for the demimonde of actors, geisha, prostitutes, pleasure-seeking gentry, crooks and bankrupts which flourished in Tokyo and other large Japanese cities of the late seventeenth century. The *Ukiyo* gave the world a brilliant genre of pictures and sketchbooks for which it is now best known. But the depredations of its crooked citizenry almost swamped the Japanese national character.

deals and ready pleasures, and he is constantly enlarging its boundaries. The fix, the bribe, the organized cheat are common in sections of American life which were once thought almost sacrosanct, like sports, art or religious activity. The more improbable his zone of operations, in fact, the better chance has the Operator to take the suckers completely unaware. He shifts his style with the ease of a stage manager adjusting the scenery—from the real-estate fraud or the crooked TV repair shop to the stock swindle to the accident insurance racket, or vice versa. But he is at least subject to a few reasonably definite categories, which follow.

The sharpers. The most readily distinguishable group of Operators, the promoters-gone-wrong who swindle the buying or investing public by taking over once-legitimate businesses and exploiting them. A sharper generally starts out in life as a reputable businessman.

The takers. Their world is the exchange of bribes and kickbacks. They proliferate in wholesale businesses that require a great deal of personal contacts between buyers and suppliers. They also populate the lower fringes of politics, where the crooked building inspector or the venal police officer is an all too common fact of life.

The boiler-room operators. Stock swindling has become such a major criminal or (as prosecutors often find out to their sorrow) semicriminal occupation that its practitioners deserve a category all their own.

The fixers. The free spenders (and freeloaders) who make their way in business by greasing palms for percentages. Seldom can a criminal charge be made to stick against them. They peddle influence, jobs and money, and they deftly drag reputable businessmen into their peculiar social and moral whirlpool.

The pitchmen. The custodians of false claims and fraudulent pretensions. Although related to the sharpers, they deserve a separate category—if for no other reason than that their activities, although equally debatable morally, seldom land them in jail. Most of them begin as relatively honest workers in advertising, journalism, business or the law.

The corporate operators. The aristocracy of the whole movement: the king-size sharpers. They represent the class least eager to see its name linked with the other types. Their lives are often symbols of respectability; but they prey on both American business and the public through their addiction to such personally profitable devices as convenient mergers, juggled assets and various forms of trade and competition. They use their employees and their stockholders like helpless pawns, but they rarely break the law clearly enough to warrant the court action they deserve.

The crooked labor bosses. Robber Barons with contempt for union democracy. Their baronies have proved extraordinarily resistant to both legal action and spurts of public indignation. (Although not specifically discussed in this book, they are allies and supporters of most of the other categories cited, in one way or another.)

The professionals. Although the most established of American operators, these out-and-out criminals are probably the least important. They include swindlers and embezzlers, forgers and passers of bad checks. They extract yearly uncountable millions (90 per cent of their victims never tell) from the people who P. T. Barnum said were born at the rate of 60 an hour. Many of them shift into the more modern categories of sharpers or even fixers.

The dodgers. Pure amateurs at first. This category, its numbers swelling hourly, comprises all those who try and succeed in evading public or business responsibility by fraudulent means. Almost everyone in it regards himself as an honest man.

The more able of this sort find it easy to become dedicated full-time operators.

Whatever the type of Operator, however thin his protective coloration, we can safely assume that the Genial Society will have a hard time catching him. Where legal catching is out of the question, it may be difficult even to identify an Operator as such. For there are three heavy road blocks which can hinder pursuit. They are: 1) the federal system of government; 2) the due process of law; and 3) the Genial Society's unthinking assumption of its own honesty.

To begin with, every effective Operator is a strong states' rights man. His activities follow the flag, wherever it may wave —an epidemic of crooked car salesmen not long ago invaded U. S. Army posts in Germany; and scant days after Congress passed the Alaska Statehood bill, the New York State Attorney General's office issued a special warning to investors against the rising number of phony Alaska mining stocks. The Operator is generally careful to run back and forth among as many different state jurisdictions as possible. Nowhere else in the world can he take such advantage of rival local authorities and play out his game with so many differing sets of ground rules. A consumer fraud regarded as criminal in Connecticut might not even be mentioned on the statute books of Minnesota. The peculiarities of state laws on banking, investment, taxes and trade are enough to delight any keen and fraudulent mind.

A murderer or a bank robber gets short shrift under any state law. And, barring the rare exception, the extradition processes are swift and sure when one state's police catch another state's violent criminal. But crimes of fraud are not so clearly defined. Most of them are too intricate and indirect in their illegality to upset a governor's or a state legislature's blood pressure. The slicker types make a specialty of American legal geography, hopping with some care from one area to another as occasion demands. Federal agencies like the SEC and the FTC grow gray trying to bring these offenders to book. Often they must resort to heavy persuasion before some state legal mechanisms can even be alerted to the danger.

There are, however, certain discernible patterns of crime, cut to areas where local conditions or sheer geography favor them. Denver, for instance, has always been known as a handy stopping place for forgers and check kiters. The reason for this is simple. Although big enough to give some protective cover, it is rather isolated, as American big cities go—a condition made to order for this sort of work. Los Angeles, it goes without saying, has been a center for numerous varieties of real-estate fraud. The general area of southern California, with its high percentage of retired people, has had more than its share of phony investment swindles, as well as a collection of heterodox swamis and nonordained soul-savers, who specialize in contributions.

Detroit's police department has not been overly troubled with fraud schemes—acute problems of race and industrial relations have been known to give the local cops enough work opportunities. Cincinnati, at the moment, is possessed of an efficient police force, and the garden variety of fraud operator, at least, has made himself scarce. Chicago, on the other hand, remains an aviary of splendidly tufted fraudsters. Their depredations are disinguished not so much by skill or suavity, as comprehensiveness. There is barely a corner of Chicago's civic life which has not been plucked clean by some variety of gangster or grafter, and the state of the city's law-enforcement facilities has been a national disgrace.*

For all the evils of Chicago, for all the temporary prominence

* In January, 1960, a series of scandals—involving bail-bond deals, egregious ticket-fixing and fine-stealing in the courts—was climaxed by the confession of a burglar that he had committed his larcenies under the direction of local police officers. Only a few days after his confession, more than a score of public officials had already been implicated.

of vest-pocket iniquity centers like Phenix City, Alabama, or Jersey City, New Jersey, or the profitable eccentricities of the corporation laws of Delaware, it is New York where the best Operators always congregate. It is no accident that a great proportion of the criminal examples noted in this book have some connection with this city. For New York fills roughly the same function in the world of white-collar crime that it fills in the legitimate theater. A crooked practice may originate in Austin, Texas, or Tacoma, Washington, but if successful it will sooner or later find its way east for the criminal equivalent of the Broadway opening. If the Manhattan "opening" proves a success, there are plenty of road-show opportunities afterward.

The one exception is political fraud, where the supreme goal, of course, lies 300 miles to the south. But cases where an entire small-town grafting operation can be transferred to Washington are fortunately few. For all the chiseling done by individuals in the Eisenhower and Truman administrations, the country will probably not tolerate again the spectacle which Warren Harding left us of Ohio's back-street politics installed in the White House. It was too embarrassing.

In dealing with white-collar criminals, crooked politicians included, the law often less than fulfills its purpose. It may be not so much a threat as a handy port in a storm. The nub of the legal problem in fraud cases was stated as well as anyone could state it in a 1917 decision by Judge Hough of the U. S. Circuit Court of Appeals: "Just when the sanguine man becomes reckless and the reckless one criminal cannot be laid down as a matter of law." The question of fraud is largely a matter of proving intent. There is nothing to stop the proprietor of, say, Sub-Arctic Tundra, Ltd., from saying in court that he honestly believed there was gold, uranium, platinum and buried treasure in those desolate flatlands. There is no stolen car or corpus delicti to prove him wrong. For the modern operator lives in a world of paper and promises, a world which Mr. Blackstone and the constructors of the Common Law could hardly have anticipated.

Every district attorney dreads a fraud case, except the reckless legal knight in armor (and these are in short supply). It is hard to prove and, to state his problem in unlegal but human terms, likely to damage his record with an acquittal. The obvious reason for this is the attitude of juries. A juror can get indignant about a murder victim, but he may feel nothing but contempt for the victim of a swindle—unless the prosecutor can produce the classic example of the woman in widow's weeds, or the orphans' trust fund. Such clear-cut cases are few and far between. In most fraud actions, jurors have the attitude of spectators at a court-tennis game, trying to determine whether the effort of figuring out the complex rules is worth it.

A deeper handicap is the state of the laws. It would be a farfetched Utopia indeed which had its laws keep up step by step with the march of crime. The best we can hope for is that they will follow close enough upon cases of novel wrongdoing to restrict their spread. In the area of fraud and corporate or personal deception, this has not happened. In New York State, to give a flagrant example, it was not until 1953 that a law finally declared that it is illegal for a union leader to accept a bribe. Even now, in a world where advertising claims can be made by subliminal suggestion, only a minority of the states have thought of revising the old basis of their consumer-protection laws: Let the buyer beware.

"You have to have an evil and it has to be pretty bad," said Warren Olney, until 1958 the head of the Department of Justice's Criminal Division, "before you get enough public pressure behind it to get legislation." The trouble with laws governing the Operators' activities is the Genial Society's lack of public indignation. Ample laws exist on the statute books, both state and federal, to insure against the reincarnation of Jim Fisk, Jay Gould, or, in his more unsavory aspects, P. T. Barnum. But the *new* kind of Operator has revised his methods. Netting him can be as frustrating as trying to capture a mosquito with a lacrosse stick.

So far, so bad. But the hopeful prosecutor has to contend with yet another obstacle, the attitude of the judiciary. To say that most judges do not get indignant over the nonviolent criminal is an understatement—at least according to most prosecutors. The Operator invariably makes a better appearance in court than his violently criminal brethren do. In any case, the sentences given for fraud, swindling or business deception are proportionately far lighter than those handed down for crimes of violence, although by volume it is the crimes of fraud which are economically and morally more expensive to society.

In January 1958 the leader of a fake insurance-claims ring in New York City was convicted on three counts of first-degree grand larceny, one count of second-degree grand larceny and three counts of conspiracy. He was convicted of swindling $11,000 from three insurance companies, the specific offense for which he was tried. The judge gave him a *suspended* sentence and ordered him to make restitution—of $3,000.*

Angered by such dispositions, District Attorney Hogan was moved to comment: "It's becoming common in General Sessions for a thief after conviction to make a fractional restitution and walk out without any penalty. It's practically like paying for a license to swindle after you're caught."

If a prosecutor gets his conviction through the judge and jury, he has then to reckon with the mechanism of appeal. The

* See Chapter V.

process of appeal to a higher court was developed to insure an accused against any possibility of judicial or factual error in his trial. The wide channels of appeal, teeming with so many varieties of legal technicalities, permit convicted criminals to argue their cases for years before final disposition. If they are patient and wealthy, the chances are that some legal technicality may ultimately intervene in their favor. Really successful Operators have ample resources for this sort of happy procrastination. Fraud cases, often involving very complicated questions of law, generally invite appeal.

The final factor in the Operator's success is the moral problem, to which we have alluded. Fraud has become noisome, destructive and difficult to punish in America precisely because of our commitment to the copybook maxim that "Honesty is the Best Policy." Generations of Americans—sales managers, union presidents and Secretaries of State—have subscribed to this principle and believed in it. Lawyers and social commentators have written volumes on that tabernacular linchpin of business society, the Honest Contract. At its best this commitment to rigid communal honesty holds our democracy together. It still enforces far more voluntary obedience than is observable in many other societies.

The trouble is that our own overprotected society takes the group commitment for granted. We believe in honesty too much and too little, for we leave the premises of honesty unexamined and forgotten. We rely on the law and our system of public order to define honesty for us, instead of going back to our own consciences, where our own honesty is in question, or critically poking beneath the fancy label or the television commercial, when it is a matter of someone else's honesty. The law cannot always tell us when a person is crooked.

The problem of an individual making such moral decisions for himself is pressing—yet it is far from a hopeless task. A handy yardstick was given us long ago by Alexander Pope in a passage from his *Essay on Man*:

This light and darkness in our chaos joined,
What shall divide? The God within the mind.
Extremes in Nature equal ends produce,
In Man they join to some mysterious use;
Though each by turns the other's bound invade,
As, in some well-wrought picture, light and shade,
And oft so mix, the diff'rence is too nice
Where ends the Virtue, or begins the Vice.
Fools! Who from hence into the notion fall,
That Vice or Virtue there is none at all.
If white and black blend, soften and unite
A thousand ways, is there no black or white?
Ask your own heart, and nothing is so plain:
Tis to mistake them, costs the time and pain.

II
NUMQUAM CREDULO . . .

A few years ago a man set up a table by the stairway in a New York subway station. He displayed a few dozen small boxes and in his hand he held a small watch. "Real watches," he chanted at the rushing crowds. "Keep time . . . only 25 cents . . ."

An occasional purchaser might inspect the small box and find inside a mere painted dial. Some of these demanded their money back. "We don't want any dissatisfied customers, no sir," the merchant would say. "Your money back, sir." With this he pressed a quarter into the customer's hand and smiled bravely. The customer rushed back up the stairs. The quarter was counterfeit.

Fate, in the person of the Manhattan East Detective Division, ultimately overtook the watch salesman's business and he was lost to history. But in his day he made quite a few quarters.

There was a time when Americans of consequence prided themselves on their classical educations, and habitually shredded their conversation with Latin quotations or allusions. The political speeches of John Quincy Adams, for one, were

23

so full of Latin that the voters rarely understood them. Moderns of the Genial Society come from schools which teach their young Homemaking or Driver Training and only a few scraps of Latinity remain in circulation: phrases like *e pluribus unum, mutatis mutandis, tempus fugit* and *et cetera*. One phrase, however, continues to be cited almost constantly as a pillar of our daily economic life. It is the old Roman caution *caveat emptor,* "Let the buyer beware."

There are few businessmen who have not made the acquaintance of this phrase and used it on occasion with telling effect. It is especially handy as a way of ending a discussion about seller ethics which has been growing uncomfortable. The *caveat* is not the immutable legal principle it once was—organizations like the Federal Trade Commission originate from a conviction that the principle is no longer tenable. Yet it recurrently finds its way into decisions handed down from respected benches. It is subject to a variety of interpretations. To the old-fashioned manufacturer, *caveat emptor* has a charismatic value equal to words like Robert Taft, Sunday School, free enterprise and golf. The younger man in an advertising agency will rarely use the phrase without a smile or a cough—and well he might. But use it we all will.

There was a time when the principle worked in practice. But in the maze of current consumer-seller relationships the phrase seems as remote as the Roman scene when the Gracchi started reforming sharp practices in real-estate sales. In those ancient days, as in the earlier history of this republic, *caveat emptor* had validity. It conjured up the picture of a man going to buy some commodity he knew about—whether a few pounds of apples, a horse, or a slave—from somebody who knew that the customer was likely to have direct knowledge of the purchased product. Sharp practices there were on both sides of the buyer-seller relationship. But it was rightly presumed that almost everybody concerned could take care of him or herself. If there were any doubts in the purchaser's mind, after all, he had the obvious right to examine the product.

This selective process is almost extinct in many areas where exaggerated codes of politeness and group trust work against the testing nature. It requires an increasing degree of courage for the well-heeled to ask for a sliver taste of the wheel of cheese he is about to buy—let alone to demand a close look at and explanation of the gas-eating mechanism inside the hood of a new Sound Barrier Eight. Granted the courage, it would require a superhuman perspicacity and technical knowledge for any buyer to penetrate the claims advanced for most products on the market in the United States today, from dentifrices to housing developments.

"The consumer should be able to buy on the strength of the representations made to him." This principle, as phrased by Assistant District Attorney Joseph Stone of New York County, is a good modern legal restatement of what *caveat emptor* ought to mean. But each year Stone and thousands of fellow district attorneys, Better Business Bureau men and officials of the Federal Trade Commission go out to do battle with a progressively tougher set of consumer handicaps. Each month thousands of new claims appear for products of dubious value: shampoos that claim to cure dandruff; reducing pills with virtually supernatural powers; health clubs which may assert that cancer, heart disease and arthritis can be cured by a set of exercises. Throughout their lives some form of chrome-plated deceit continues to work on citizens of the Genial Society, through TV pitches, newspaper ads and personal sales talks, on behalf of tired tires, unworkable "transistor" radios, fake "luxury" furniture or teacherless correspondence schools. In the end, it may even bury us, through the courtesy of a phony cut-rate funeral.

In considering misrepresentation, incidentally, I have deliberately steered clear of the crimes against mere taste and
decency perpetrated hourly, mostly on television: the smiling
young career girl who achieves "important regularity" with the
new all-purpose laxative; the cosmetically freckled children
pestering their mother to build muscles or forfend tooth decay;
the vats of stomach acid that burn their way through table-
cloths, containers and anything that is left of their viewers'
sensibilities. If this type of advertising is found effective, the
more blame to us all for buying the products it promotes. But
clear, cold misrepresentation of fact is not excusable on the basis
of popular attitudes.

Product misrepresentation is increasing. We hear of a new
high in bait advertising, the device of getting a customer into a
store with the lure of an item falsely announced as available.
Pre-ticketing—the falsely high list price of an article, drastically "reduced" for quick sales—is sweeping the country. The
"puffs" of normal advertising, even when they do not reach the
level of out-and-out fakery, constantly scout the spirit if not
the exact statute letter and number of the law. All these make
a formidable total of "operatorship," when added to the normal
pedestrian chicanery of false weights, fictional repair bills, fake
bankruptcy sales and the like. Nothing is safe from the Operators' misrepresentations. In September 1958 the U. S. Customs
Service confiscated a load of contraband arms sold by some
American entrepreneurs to Fidel Castro's revolutionaries.
When the agents went to examine the hand grenades in the
shipment, they discovered that they were phony, practice
grenades. The holes from the powderless interiors had been
plugged and painted over, to make them look like the real
thing.

The statistical evidence for the rise in consumer frauds is
at best the visible part of a huge iceberg. The very business of

making a complaint is tedious, at least by current standards. Since the individual is losing a relatively small amount of money when he buys that disguised $9.95 electric fan for its new "sale" price of $15.98, the incentive for complaint is in most cases not too strong. Despite such impediments to fraud's discovery, and the limitations of agencies empowered to deal with it, the rise in consumer trickery can be charted from their records. Between 1955 and 1958 the number of formal FTC complaints about business deceptions doubled. The consent orders, once a rarity, rose from 82 to 228. At this writing there are well over 1,000 complaints on file in the FTC offices— all of them necessarily against firms dealing in interstate commerce. State agencies have shown the same tendencies. In 1957 the rise of consumer fraud in New York State led to the establishment of a Consumer Counsel in the Governor's office and a special Division of Consumer Frauds and Protection in the state Attorney General's department, which has been forced into a continual expansion ever since.

If the increase of consumer-fraud Operators were solely a quantitative one, it might not pose so many problems. Misrepresentation of products is as old as business. The alarming thing about this sort of fraud today is the preponderance of weight on the seller's side. The more complicated life grows in the Genial Society, the more luxuries turn into necessities, the less an individual is able to check up on their value. A decade past the mid-century mark in the most opulent of the world's civilizations, we find the well-equipped American consumer uncertainly fingering his wallet (because that's where the credit cards are) as he tries to figure out the true value of a product against the massed forces of blanket advertising, salesmanship reinforced by depth psychology, and a national mentality that views installment buying as the key pillar of the economy and scorns the man who hangs on to his money.

Despite fitful political sermons in favor of saving, the national mood reflects the rule of thumb laid down by the paladin of cigarette merchants, George Washington Hill, in 1928: "The more the consumer buys, the more he feels the need of having."

It is the purpose of this chapter to suggest how plucked and featherless the American consumer really is, standing out there in the cold with nothing to protect him but *caveat emptor,* word of mouth and an unread file of consumer magazines. It would accurately describe his situation, if we want to stick to Latin tags, to substitute for *caveat emptor* an archaized version of the old P. T. Barnum motto: "*Numquam credulo aequus jactus* —never give a sucker an even break."

A federal court decision in the case of Whitehead vs. U. S. is a good legal restatement of Abraham Lincoln's dictum about fooling people. "It is probable," the judge wrote, "that no one who has not given the matter serious study for practical ends can fully realize the different degrees of ignorance and gullibility represented by the population of America. No scheme to defraud, however well-conceived for evil results, would probably reach all the people; and few schemes, however transparent, would fail to find some victims."

The operators behind consumer fraud are out for the lowest common denominator of gullibility. The more numerous the goods, and the less verifiable their claims, the wider the chances for herding the customers into the barn and milking them. Opportunities for this process exist almost without limit. A compilation of recent Federal Trade Commission actions is like a shady business Baedeker. A California furrier offers his wares at regular prices to customers who believe they are getting them as bargains in a radio quiz-show "contest." A New York asphalt company is caught outrageously padding the price of its roofing products. A Michigan furnace company sends out its salesmen posing as government inspectors, who dismantle furnaces as a setup to expensive repair jobs. A New Jersey supply company represents factory rejects as first-class television tubes. A tire company in Chicago passes off used tires as new ones. A Florida cigar company advertises low-quality cigars as coming from a government-bonded warehouse. And so it goes.

Most of these false claims depend for their effectiveness, in the Barnum tradition, on the imagined shrewdness of the consumer himself. This is what makes the consumer fraud so difficult to prosecute in a court of law, where in fact it seldom ends up. It holds true especially for the current Big Three of consumer fraud: bait advertising, pre-ticketing and the fake "comparative price."

Bait advertising, in its simplest form, is an enactment of the old carnival watchword to get the sucker "under the tent." To the accompaniment of much publicity, a store manager announces a number of items priced absurdly low. If he is legalistically inclined, he carefully advertises a "limited" number. When the customer arrives, he finds that the handsome $39.95 air-conditioner, or the sumptuous $49.98 TV set, has either disappeared in a rush of early morning orders or is—in some cases literally—nailed to the floor. ("Sorry, sir, that's our sample, and the rest are all out of stock.") But there are several vastly more expensive models. "Now over here," says the salesman, "we have a really new thing in TV sets. This model, with built-in refrigerator and folding bed, has just been marked down to $319.50." "Well," says the customer, "I didn't really plan to spend that much . . ." The rest is familiar history.

In the mail-order field, this play works even more smoothly. When the customer answers an ad offering a princely storm window for, say, $9.99 ("guaranteed as the result of scientific experiments to reduce heating bills by at least one third"), he gets a visit from a salesman. The bargain-conscious customer signs an order and forks over his deposit after a look at the model.

"By the way," the salesman adds as a parting gesture, "remember that you have to clean that window with steel wool and simonize it at least once a week." This causes some consternation in the customer, possibly even to the point of demanding his money back. With the correct look of astonishment the salesman says that he's sorry, but of course a deposit is a deposit. ("After all, what do you expect for $9?") Then, as a last thought, he becomes confidential. Those rascals at the factory, he allows, just don't know the score on dealing with decent people. He does happen to have, right out here in the car, a very good, really de luxe job that sells for $29.95. With this, no homeowner could ever go wrong. And it's a steal. "Now, just an extra deposit, and . . . yes, delivery can be assured in a matter of days."

This subversion of morals and economics sounds transparent and naïve. But the agencies concerned with consumer fraud can vouch for the fact that it is virtually a way of life. Every week honest Americans are writing in by the thousands to get a chance at similar schemes—a fact which in itself constitutes one of the great arguments against the theory that our new leisure time is turning out an enlightened citizenry. The number of customers who are reeled in directly with bait advertising in store windows, TV and newspapers is incalculable. As New York State's Attorney General Louis Lefkowitz put it:

In the world of business, there is an appalling scope to the frauds and deceptions which are practiced upon the consumer. Shady operators and their slick schemes not only rob the public of millions of dollars each year but give an economic black eye to the legitimate businessman. Bait advertising and misleading sales tactics rank high among the clever devices which are used to victimize the consumer; unconscionable overcharging; misrepresentation as to the merit or quality of a product or service; false advice as to the needs of the product or service—all these and many more gimmicks are used to add to the plunder.

Some consumer fraud schemes are, of course, run by out-and-out sharpers whose only business is the extraction of money, without return. All of the devices we are now discussing, however, are used by people who consider themselves not sharpers but legitimate businessmen, and who plan to stay in business. They often say—and in some hotly competitive markets with validity—that cutting corners is the only way they can keep their business solvent and competitive.

Take fictitious pricing. A remarkably large number of American businessmen indulge in this practice. It is the inevitable excess of a competitive free-enterprise system, and we shall never wholly extirpate it. But the evidence suggests that modern merchandising techniques, devised to advertise the fair price, have ironically put the padded price further and further away from restriction or even exposure.

The simpler form of this evil is the comparative price. That is the technical term for the attractive sign in red: "Formerly $79. Now for a limited time this electrically heated towel rack, with solar radio attached, can be yours for $49.95." In many cases comparative prices have validity. But their success as legitimate selling devices has led to their wholesale exploitation by merchants not so scrupulous. Many a shopper going to a close-out sale (*Clearing our entire stock. We must vacate our premises by July 1.*) has found out (or not found out) that the "bargain" prices advertised are as old and well established as the laws of the Medes and Persians.

With other operators in this field, we can detect the faint beat of conscience. They are the people who put out advertising of "Savings at one third of former prices" or "One half to one third off . . ." No customer of course is expected to ask,

"Off what?" and the seller is not eager to explain that "former prices" may refer to the price of the article when it was in the handicraft stage.

If the simple "one third off" dodge has been slipping in popularity among retailers, it is probably because the public does catch on, occasionally. In 1956 Duquesne University and the Better Business Bureau of Pittsburgh undertook a survey on public credence in reduced prices. Their sampling showed that the curve of acceptance dropped sharply as the alleged reductions grew higher. Almost 85 per cent of the sampling had faith in a 20 per cent savings. By the time the "savings" got to the "one third off" level, slightly more than half the customers questioned really believed it. An advertised savings of "one half off" found only about 12½ per cent takers.

The amount of public discrimination may not have been this high in actual practice. There is a considerable difference between showing your consumer's wisdom before a poll-taker and testing it in practice among the enticing riches of an all-out September Sale ("Never before in history has such an opportunity . . . Only two to a customer . . . Doors will open at five minutes after nine . . ."). But ten times bitten is at least twice shy. It can be said that the simple "one third off" gambit is in something of a decline.

Nonetheless, the existence of surplus stocks after World War II and the growing familiarity of the public with hitherto arcane facts of life like factory rejects, "seconds" or "surplus stocks," produced a new galaxy of come-on advertising, which shows no signs of abating. Its more recent bargain hunts have featured gleaming new power mowers, conspicuously labeled "from the factory to you," thus wrongfully hinting that there were no middleman charges for shipping, jobbing and wholesaling. Then there is the shoe sale of "marked-down factory seconds" (again, marked down from what?) which, the salesman explained, had only minor defects. Actually they were just inferior shoes, slightly overpriced. Patrons of many a Kar Korner in hardware and appliance basement stores were able to purchase impressive bargains, as it seemed, in "change-over tires," "new car take-offs" or well-wrapped "New Tread" tires. Their enthusiasm was dimmed when they found out, inevitably, that all these varieties were actually simple used tires or retreads.

Each week the advertising copy and the sales pitch of such stores perform new semantic marvels. In a case of recent note, some furriers in the New York area, scorning for a time the old stratagem of labeling various humble pelts with the names of exotic (and often nonexistent) animals from the wrong places, came up with a fine entry: "below original wholesale prices." This was in addition to the usual expedients of "one third to one half off," "no middleman's profits," or "Now it's here . . . the entire stock of a famous New York manufacturer . . . at unbelievably fabulous prices."* All of the foregoing, to say nothing of thousands of others like them, proved unpalatable to the FTC inspectors.

The most elaborate edition of the current price fiction is the pre-ticketing scheme. As now practiced, this goes far beyond the primitive device of, say, a New York clothing chain advertising its "originally priced" $55 topcoats knocked down to $24.88 (which was something more than their value), or the Philadelphia suit-makers who tagged their jackets at $60, then immediately brought this down to the true price of $19.85. At its most sophisticated, pre-ticketing involves a deal between

---

* Working in the older tradition of misrepresentation, another furrier drew the reluctant admiration of Federal Trade Commission inspectors for the completeness of his chicanery. As the Commission later noted: "The complaint charged that the firm's ads did not give the names of the animals producing the furs, did not reveal that furs were artificially colored, neglected to mention when they were composed of paws, tails, bellies and waste fur, and did not identify the country of origin of imported furs."

the manufacturer and the retailer to ticket goods from the factory at prices far above true value. One large manufacturer even sent its goods, in this case women's belts, to its retail outlets with tags already marked "$1.50. ———'s price 87¢." In the fields of clothes, appliances and luggage this sort of thing proliferates. The really "obliging" manufacturer makes a big thing of stamping the inflated price on each of his products, sure in the knowledge that his dealers will attract more than their share of bargain-hunters thereby.

Many practiced pre-ticketers use national advertising to establish their ambitious values for them, whether the pre-ticketing has been done by local or national manufacturers. Take the overzealous perfume manufacturer. Equipped with his vats of home-brew, with just a wisp of Grasse fragrance in the pot for seasoning, he inserts an ad in a few national magazines offering his new "imported" perfume—*Je m'excuse*, let's call it—at heavily loaded prices, something like $30 an ounce. This offering may never have swum into the ken of retail store managers. If it did, it was probably on the crest of some dozen spirited phone calls to a few large drugstores, demanding to know whether a whiff of *Je m'excuse* was in the house. Not long after, a salesman would pop by, suggesting a few bottles on consignment. So far, so good.

Comes the Christmas season, with the passage of a few months, and an almost universal urge impels casual male shoppers to order flagons of perfume. What better remembrance than a few bottles of *Je m'excuse*, which is now advertised as greatly reduced from its original price—in fact down to a tidy $5 an ounce? Salesmen already have shown druggists and other retail dispensers big mock-ups of the original ad in the national magazine. By the canons of the Genial Society, therefore, a major price reduction has occurred, for if a price was nationally advertised, it must have been real. It goes without saying that the real worth of *Je m'excuse* is something under $2.

A variant of this plot, which also came under the FTC's fire, was used by the hosiery firm which first put a $1.95 price tag on its ladies' stockings and advertised this fact widely, but briefly, in national magazines. The company's retail outlets were then forced to buy small quantities at $12 per dozen pair, to be offered at the nationally advertised asking price. After an interval, the stores were allowed to put on "half-price" sales at 99¢ a pair—the wholesaler having meanwhile dropped its price to a normal $7.25 a dozen. Just another run in the economy's stocking.

In almost every retail field, pre-ticketing has slain its ten thousands in illicit profits. It flourishes best in new luxury items or appliances, like power lawn mowers, where a general price level is still in the process of being established. But once begun, the practice works swiftly enough to gratify anybody who still remembers Gresham's Law. The more the phony price is paraded, the more the real price is suspect. With all prices suspect, the honest merchant would have depressingly little incentive to sell his goods at just rates. On the contrary, he could have a compelling incentive to adopt the prevailing phony price system. Otherwise, he might not be in business very long.

A hallmark of consumer frauds is their cyclical or concentrated nature, and the ease with which they multiply in areas of new industry or invention. Take television sets. Nothing less than gross public unfamiliarity with the medium could have produced the steady profits of the firm which first measured its widely advertised inexpensive picture tubes *diagonally* (as a microscopic footnote in the ad explained). Similarly, the commercial development of transistor radios produced a small plague of fly-by-night bargains, purporting to be legitimate versions of the transistor principle. Most of them sold at prices between four and eight dollars—considerably less than one expects to pay for a workable transistor set. In all cases that were investigated, the bargain "transistors" proved to be about as advanced as a primitive crystal set and often even less efficient.Yet they sold marvelously, thanks to the official-sounding claims made for them. They are selling still.

One "transistor" outfit, impressively titled as Borg-Johnson Electronics, Inc., was shut down by New York State authorities after having cleaned up $1,270,000 in two months of whirlwind sales. Borg-Johnson's "Lifetime" Germanium Diode Pocket Radio sold at $4.95 with a money-back guarantee. Wrote the U. S. Post Office Department's judicial officer who also reviewed the case: "The device falls so short of the claims made for it in the advertising that to hold that merely because a refund was offered no fraud is involved would do violence to the historic concept of fraud and the enforcement of the postal fraud statute."

There are whole areas of commerce where the untrained customer can make intelligent value judgments about as easily as he could construct a transistor by himself—the hirsute tangle of the fur industry, for example. Alternatively, there are fields where the lack of goods or services offers an open invitation to the Operators' talents. The excesses of garage mechanics in this category are by now so well known that many Americans would as soon leave their wives alone in a Gashouse District café as put their cars in a strange garage. But the price exacted by crooked appliance mechanics is even larger.

There is no intention, in saying this, to impugn the honesty of the few good mechanics and repairmen left in the country. They are the nation's most valuable assets. The day will assuredly come when one of them will find himself the only person left in the republic capable of turning the switches, adjusting the levers, and manning the mechanisms that operate the nation's power stations, steer the remote-control cars and aircraft, make the movies, bake the cakes and adjust the minds of the school-age population. (The rest of us will be watching him.)

Yet almost everyone has suffered the depredations of one or more bad repairmen, if for no other reason than the impossibility of checking on their performance and our native diffidence in setting a price beforehand. In New York City, the hub of the fraud world, the District Attorney's office of New York County recently uncovered a classic of this new genre. A few southern sharpers, who had just pulled off a similar stunt in Birmingham, Ala., dropped into Manhattan and set up a Bowery store labeled "City Television Repair." They circularized as many Manhattan housewives as they could, with an ambitious ad program speeding their path ("No charge if we don't repair your set . . . First call free . . ."). Once they obtained a set to repair, their bills would run from $40 to $90. The repair work done was mythical. Complaints began pouring into the D.A.'s office.

The process of tracking down evidence on these Operators was illustrative of the complications in fighting consumer fraud in general. They stem principally from the physical scarcity of men and machines to pursue each violator and procure enough evidence to stand up in court. Four detectives tailed City's servicemen's cars, and a legal wiretap was put on their telephones. "In five different instances," as one detective tells it, "we got an apartment where a detective and a policewoman represented themselves as man and wife. We'd have a TV set that had been given by the manufacturer and was guaranteed perfect. We deliberately disabled the set, made secret markings on the chassis, on the picture tube and other components of the chassis. These were made by an electric vibrating tool, and we sprayed the parts with metholine (visible only under ultraviolet light).

"In each case the most the bill should have been was the cost

of a new tube and the charge for service; the tube should have
been about $5 to $8. But within a few hours the housewife
would get a phone call from this character, saying the big
picture tube was defective, that the tuning controls were out
of order, that various circuits were short-circuited. The bills
ranged from $45 to $71.50. When we did get the set back we
found they'd only replaced the one defective tube and that
they'd sprayed the big picture tube with a black solution to give
the appearance of a new one.

"When the serviceman came into the room with the set, we
had the room wired and all our conversation was recorded, and
he was photographed . . ." The result was two convictions, and
a remarkable decrease in the number of similar establishments.

In the same city another television outfit, Eagle Radio and
Television Service, Inc., advertised widely that it would fix
TV sets on credit with no down payment—nothing to pay in
fact until 30 days after completion of repairs. Then the customer
would pay 50 cents a week. But after a serviceman removed the
set to Eagle's roost, the story was different. No sets were returned until after the customer had made a down payment
ranging from $15 to $35, with the balance to be paid in $5
installments. In the matter of replacements and needed repairs,
Eagle's charges were, if anything, more fraudulent than City's.
In this case the state Attorney General's office succeeded in
putting the "firm" out of business.

Crude repair frauds like this, perpetrated on the poor and
relatively friendless, may ultimately find their way into the
District Attorney's office. The really scot-free operators are
those who prey on the more sophisticated higher-income levels
of the community. Enough writers make their living by demon-
strating how the inhabitants of "Suburbia" are gypped (or
sociologically frustrated, or mutually seduced, or burnt at
barbecues) without adding to the toll here. Indeed, even at

higher literary levels, the grim biographies in the folklore of
Louis Auchincloss or John Marquand are enough to steer a
growing boy away from Old Westbury or Westport forever.
The fact remains that the guilelessness of suburban homeowners
has necessitated a whole library of Better Business Bureau publications, warning of modern countryman's perils like the fake-
humus racket, the bogus termite expert, the phony tree surgeon
or the fly-by-night roofer.

The door-to-door salesmen who specialize in the suburban
trade start poking their briefcases aboveground with the first
hint of spring. On their calls they stress the need of immediate
household improvements, and the advisability of signing a contract for them immediately, if the housewife wants to make that
"extra saving." In general, the hastier the sales pitch, the more
crooked the terms of the contract. Such high-pressure docu-
ments almost invariably involve the homeowner in heavy
expenses, with only a fraction of the talked-about work actually
provided.

The worst of the lot are those professional prophets of disas-
ter, the crooked fire-alarm "demonstrator" and the glib furnace
"repairman." Like the German generals of the early *Blitzkrieg*
days, these craftsmen rely on speed and shock to achieve the
maximum tactical advantage. The fire-alarm specialist will
represent himself as a demonstrator of alarm devices, broadly
hinting—or stating—in the process that he has been commis-
sioned for this job by a local fire department. He intersperses his
demonstration with an account of recent fire victims—all of
them people who had heedlessly neglected to have alarms installed—and comments on the inflammable nature of the house
he is visiting. The alarms which a scared homeowner may then
order will probably work; but time will reveal that they are
vastly more complex and expensive than the size of the house
warrants.

The furnaceman's technique is to come to the householder's door, mutter something about "gladly inspecting the furnace" and get downstairs fast. As quickly as possible, he dismantles the furnace, spreads its parts over the basement floor and begins a vivid scare routine about how menacing the condition of the old furnace has become. The net result is generally a new plant, at exorbitant prices. The more blessed of suburban householders never find out that their old furnace was good all the time.

Sometimes the fraud or the corner-cutting is performed by local contractors. Familiar is the plight of the new homeowner who half-wittingly gets himself into a major floor-surfacing job under the impression that the contractor was just going to put some varnish on the bare spots. Even more familiar are the casualties of the artful mail-order invitations to the city boy with the new green thumb. "You can almost see green beauty spreading," ran the prospectus of one Maryland firm, which promised that its grass would multiply itself 50 times in a few months. In this instance, some of the buyers complained. The Federal Trade Commission was able to remind buyers and seller that it takes two or three growing seasons to make a grassy lawn out of a bare plot.

Yet this kind of fraud rarely gets itself into the papers for the reason that only a few people bother to complain about it, and even the complainants seldom seek legal redress. In this diffidence they are only holding true to the customs of the Genial Society which deplores outcry per se. There is also the closely knit nature of their community, which makes it inevitable that any sucker who makes a fight of it must be revealed as such in the eyes of all. This is one of the reasons why the second generation of Suburbia shows such a marked tendency to move back to the wicked, anonymous old city.

In one major department, for a time at least, the suburban American *has* been forced to make some kind of outcry. That is the matter of his house itself. The urge to get a good-looking bargain, and the evils of finding it bad, are nowhere so forcefully displayed as in the real-estate and housing business. The disillusionment of the man who bought his quarter-acre plot at the legendary "Sun 'n' Sky Homes" housing development (it took years of roofing repairs to make him realize how apt the name was) has become an American epic. The door handle that comes off in the hand, the half-cellar that wholly leaks, walls with the soundproofing qualities of mosquito netting, the fake bathroom tile that really peels, the open closet masquerading as a "dining area"—all these defects have been well exposed and authenticated in the works of the less scrupulous builders.*

This book has no ambitions to explore the Stygian complex of architects, builders, suppliers, government agencies and finance men which compose the American housing industry, or to distinguish in detail between the less scrupulous and the more scrupulous builders. For our purposes the lesson at hand lies in the unreasoning craze of the consumer to get attractive *terms* for his house-buying effort, with conditions of quality, livability or economic soundness far secondary.

Since the end of World War II, real estate has been one of the Operator's most profitable stamping grounds. In the postwar housing shortage, the desperate need of families for roofs over their heads fostered the rise of the most unscrupulous kind of housing operator. Where the new "development" idea of mass housing, as exemplified in trail-blazing operations like the Levittowns or Park Forest, Ill., did give value to the customers, they made it all the easier for shoddy imitators. Taking advantage of the housing shortage, and the postwar financial straits of so many families, a tendency emerged to deck out a poorly made house in the fanciest possible financial trimmings.

* John Keats' well-known book exposing this situation, *The Crack in the Picture Window*, has been widely condemned by contractors since its publication; but there is a great deal of truth in it.

Installment buying was extended to this area with a vengeance. The 30-year mortgage became as much a staple as the 30-month car-payment plan, and more dangerous because it was far harder to escape from.

Operators in this field were quick to notice the curious inability of the American public, whether in buying a house, car, vacuum cleaner or making a loan from the bank, to add up the total amount it is paying. For the most part, the builder had only to put insurance mortgage charges, handling *et al.* into a nice monthly package. The consumer would be likely to sign the papers forthwith, with little thought about the huge interest payments he might be incurring, the future repair bills or the future negotiability of the modified Cape Cod patio-style ranch house, which Wyatt Earp could probably have pulled down with his lariat.

In an odd way the government itself perpetuated this business of "selling terms, not houses" through the very agencies devised to protect the would-be householder. The system of appraisals and mortgage insurance devised by the Federal Housing Administration was begun in the "third-of-a-nation" thirties, when most people had the price only of a very cheap housing product, if they had the price for any at all. In 1959, when most of the country had the price, the system of FHA mortgage insuring still tended to put a premium on cheapness. The down payment and financial guarantees required for a $12,000 house remained disproportionately heavier than those asked for a $9,000 house. And the builders who put quality materials in their houses were sometimes penalized for this by a rule-of-thumb method of appraisals. One California builder, to cite a much-discussed example, who had put good fixtures and sound, long-lived materials in his house was granted no higher a value by the local FHA appraiser than a competitor who filled his model with gimcrackery. Nor did purchasers notice any real difference.

Such a flat-footed appraisal system would not have existed so long if the public had not manifested an all-consuming emphasis on "terms" as such. There is no law against this emphasis. No Better Business Bureau could quarrel with it. But it is directly or indirectly responsible for some distinguished sins against quality and fair dealing in the business life of this country.

Thus far we have emphasized the flagrant crookedness of the fly-by-night operator, the disreputable merchant, the man who cuts corners as a way of life. It must be admitted, also, that charges of one form or another of consumer deception have been made against some of the largest and most reputable firms in the country. For example, the FTC has taken actions against such reputable department stores as R. H. Macy and B. Altman in New York.* The Firestone Tire & Rubber Co. agreed to stop labeling its second-grade tires Deluxe Super Champion, as opposed to a mere Deluxe Champion for the normal first-line variety. Its spokesmen have pointed out, with justice, that their competitors in this most competitive industry have done as bad, or worse.

Other major American industrial colossi have been caught clay-footed in more complicated raids on the consumer in the field of price discrimination and illegal merger activity. At this point we are concerned only with the effect of direct misrepresentation on the American consumer, whether he is paying an all too concrete price for a fictitious markdown, getting a "Swiss" watch movement which happens to have been made in Hong Kong, clothing himself with a "British" sweater actually made in Philadelphia from Japanese yarn, or relaxing in the comfort-

---

* There were consent orders in both cases—two orders against Macy's (1956 and 1959) for fictitious fur labeling and misleading pricing of automobile seat covers, respectively; one against Altman's (1959) for fictitious labeling of furs. It must be remembered that, in accord with long-established practices, the fact that a firm signs a consent order implies no admission of guilt for the practice noted.

able delusion that the clever composition chair he occupies is made of real leather. Few of these misguided customers acquired their goods without some sort of advertising intervening. It is no novelty that the best of American businesses step over the line a bit when they are advertising.

The seventh of October 1958, placed just five days before Columbus Day, may go down in American advertising circles as a discovery of almost comparable importance: the Federal Trade Commission declared its findings that Chesterfield cigarettes were not really "milder." The decision may not have been relevant to the particular advertising pitch of the time. Liggett & Myers executives were at pains to say that the offending claims cited in the FTC ruling had been banished since 1953, when the first FTC action began. But no better example could be found of the way in which reputable corporations have made a shambles of their public communications, in the free-for-all of conflicting verbalisms that pass for advertising.

The background to the cigarette order had been some months building. In February the FTC's Bureau of Consultation declared itself unable to find any common denominator in all the heavily publicized "tests" for relative lack of nicotine and harmful tars in American cigarettes. (Among other things, the tests "smoke" cigarettes at lengths ranging from 20 mm. to 38 mm.) A congressional committee, dealing with FTC practices, had gone further and suggested that the Commission put a stop to the "deceptive" advertising practices of the cigarette manufacturers. And the hard-breathing crusade of the *Reader's Digest* magazine had helped make the cancer-cigarette-filter association one of the country's Most Unforgettable Characters. It was a milestone when a generation of cigarette ads finally drew official rebuke—because in a situation increasingly fraught with medical doubt, if not danger, they had grown steadily more misleading.

"We are in trouble," Vice President Edwin W. Ebel of General Foods Corporation said to an advertising group in 1958, "when the public loses confidence in the statements made by advertising. What we print, what we voice over the air, its believability in detail—that is the heart and soul of advertising. To preserve confidence in what advertising says is where your and my energy should be spent."

Even the most elementary side of confidence-preserving has its problems. Although the beginnings of countless consumer frauds occur in the pages of newspaper or magazine advertising, newspapers and magazines have still not worked out a good scheme for checking on the authenticity of the wares peddled in their pages. Some of them set high standards, and they have had to work hard to keep the standards high. *Life* magazine, which originated the legitimate "Advertised in *Life*" label for its customers, had to resort to legal means, notably between 1955 and 1957, to prevent the unscrupulous from using it. A few other magazines and newspapers are equally vigilant in checking on the wares for which potential advertisers are responsible. But in a large area of the press the tendency persists to sign 'em up and ask questions later.

Television, it would appear from some advertised products, only rarely asks questions either about the product or the manner of its advertising. From time to time it institutes belated policing operations. It was a start at least when the National Association of Broadcasters agreed to stop passing actors and models off as dentists, doctors or nurses in commercials, beginning January 1, 1959. (Unfortunately, this restriction has only resulted in the same white-coated actors pointing to impressive-looking folders which they refer to as "doctors' tests.") Later in 1959, under the influence of what amounted to a national probe of the medium, the TV proprietors at least began to distinguish between "live" and taped programs, and instituted long and searching debate about the ethics of canned audience laughter.

Perhaps it is illusory to expect any sort of high standards. The small retailer or manufacturer can scarcely be expected to crusade for fair prices and honest competition when giants of the oil, steel, drug and electrical goods industries—to note some of the 1958 and 1959 cases—were under heavy attack in the courts for price fixing or various forms of restraint of trade.

The final word might be said here about those pace-setters of the economy, the Detroit automobile companies. There was an ancient time (*i.e.*, 1939) when each year's new cars were proudly ticketed with their prices, as a matter of course. Even the casual billboard carried the ever-present label "$700 F.O.B. Detroit." Modern life, and the exigencies of competition, took this price notation off the billboards shortly after World War II. For the next ten years, until Congress finally passed a law about prices in 1958, the car men puffed along merrily with their ads extolling everything under the dashboard and over the fins— except the price. For it became recognized that car dealers, to exist in their own intense form of competition, had to make free with their own individual combinations of prices and trade-in values—adjustable on the customer's demand (or so the customer thought). This was known in the trade as "packing." With this lack of general published prices (as noted in a 1956 Senate investigation), the consumer ended by paying a price for his car—the result of the trade-in allowance, the dealer's need, and variations in financing and insurance terms—that was about as stable as the price scale of a Damascus rug salesman. After some public discussion, the worst of these packing abuses were corrected.

Given the high-pressure sales tactics of the car companies, who rarely show mercy to the hard-pressed, overstocked dealer, it is small wonder that the crooked car salesman became a

national legend, well-founded in fact. The scope of his depredations is still hard to believe, but some of them are down on
public record.

In 1958 a West Coast merchant was sentenced to a year in
jail and fined $10,000 after a trial involving charges of grand
theft and forgery. The hero of this classic operation, up to the
moment of his downfall, was a car dealer. His company had its
headquarters offices and showrooms in a thriving suburban
area. Several other nearby car companies were either wholly
or partly owned subsidiaries. (A condition of the sentence,
needless to say, was a period of probation, during which the
merchant was forbidden to go near the automobile business.)
For some years it had been virtually impossible to escape hearing about him, if you lived in his area, for the volley of newspaper, radio and TV publicity. It was also difficult to avoid
losing money on a car purchase, once you stepped into the
financial house of mirrors beyond the neon-lit threshold.

The dealer's forte, necessarily obscured by the legal pigeon-
holes of his indictment and conviction, was a tendency to take
the technique of the salesman to a ruthlessly logical extreme.
His journey inevitably carried *him* over the threshold of pure
and simple fraud.

As with the humbler variety of bait advertiser, the first rule
of his operations was to "get 'em under the tent." The customer would be quoted an unbelievably good figure on a
new car, and offered a trade-in allowance beyond the dreams
of avarice—or at least far beyond the price he could get for
his old car elsewhere. Similar good "deals" were proposed on
financing terms. Then the salesman, who was invariably about
to go "off duty," would wind up his breathless pitch with a
suggestion that the customer need only *sign* a few forms and go
home sure in the knowledge that he was the *de jure* if not
exactly *de facto* possessor of a powerful new vehicle.

A return visit or the next morning's mail almost always brought disillusionment. The amount written in on the blank forms for a used car's trade-in value seemed to have shrunk alarmingly. The price of the new car was correspondingly higher, embellished with all the extra arm-rests, radios, clocks, heater, steering-wheel attachments, etc., which the customer had thought to be included in the general package. Financing contracts were "rewritten" or reneged on. One wavering customer, persuaded to take an attractive used Oldsmobile on a tryout basis, found out that his old Ford had disappeared overnight. A few "insurance" papers he had signed turned out to be a perfectly legal trade-in agreement, with an appallingly low figure allowed for his car.

Another typical case of customer relations was the sad awakening of a gentleman who was unable to keep up with a $90 monthly payment. When he fell behind, his car was repossessed by the direct expedient of stealing it out of a locked garage. The dealer then sent his ex-customer a short communication noting that the car had been sold at auction, but had not realized enough to pay off the agreed purchase price. A bill for several hundred dollars was enclosed to cover the gap.

This sort of sharp practice is regrettably not rare. At least it used to be prevalent when the car-buying stampede was on through the early fifties. But here it was systematized to a science. Salesmen coming on the force first went through the normal indoctrination given by reputable car dealers. Then they often received a further set of instructions in really aggressive salesmanship.

The first rule was simple: "Get his keys." Most customers drove to the showroom. If they drove they had a car; if they had a car, it could be traded in for a new or bigger used model. The salesman's job was to get the customer's keys, on the pretext of having his old car "appraised." What good American, after all, objects to having his old car appraised, with no obligation to buy? In point of fact, the old car was hidden in another corner of the lot, if necessary, just to get it away from its owner. From then on, the salesman's job was to see that his man walked out of the showroom with a new car and a contract, never to see his old model again.

There were other instructions: "Never leave the customer alone—he might start checking the accessories in a car he had been shown, or might even take time to think." "Get the man's pen or pencil away from him on some pretext—he might want to take notes on what he was offered."

The small, glass-walled sales booths were apparently wired for sound, so that from his central command post the boss could listen in on the progress of any sale. If a salesman showed signs of moral qualms, one of the firm's veteran deal-closers would step in the breach. This breed is called a T.O. man (for take-over) in certain automobile circles. His specialty is to supply the peroration to the conversation between salesman and customer, ramming home the hard sell in a verbal maze of glib figures and enthusiastic predictions.

Occasionally there was trouble. The man who lost his Ford overnight and gained the attractive used Oldsmobile finally made a complaint. Detroit cracked down as fast as a TV network decrying a rigged quiz program. The boss was impelled to renegotiate this "agreement."

He blamed it on inexperienced salesmen; and he also put so much reverse English on the final contract that the customer remained cheated. "At the time [we signed the insurance papers]," a grand jury witness recalled, "the man gave me his word of honor. Maybe I am one of those fellows that take the word of honor seriously. But I don't any more, thank God, and from now on I do take time and read."

These sad words struck at the heart of the big problem in consumer crookery: the consumer himself. Granted that crooked car merchants, like the crooked furnace salesmen and the devious bargain-touters, thrive at periods of great buyer demand. (The great Texas cattle drives are the only historical phenomena to compare with the headlong storming of automobile showrooms in the years after World War II culminating in the Big Drive of 1955.) Yet in good years or lean, the sharper's success depends only in a limited tactical sense on the dodges he practices. His strongest and unfailing ally is the abnormally high boiling point of the American consumer. The Genial Society does not bargain. It has been surrounded by such plenty that bargaining gradually seemed to grow superfluous. It is timesaving to believe outright in a neighbor's untested "word of honor," especially when the word is given in an opulent showroom.

It is automatically presumed that a car dealer must be honest, because he has such a "big company" in back of him, or because "they're all the same anyway—they have to be." This is a strange attitude, especially in such an automobile-conscious country. Yet the same people who display this automobile obsession sign blank contracts in dealers' offices without investigation,* and sit by placidly watching Detroit raise its prices each year, with disregard for either economic conditions or consumer demands. When revolt comes, as in the rise of the small car, it begins not with technical or economic objections, but *primarily* because of European snob appeal. Perhaps there is some inner connection between the new car models and the men who drive them. What do we make of the basket-

---

* I do not question the fact that the great majority of car dealers are honest. This is no excuse, however, for their customers' lack of discrimination.

case driver, as he drives along the highway pushing the two or
three automatic buttons necessary to give him the illusion, at
least, that he is controlling his vehicle? Have his self-reliance
and critical faculties diminished with every new physical labor-
saving device? The widening range of our gullibility suggests
that they have.

What protective forces does the law mobilize against the
Operators' war on the consumer? There is, specifically, the
Federal Trade Commission, an organization under a thousand
strong, which has control, of course, only over matters involving
interstate commerce, and as peculiar a set of ground rules as
any agency in Washington. It is not, in the first place, a law-
enforcement agency. It is a regulatory agency, which can enforce compliance with its own regulations—after a time-con-
suming interval. If the FTC can prove to itself (since the
Commissioners, themselves, are judges of what their field agents
report) that a firm has violated fair trade practices, lied in its
advertising or attempted illegal mergers, it can: a) bring the
company concerned to accept a consent order, agreeing to stop
the offending practice in the future; b) fight out the matter at
a formal hearing, after which a cease-and-desist order may be
issued against the company. If the company still flouts the
law, then and only then can the FTC go to court and c) secure
an injunction against it, with a civil penalty of $5,000 for each
violation of the order.

When the operators use the U. S. mails for any type of consumer fraud, the penalties are far stiffer, often involving heavy
jail sentences. The Postal Inspection Service, like the FTC, is
limited in its scope by the number of its personnel—although
not nearly so drastically. (Its strength in 1958 was 1,402.) But
it has a high record of convictions. In the fiscal year 1958 the
inspectors got convictions in 98.7 per cent of all the cases they
had brought to trial.

Besides such specific agencies there is the threat of several fraud provisions on the federal statutes, including the false claim (18 USC 287), the false statement (18 USC 1001) and conspiracy to defraud the government (18 USC 371). As earlier stated, U. S. Attorneys often have their troubles prosecuting under these generalized auspices, although they are more successful in enforcing the "fraud provisions" for violations of specific federal programs.

On a local level, the protection of the consumer depends on the vigilance not only of district attorneys, but of officials in charge of markets, licensing and other forms of merchandising inspection. Occasionally, an Operator is trapped less by his fraud than his own *modus operandi*. A few years ago, the owners of a body-and-fender-repair company in Baltimore were convicted of violating the federal law against wire tapping. In their pellmell pursuit of accident business they had been intercepting radio communications of the Baltimore City Police Department.

The difficulty of enforcing almost any law for the consumer's protection, in fields where he can hardly be expected to estimate true quality, was illustrated not long ago in New York City, in the matter of ladies' cashmere sweaters. Some complaints had reached the New York authorities that the attractive $49.95 sweaters on sale were far from the advertised 100 per cent cashmere. The city investigators, who shopped twelve New York City stores, found serious discrepancies in all twelve's products. They were confirmed in their analysis, moreover, by a fabrics expert. He pointed out that the world's supply of marketable cashmere, at that moment, was not sufficient to put 100 per cent cashmere sweaters in all the city's department stores.

Called on the carpet, the store managers produced manufacturers' invoices showing that the material was indeed 100 per cent cashmere. Representatives of the New York District

Attorney's office then questioned the manufacturers. They in turn showed 100 per cent cashmere invoices from the six mills which had supplied them with the material. There was, apparently, skulduggery at the millrace, and the New York lawyers raced to prove it.

After *two years* the case came to trial. The Court of Special Sessions ruled that there was no violation of the state statute involved, which declared it a misdemeanor to misrepresent a product's quality in advertising, since the mill was not at all in contact with the consumer. It is only the agency which offers a product for sale that is, by current state law, liable to prosecution. Since these agencies, the department stores, offered convincing proof of their innocence in this matter, the case was dropped.

The enforcement agencies may grow stronger—or at least larger. The laws may proliferate in their complications. Injunctions may crowd the court calendars. Police and markets inspectors can test scales or administer warnings, backed by the threat of court action, to merchants who advertise nonexistent $25 TV sets, or claim to sell a $4 brand of olive oil for $2.85 (but don't really). They can advise the crooked furniture-store proprietor that he had better start labeling his "mahogany bedroom suites" for the gumwood they really are. They can take swift action against the gas-station owners who make small but steady profits (and incidentally stimulate whooping cough in the motors of 325-horsepower fin jobs) by putting regular gasoline in the "special high-octane" gas pumps. But no one in the field believes they can keep the Genial Society safe from anything like all the consequences of its own economic and moral laxities.*

"How far," asks one hard-pressed consumer-fraud specialist,

* In fact, the custodians themselves sometimes sabotage the law instead of enforcing it. In New York City in 1959, complaints about short weights in meat markets led to a series of arrests, suspensions, and transfers among officers of the Bureau of Weights and Measures, and the exposure of a city-wide system of graft and extortion.

"can government go in protecting and leading around by the hand people with money in their pockets who have a burning desire to spend it?"

The old service motto, "Let George do it," seldom finds itself quoted in the speeches extolling our national progress and advancement, but it might well be an unexpressed national slogan. The average consumer armors himself in the presumption that "all those government agencies," the city and state administrations, the police, the courts, the Better Business Bureaus, the credit associations, will tend to take care of all the *really* crooked businessmen. (As for mere sharp practices, he may cut a corner himself now and then.) So it is that, given the presence of a real commercial hit-and-run driver, the pedestrian consumer generally ends with his wallet splattered on the pavement at the first intersection. He hadn't even bothered to look.

Modern advertising conditions the individual to be diffident about searching questions. Who is he to buck the opinions of all the thinking men who smoke filters, all the discriminating executives who drink Old Red Eye after each board meeting, all the women-who-care who clean their teeth with super-annuated Foamex or tear their stockings climbing into the turret of a Springless Six (the car that rides lower than sea level)? Who is he to question the retailer who offers him dubious bargains, backed by all the weighted influence of the "national manufacturers" he sells? The only point at issue, actually, is that he is a thinking man, or should be, and that it's his money.

A little *caveat emptor* can help mightily to stiffen the individual, and hence the collective backbone of the Genial Society. The alternative principle is in the last analysis destructive of consumer, seller and producer alike. But it yawns before us: *Numquam credulo aequus jactus.*

III
PILLS, PRIDE, PROFITS

Tired? Sick? Overweight? Overtense? Undersexed? Arthritic? Bustless? Bald?

If any, or (conceivably) all of these complaints are yours you can for the first time banish worry— and fear. Just try a new laboratory-tested wonder drug compounded of analgesic elements approved by America's foremost medical authorities. Modern science's newest miracle remedy for the relief of pain, worry, personal discomfort and emotional distress, it is pleasant-tasting, non-habit-forming and now available without a doctor's prescription. Get it today. And remember, its amazing new ingredients have been released for use by U.S. health authorities . . .

This fugal theme has become so much a part of the American scene that most of us take its drone for granted. We shouldn't. The gray area of spurious medical claims and outright fraud it represents makes up the most immediately dangerous part of the Operator's realm. Medical, health and other welfare frauds are astonishingly expensive, and they are multiplying faster than any other variety. The American Medical Association recently reported that unscrupulous "health and nutrition experts"

55

take $500,000,000 yearly from their customers. The phony reducing merchants are equally aggressive. In a 1958 report, Representative John Blatnik's subcommittee of the House Committee on Government Operations said flatly: "The American consumer is being bilked out of approximately $100 million annually which he spends on these preparations." The additional yearly amount of money thrown away on fraudulent or half-fraudulent medications has been tabbed as anything from $50,000,000 to $200,000,000.

A more striking sign of how medical fraud has grown can be derived from the files of the National Better Business Bureau. The Bureau and its local affiliates get five times as many inquiries on this subject as they did three years ago. Worse yet, they receive twelve times as many complaints. An outfit in Ohio offers a mild laxative as a sure-fire cure for obesity. A Midwestern brace company exaggerates the curative effect of its rupture trusses. A Massachusetts manufacturer suggests that its bouillon cubes will prevent Asiatic flu. A Louisiana scalp clinic claims that its preparations will prevent baldness, dandruff or scalp itching.

Needless to say, the victim of a welfare fraud often loses more than his money. He is likely to spurn medical attention, in the belief that he is getting it. He may undermine his health, in the belief that his new health or body-building cure is "harmless," just the way the ad said. It is no longer an oddity to see newspaper headlines like "Pep-pill firm sued for $75,000 in death." But most such fatalities elude the tabulators as surely as the quacks involved elude justice. "Unfortunately," says Chief Postal Inspector David H. Stephens, who has prosecuted a great many of them, "the ghouls who trade on the hopes of the desperately ill often cannot be successfully prosecuted because the patients who are the chief witnesses die before the case is called up in court."

The "cures" that end in fatalities admittedly stand at one

extreme. They are purveyed generally by hardened crooks—
like the Midwestern "doctor" with a record of confidence
games dating back to 1925, who has lately posed as an eye
specialist, curing cataracts (whether real or fancied) with what
he advertises as "radium water," sold at as much as $1,400 a
splash. At the other end of the line stands the assurance-plus
TV announcer. His purpose is simple: to plant the impression
that no one who litters his ash tray with Goldenrod Emperor-
size Super-filter tips need ever worry about lung cancer. His
sponsor is "respectable" and rich; but the sponsor and the fake
eye doctor, for a moment at least, are in the same league. The
"doctor" in question was picked up in Missouri, in January 1959,
on a swindling charge, and temporarily put out of the way.
Nothing has happened thus far to any one of numerous cigarette
companies involved in the second play. Nothing probably will
happen to them, despite a flurry of actions recently begun in
Congress and the Federal Trade Commission on this score.*
Congress and the FTC will have to face the facts that people like
to smoke, come what may, and that the smoking trade is most
competitive. They will at least have the advantage of bringing
their regulatory actions in the clear, against business organizations which must necessarily operate with some display of a
public conscience.

It is, however, in the area *between* the quack killers and
legitimate businesses that the worst problems of welfare fraud
occur, and the most widespread. These are the fly-by-night
Operators who run plausible businesses on the thin edge of
the law in those major American industries: the curing, preservation, and beautifying of bodies, and to a lesser extent (in line
with the Genial Society's general value standards) the acquisi-

---

* In the end, however, the hue and cry did have some effect. In February
1960, the FTC was able to announce that the tobacco companies had agreed
to drop all "low-tar" and "low-nicotine" claims from their advertising. *Fiat
justitia, ruat filter.*

tion of skills and education. They represent the greatest danger to the public, and they reap the bulk of the illegal take.

We can begin with the "medical" men. For all the scientific jargon they now use, the appeal of these modern medicine men is traditional. It is little different from the lure of the hawkers of patent medicines, or worse, at bygone country fairs and carnivals. Unfortunately, it is by comparison credible, widespread and far more dangerous. As the *Journal* of the American Pharmaceutical Association once put it (in March 1958): "The patent-medicine man, with his spiels and mumbo-jumbo, of 50 or 100 years ago was a neophyte in bilking his ignorant and trusting customers compared with the modern charlatan."

Where the gallus-snapping hawker could get only a passing carnival audience for his snake oil (until he grew prosperous enough to advertise), the modern medicine operator can put his product in front of millions, instantly, by every device of modern communications. Where the hawker's crude snake oil appealed only to the gullible or the less educated in a community, the new Operator's approach is designed to trap the normal consumer, who has enough of a nodding acquaintance with scientific jargon to stimulate his interest.

The threat may lie in the nature of the product, or in the fraudulent claims made for it. A harmless potion can be the equivalent of a killer if it is purchased as a cure for a serious disease. The old-time quack operators were nothing loath to tout their products this way. Dr. King's New Discovery was the "Sure Cure for Consumption." Dr. Rupert Well's Radiatized Fluid for Cancer would "cure you at home, without pain, plaster or operation."*

Most of these old-fashioned remedies were relatively harmless, if taken in small quantities; although increasing fortification

---

* For these and the following old-time examples I am indebted to Stewart Holbrook's wise and entertaining book, *The Golden Age of Quackery* (Macmillan).

with alcohol and narcotics made some of them dangerous. A man of temperate habits could transport himself to a temporary state of euphoria with liberal draughts of medicinal Duffy's Pure Malt Whiskey ("Clergymen Endorse Duffy's"). Sears' White Star Secret Liquor Cure contained a heavy narcotic. And in 1905 a two-year-old child died, in the words of a Cincinnati coroner's report, "from the poisonous effects of opium, the result of drinking the contents of a bottle of Dr. Bull's Cough Syrup."

By the turn of the century, some of these out-and-out frauds had aroused a public outcry. Doctors and a few courageous magazine writers (courageous since the fraudulent patent medicines were such heavy advertisers) led the agitation that ultimately forced passage of the Pure Food and Drug Act in 1906. Although this legislation had its effect in curbing flagrant misrepresentations, it could hardly have anticipated either the flood of modern medicine-man advertising or the gullibility of a public that knew a little, but not much, about new scientific advances.

The country received grisly proof of this in 1937. A Tennessee doctor and drug manufacturer had heard about the new wonder drug sulfanilamide, and it occurred to him that such a well-publicized scientific remedy might do well on the market in bottled form. After experimenting with various solvents, he found that the sulfa powder dissolved nicely in diethylene glycol. He prepared some five hundred gallons of the mixture and began selling it as a patent medicine under the name of Elixir Sulfanilamide. The rest of the story was summarized by Professor Otis Pease of Stanford University, in his recent book, *Responsibilities of American Advertising:* "Within a few weeks of his first sales sixty people had died from it and ultimately it was to account for seventy-three deaths in seven states. The entire inspectors' staff of the F. and D.A. was required to track down the dispersed product before what remained of it was finally recovered and impounded."

It developed that no tests whatsoever had been made of this product before it was put on the market. Yet the case came under the provisions of the existing law of 1906—still the only one on the books—only because of a technicality, the fact that he had not put alcohol in his "elixir." The ingredient was necessary to justify the name. The manufacturer was fined $16,800 —a sum arrived at because of the repeated sales of his product. He was not liable to any more severe penalty.

In June 1938 a new food, drug and cosmetic act stiffened the sagging whalebone of the original 1906 article. It banned deceptions on labels and containers and laid down an impressive set of ground rules for testing of new drug products. Yet the Food and Drug inspectors often meet the same difficulties in making the modern law stick as do their opposite numbers in the Federal Trade Commission offices. For the most successful of the borderline Operators rarely tamper with directly dangerous mixtures. Their products generally have useful chemical ingredients. They may be analgesics of a sort, and they probably contain just enough of the advertised components to make prosecution under the Federal Pure Food and Drug statutes difficult. They do their damage principally through the gap in what the wonder remedy says—or broadly hints—it will accomplish and its actual effects.

Serious harm can come to sufferers from real ailments, from arthritis to cancer, who delude themselves that they are under treatment when they use the Operators' drugs, firm in the corollary delusion that "the government" has somehow inspected everything on the market. Others can get into trouble merely by taking the advertised dosage. They rarely pause to read the caution on box or bottle warning, for instance, that the miracle-formula reducing remedy is dangerous to people with high blood pressure (which includes many of the obese)

or that the soothing remedy ("better than an expensive prescription tranquilizer") is actually a garden-variety sedative,
not to be taken repeatedly.

The most popular of these products, and the one most
heavily ballasted with those catch-words "wonder drug," "miracle remedy" and "clinical tests," is the sure-fire remedy for
obesity. It is the one cure which hits the Genial Society—to be
unsparing—where it lives. Enough armchair philosophers have
commented on the interesting obsession of Americans with reducing, at a time when most of the world's population is more
concerned with the problems of getting fed. But even more
interesting is the national conviction that one can reduce overnight, while still overeating.

Individual doctors, the American Medical Association and
almost everyone else concerned with the problem never tire of
warning that to reduce means to stop eating so much. No jiffy
preparation, if taken without an accompanying diet, can do
the job. As Miss Maye A. Russ, director of the National Better
Business Bureau's Food, Drug and Cosmetic Division, testified
to the Blatnik subcommittee: "According to our information,
none of the known products available for over-the-counter sale
will, in themselves, cause a reduction in weight. This can be
achieved only by reducing the caloric intake in relation to
maintenance requirements. Probably the most that such products can do is serve as an aid, possibly more psychological than
physiological, in helping the user to adhere to a low-calorie
diet."

There is no doubt that some makers of nostrums in this $100,-
000,000 industry are acutely aware of their products' limitations. A good illustration was the evidence submitted by one
manufacturer to back up the "medical tests" cited in his advertising. He claimed to achieve a striking poundage reduction in
a specific number of days. To substantiate this boast, he had a

physician administer regular doses of ammonium chloride, one of his ingredients, to 27 people over a 72-hour period. One man did lose six pounds in three days. To do this, however, he had been put on a diet of 1,000 calories daily (some 2,000 calories beneath the American average) in addition to the magic tablets. His original weight, by the way, was 223.

Yet the "wonder remedy" specialists go on turning out their products and their ads with bewildering profusion. As fast as government agencies close them up by consent order or injunction, others go into business. They run in packs and in cycles. And they take care always to keep some grain of truth or plausibility tucked in among their ingredients. Their range is impressive—from steam-bath reducing suits to candy especially designed to swell in the stomach. But pills are the most popular. In this field the recent epidemic of propadrine compounds makes a revealing and typical study. (Congress—and the public—had its first good look at propadrine and the preparations that trade on it in the testimony of Miss Russ and others before the Blatnik subcommittee in 1957-58.)

As medical authorities testified, propadrine (phenylpropanolamine hydrochloride, to give it its due) have been known for 20 years. It has been used in the treatment of hay fever and other allergies. It has been on occasion an adjunct to medical treatments for obesity, but only in connection with strictly controlled diets. In these cases it was dispensed in tablets aggregating a dosage of 100 to 150 milligrams daily, always under a doctor's direction. Some doctors reported success in using it this way as an appetite depressant. But it has not been regarded as safe for indiscriminate consumption. The U.S. Food and Drug Administration insists that the following *caveat* be fixed on every product containing propadrine: "Individuals with high blood pressure, heart disease, diabetes or thyroid disease should use only as directed by a physician. Do not exceed recommended dosage."

Fat people, of course, are prone to suffer from these ailments.

In the summer of 1956 a firm called Otis Laboratories started pushing a product called E.E.D.R. ("Flushes fat right out of your body") and cited 16-year-old articles by doctors on propadrine tests to prove their point. (As consultants to the New York Academy of Medicine were soberly quoted by the Better Business Bureau: "There is nothing in this formula that would flush fat out of the body. If so, it would not be permitted to be sold without a doctor's prescription.") By October 1956 another concern, the North American Stevens Corporation, popped up with a weak propadrine compound called E.H.P. (Eat Half Plan). E.H.P. was preceded by a fanfare of advertising, e.g., "Now, Released to you! The First wonder drug for reducing . . ." Fortified by "medical proof," the ads claimed that users could slough off 33 pounds of "ugly, excess fat" without giving up a single helping of mashed potatoes. (On May 14, 1957, this outfit signed a Post Office Department stipulation agreeing to discontinue use of the mails.)

On the heels of the E.H.P. people (who later reissued their product under the catch name of No-Di-Et), the Alleghany Pharmacal Corp. started turning out a slightly stronger propadrine compound called Hungrex. "Announcing the most powerful, yet safe reducing drug ever released for public use," the spiel ran. "Federal Health authorities now release safe drug for reducing that limits the ability of your body to produce sensations of hunger. . . . Clinical tests on 1,880 fat people show fantastic weight losses. . . ." Hungrex made its peace with the Post Office in July 1957.

N.D. 17, put out by Fisk Research, Inc., in January 1957, touted the "first no-diet reducing wonder drug used successfully by thousands of physicians! Lose as many pounds as you like without diets of any kind, without exercise, without giving up the kinds of food you love to eat." (Fisk agreed to discontinue mail advertising a half year later.) The makers of a similar compound cried out: "Now! Reducing Wonder Drug Used by Thousands of Doctors Available Without a Doctor's Prescription." The "doctors" remained anonymous.

Next reducing pill to appear, and probably the most heavily advertised, was Regimen tablets. These products of the Wonder Drug Corp. were preceded by a thunderous drumbeating for "no-diet reducing." "Doctors," ran the ads, "know what's good for you. They know all the different methods to reduce—the scientific way to attack excessive weight. They normally prescribe—not one—but a careful combination of drugs, which is the basis of Regimen tablets . . ."

The new "no-diet reducing wonder-drug," according to its sponsors, was born of intensive clinical tests and its medical effects were new and revolutionary ("works through the blood stream, directly on the cause of your overweight . . ."). Dr. Leon S. Hirsch, of Cincinnati, Ohio, one of the first doctors to use propadrine experimentally—and, even more pertinently, one of the medical authorities cited in the Regimen ads—had a more pessimistic view. Testifying before the Blatnik subcommittee, he said: "There is no such thing as no-diet reducing as advertised by these promoters." He pointed out that neither Regimen nor other manufacturers had any right to use his tests as basis for their claim. Not only were the tablet dosages far weaker, but the ad copy continued to overlook the fact that his patients in the experiment had been on a strict diet at the time. "I do not endorse these worthless and dangerous products," he said, "and consider their promotion for over-the-counter sale to be a deliberate attempt to exploit for profit the unfortunate persons who are afflicted with the disease termed 'obesity.'"

In 1957 the Post Office filed a complaint against Regimen,

for advertising based on "false and fraudulent" statements. (In June Regimen signed its affidavit agreeing to discontinue use of the mails in this enterprise.) But over-the-counter sales continued. In July 1958 the F.T.C. brought its own action against Regimen. Regimen's makers contended the F.T.C. complaint quoted their ads out of context, but in April 1959 they consented to an order banning certain claims. (The F.T.C. later vacated this order, a comparatively mild one, and continued to investigate the product.) In November 1959 the New York District Attorney's office seized TV film commercials, various books and financial records pertaining to Regimen for its own investigation.

Through it all many TV viewers could still see the magic sales pitch between the truncated segments of their old movies —in 1959 Regimen was among the top fifty TV advertisers nationally.* The same people smiled through their "before" and "after" routines, displaying the svelte dress sizes they were *now* able to wriggle into. The only discernible difference in the sales pitch was that the exact reducing time limit no longer appeared, e.g., "I lost six pounds in *days* with Regimen." Over-the-counter sales were apparently excellent.

Meanwhile, other contenders had entered the field. An item called 7-Day Reducer ("Friends, from government health authorities in Washington, D.C. . . .") was followed successively by Trimet (". . . you too can lose weight safely . . ."), Curb-wate ("U.S. Health authorities release amazing doctor-approved ingredient. . . .") and others. The *reductio ad absurdum* in the activities of the reducing merchants was a reducing cigarette. "Trim," ran the TV promotion, "is will power in cigarette form."

Hunger, Trim's inventor argued, is mostly psychological in our civilization (an interesting sidelight on the Genial Society's

---

* In November 1959, the National Broadcasting Company, for its part, notified Regimen that it was unwilling to accept its current advertising copy.

success in remodeling traditional concepts to suit its own situation). He submitted that the best way to cut down on hunger pangs was to cause a puckering sensation "similar to what would be felt by taking alum in the mouth." The concurrent smoking pleasure could help alleviate any desire to eat. The wonder ingredient of Trims was none other than tartaric acid, the same substance, when mixed with Rochelle salt and bicarbonate of soda, which gave us the old-fashioned Seidlitz Powders.

A group in New York and Cambridge, Mass., known as the Cornell Drug Company brought Trim out in 1957. In July 1958, long after operations started, the U.S. government confiscated a shipment of Trims as a violation of the Federal Food, Drug and Cosmetic Act. Among the alleged mislabelings to cause the government action were these: 1) "smoking three Trims per day will bring about a definite weight loss over a given period"; 2) Trims are safe for "everybody"; 3) "doctor-approved"; 4) "after years of clinical tests." The misrepresentation involved was more than enough to convince the regulatory agencies that Trim was something less than "the miracle-reducing discovery of the century." Tartaric acid, furthermore, is a combustible. The government added dryly that Trim's manufacturers used it without having submitted any data on its safety.

Such tales could be told equally well about the other corners of the medical operator's world. The cure artist has no hesitation in taking on more meaningful claims for his products than mere weight reduction. Arthritis is perhaps his most popular target. It should now be well known that this is a serious condition, which needs the personal examination of a physician. The National Better Business Bureau, for one, has recommended that no product be advertised for the home treatment of arthritis. But each year "new medical compounds" keep coming down the pike. They are all purportedly guaranteed to make arthritics feel like circus athletes scant days after the first dosage. A random look at the files of the Federal Trade Commission will indicate the scope of the arthritis cure-alls. A man named Ivan D. Hussey, Atlanta, Ga., agrees to stop palming off Ar-Thry-Go, a run-of-the-mill painkiller, as a remedy capable of arresting the progress of arthritis or any rheumatic condition. The Reed Products Corp. in St. Louis, Mo., is prohibited from claiming that its product Ar-Pan-Ex is effective in treating arthritis—to say nothing of rheumatism, sciatica, lumbago, neuritis or neuralgia. Another St. Louis enterpriser is prohibited from claiming that his Warsene Capsules are effective against arthritis and rheumatism, and contain the same ingredients as a doctor's prescription.*

Like the reducing pills, the arthritis cure-alls are advertised as the product of some "revolutionary new formula, medically approved . . . clinically tested . . ." Their pitch has a familiar ring: ". . . acts fast. Take one tablet tonight and wake up tomorrow morning without arthritis—rheumatism pains . . . or pay nothing . . ."

In their breathless approach the arthritis "cure" salesmen resemble the "fast fast fast relief" billings of reputable analgesics like aspirin, Bufferin and others, whose TV announcers, at least, tend to give the impression that pain is banished the minute you set eyes on the bottle. There is one significant difference. The reputable advertisers must point out that theirs are merely painkillers, which will give only "temporary" relief to "minor" ailments. The frauds go a deadly step further, promising a cure which no medicine is yet capable of giving.

Anemia, epilepsy, tuberculosis, stomach ulcers and cancer are among the ailments which the cure-all makers claim to heal.

---

* These examples happen to be taken from FTC releases of February-March 1958. Similar cases can be found in any period.

Doctors can tell their patients the sad truth that no magic remedies have yet been found for these diseases, but the number of people who buy cure-alls with this expectation steadily increases. Some of the devices offered to the gullible are bizarre in the extreme—notably the popular "atomic" or "electronic" cures that lean heavily for their impressiveness on systems of flashing light bulbs and mysterious electric buzzes. If most of them are harmless in themselves, they continue to divert sick people from proper treatment.

Of all medical frauds, the cruelest is the fake cancer cure. The National Association of Better Business Bureaus recently made a conservative estimate of the amount annually tossed away on cancer "cures" as $10,000,000. The real toll, medically speaking, is impossible to assess. Some cancer "experts" like Harry M. Hoxsey stayed in business for 30 years. At the two Hoxsey "clinics" in Portage, Pa., and Dallas, Tex., cancer sufferers paid a base fee of $400 (extras added) for an "examination" followed by the administration of various Hoxsey medicines and pills. All of them were declared worthless after examination by government laboratories.

Twice, in 1953 and 1956, federal courts ruled that Hoxsey's cancer pills were illegally misrepresented as useful remedies. In 1957 the Food and Drug Administration issued a public warning against the treatments, which consist "essentially of simple drugs which are worthless in treating cancer." The warning continued: "Cancer can be cured only through surgery or radiation. Death from cancer is inevitable when cancer patients fail to obtain proper medical treatment because of the lure of a 'painless cure' " Yet Hoxsey did not cease operations until late in 1958.

There are institutions, some of them long established, with more modest claims, which do not offer fraudulent pills, but whose theories are not accepted by the medical profession. The

Ball Clinic, for example, at Excelsior Springs, Mo., specializes in arthritis, rheumatism "and all chronic states of ill health associated with, or attributable to rheumatic conditions." This institution relies heavily on attractive ads. Respondents receive a free 36-page booklet about arthritis and rheumatism, along with a "personal case history" form, to be filled out. If they are judged suitable, they are urged to get on the next plane or train and avail themselves of the "Ball Clinic Free Physical Examination and Free Diagnosis."

Once under the tent in Excelsior Springs, would-be patients are persuaded that only a well-equipped institution (with a record of 70,000 "successfully treated") can hope to get at the cause of serious ailments. These include kidney diseases, gall-bladder diseases, liver trouble, jaundice, migraine headaches, colitis, high blood pressure, low blood pressure, obesity, malnutrition [sic], neuralgia, and many others. Surgery, Ball warns, is no answer. Nor can a local doctor "successfully assume full responsibility for your physical welfare." What they need is Ball's equipment and its high-powered staff of "medical doctors, osteopaths and chiropractors."

The efficacy of Ball's remedies can be gathered from the claims set forth for them. They include the "health-giving mineral waters" of Excelsior Springs (equally effective through bathing or internal use) and theories such as these: chronic colitis is a prevalent cause of rheumatism; constipation generally results in more sickness than any other known cause; massage not only develops the muscles of the chest but stimulates the bowels, glands and digestive power. The American Medical Association commented: "We cannot recommend the Ball Clinic in Excelsior Springs, Missouri. . . . It does not appear on our register of approved hospitals."

Indigent or thrifty sufferers, who dislike doctors and prefer to avoid fatiguing travel, might still solace themselves—and all too frequently do—by investing instead in one of the numerous mail-order plastic "steam bath suits" or one of the many available "wonderful new pain-relieving therma-mineral preparations" for banishing their rheumatic aches and pains.

The newest and fastest-growing of the medical merchants' products is the nonprescription tranquilizer. The regular tranquilizing pill, barely five years after it appeared on the market in any quantity, is now a staple. The tranquilizing drugs, of which the best known are meprobamate, reserpine and chlorpromazine, have jumped from a $50,000,000 business in 1956 to a booming $300,000,000 worth of sales in 1959. The principal tranquilizing ingredients are authenticated as effective soothers of tension and anxiety among the neurotic. But doctors are understandably cautious about their use. As early as 1956, the American Psychiatric Association warned that the "casual" use of tranquilizers is "medically unsound and constitutes a public danger." The Association asked its members to resist pressure both from their patients and high-pressure drug salesmen* and to be sparing in their allotment of tranquilizer prescriptions.

Warnings like this struck certain drug manufacturers in the manner of a fire bell awakening a sleeping Dalmatian. Since that time they have tried their best to scatter their own substitute or "semitranquilizers" among the public, with no prescriptions needed. Preparations containing ingredients such as ordinary bromides, or antihistamines, were dusted off and paraded behind a barrage of impressive advertising—and they

---

* Drug salesmen need not be "high-pressure" to net their employers huge returns. Quite aside from the question of fraud in its imitators, the legitimate drug industry has been accused of heavily swollen profits. In 1960 a Senate subcommittee uncovered the fact that major drug companies charge 15 per cent of a pill's cost to profits, and another 15 per cent to the cost of promotion. The average profit of the leaders of the drug industry is more than twice that of industry in general.

still are. "An amazing new medical formula," runs the prospectus for one pill, "scientifically formulated like a doctor's
prescription . . ." Furthermore, it can be used with absolute
safety, the ads say; just follow the directions on the box.

As with so many similar preparations, the directions on the
box tell a different story. "Do not," the label reads, "exceed more
than 5 tablets in 24 hours except upon doctor's advice. If
symptoms persist after 21 days discontinue use and consult
your doctor. Some drowsiness may occur as part of the relaxation process; if it does, do not drive or operate machinery.
CAUTION: use only as directed. Continued use or dosage in
excess of that recommended may result in serious effects. Not
for use by children or persons with kidney disorders unless
advised by doctor. Discontinue use if skin rash occurs, if dizzi-
ness or blurring of vision results, or if nervous symptoms persist, and consult your doctor . . ."

The Food and Drug Administration sometimes accomplishes
a formal seizure on the understandable grounds of misrepresentation. But for every such bromide knocked out of the
market, many others proliferate. There is, we seem to believe,
a solution for almost any ill, obtainable in capsule form at the
corner drugstore.

Which leads us to vitamin and nutrition frauds, a branch of
commercial chicanery that makes the fake-tranquilizer business
look comparatively harmless and sophisticated. The self-appointed "health and nutrition" experts operate on a larger scale
than any other variety of cure-all enterprise. The Secretary of
Health, Education and Welfare, Arthur S. Flemming, noted in
1958: "Unscrupulous operations in this field have become the
most widespread and expensive form of medical quackery in
the country today." Their products include vitamin pills, mineral compounds, special diet aids, tonics, varieties of health

foods, elixirs, magic vibrators and other mechanical devices like the pressure-cooking pan (price: $180) which allegedly "vaporizes" food to make it easier on the stomach.

Nowhere else is it so difficult, also, to distinguish the reputable producer or even the honest and well-intentioned food faddist from the operator out to make a killing. The preparations of the first, e.g., vitamin pills, are useful for specific purposes and often ordered by doctors as necessary in the cases of patients suffering from certain disorders. The special diets of the food faddist rarely produce the euphoria of mind and body claimed for them; but they are seldom harmful. Many Americans get valuable exercise at least from their daily pilgrimages to obscure stores purveying varieties of special breads, herbs, etc., and Anglo-Saxon civilization in general would be lonesome without its quota of individualists who eat raw vegetables for breakfast.

Yet the reputable manufacturer may have little control over the unscrupulous salesmen, working through jobbers or dealers, who may dispose of his product. The original food faddist may not even know about the "health-food lecturer" who transforms nutritional hobbies into high-pressured cure-alls for actual diseases. There are no less than 50,000 salesmen of diet and health products in action today. The records of local health authorities and the Food and Drug Administration indicate that an alarming percentage are either crooked or notoriously loose in the claims they make for their products. In New York City, the Board of Health has received so many complaints about their abuses that a 1959 regulation is being enforced, banning house-to-house sales of items with therapeutic claims.

In Rochester, N.Y., according to an article in the *Wall Street Journal*, a man and his wife were successfully prosecuted in 1958 just for this sort of advertising. "Mine is an amazing case," the man's door-to-door message used to begin; "I had an ulcerated stomach, arthritis, neuritis, pyorrhea. I wore glasses. I had a 44-inch waistline and high blood pressure. Well, I was finished. When everything else failed, doctors and medication, I still knew that God wanted life in this body. . . . So I asked along these lines and I got one word: food. Now I can trace everybody's unnatural condition to malnutrition. There is no cure except the body does its curing if it gets what it needs to do it with."

What he claimed the body needed was his own dietary aid, a mixture with a tasty alfalfa-and-watercress base. He advertised it as effective for curing 22 diseases or medical conditions, from "that let-down feeling" to multiple sclerosis. He and his wife were fined $500 apiece, but not before they had exacted a vastly heavier toll from their health-conscious customers.

Such an appeal, as recorded by a Food and Drug Administration inspector, sounds primitive, and it is. But its success is amazing. The FDA never tires of pointing out that "Americans have to go out of their way, nutritionally speaking, to avoid being well nourished. . . . The normal American diet now includes such a variety of foods that most persons can hardly fail to have an ample supply of the essential food constituents." Yet for millions the fountain of youth and health continues to sparkle just around the corner.

There are four basic myths that keep the fountain bubbling. They bob up again and again in the revivalistic speeches of the "health-food lecturers," the door-to-door salesmen, or the come-on ads. They are:

1. The myth that all disease is due to faulty diet, or supposed "chemical imbalances." The exponents of this one hold that it is next to impossible for the average person to eat a completely adequate diet. "Now, to remedy this imbalance, we have here a scientifically tested preparation . . ."

2. The myth that soil depletion causes malnutrition. This is founded on the argument that repeated cropping has taken "vital nutritional elements" from the soil, etc. Actually, the only disease known to be linked with soil or water deficiencies is goiter, due to lack of iodine. This can easily be remedied by the use of iodized salt.

3. The myth of overprocessing. Starting with a small grain of truth, the cure-all salesmen claim to replenish all the "natural" elements normally removed by cooking and food processing through special foods, cookers, etc. In point of fact, most of these elements are replenished by healthy added vitamins, or minerals. The best evidence of this, the FDA notes, is "the fact that once-prevalent deficiency diseases such as rickets and pellagra are now so rare that it's difficult to find a case for clinical study."

4. The myth of subclinical deficiencies. There is no basis for the claim that "that tired feeling" or various unexplained aches or pains can be cured by dietary supplements. Young children and pregnant mothers need special attention like vitamins C and D, or calcium; but these are special cases, to be decided by physicians.

Tricked out in varieties of pseudoscientific finery, the myths reinforce the body of ancient inherited superstition about foods and their uses. They can be dangerous, when believed. It is harmless, as an FDA study notes, to think that fish and celery are "brain foods" or that oysters increase fertility, "but when garlic pills are promoted for high blood pressure, or grapes for the treatment of ulcers and cancer, the price of ignorance may come high." Despite the high-pressure advertising on their behalf, maté, or Paraguayan tea, has no special healing properties; kelp is not a cure for stomach ailments or obesity; honey will not banish whooping cough; root beer does nothing for the nerves; baking soda will not cure colds; grape juice will not reduce weight; blueberry juice has no effect on diabetes; and olive oil will not prevent appendicitis.

That people can obtain "blessed relief" from mechanical devices is just as illusory. The FDA spent a good deal of its energies during 1958 blowing the whistle on certain makers of vibrators. These range from small portable cushions to big upholstered chairs. The manufacturers claimed that they would not only reduce weight, but also cure or prevent arthritis, rheumatism or bursitis. Already doing a land-office business, they grew increasingly careless about the nature of their advertising. "One machine promotor," wrote the FDA Director of Enforcement, Malcolm R. Stephens, "claimed his device [a rigid cushion containing a small electric motor] would relieve menstrual cramps, backaches, headaches, hypertension and nervous tensions of the heart. According to expert medical opinion, the benefits of vibrators are limited to *temporary* relief for *minor* physical conditions. They may be soothing and relaxing to the user and help to relieve minor aches and pains due to fatigue or overexertion. They should not be represented as effective for treating diseases or weight reduction."

One of the worst capers in the nutritional field, in recent memory, was the campaign of a New York firm in 1957 and 1958 to sell compounds of a "royal jelly." Known in certain incarnations as "Royal Jelly Capsules" or "Beauty for Life Capsules," this preparation was based on a widely advertised "scientific" discovery that human beings could profit greatly from the substance prepared by worker bees for the particular nourishment of the queen bee. The queen bee, quite possibly because of this food, lives longer than the worker bees, grows larger and lays millions of eggs—facts well known to biologists. The purpose of this company's nationwide advertising campaign was, in a word, to persuade numbers of American consumers that what was good for the queen bee was good for the country.

"Royal Jelly," the ad headlines read, "the Queen Bee's Special Food . . . Its Secret of Prolonged Life . . . Doctors Report 'Miracle' Royal Jelly May Change Your Whole Life. . . ." As first advertised, one product promised to cure: impotency or "lost manhood," Parkinson's disease, heart conditions and disabilities of the motor nerves. It offered fertility to women during the period of menopause and insured longevity for anybody. The jelly also claimed to "produce a pleasing state of relaxed well-being . . . permit prolonged intellectual work without tiring . . . give a feeling of increased sexual drive and energy, especially to men and women over forty." ("All orders rushed to you in plain wrapper.")

A battery of doctors was summoned into print to support the claims, but none of them was quoted or described with what might be called accuracy. The most complete scientific report on Royal Jelly was allegedly prepared by Dr. Frederick Banting, the discoverer of insulin. Actually, Sir Frederick Banting had been dead 16 years by the time the Royal Jelly people set up shop. What work was done in his laboratory investigated only the chemical composition of the queen bee's jelly, without reference to its use on human beings. Other claims were similarly vague or uncheckable, e.g., "reports from Europe tell of an 80-year-old Gentleman whose physical condition would make a 50-year-old envious. The man regularly partakes of Royal Jelly . . ."

After a year's work by the Post Office Department and the Food and Drug Administration, some blessed relief to the consumer was given by the federal courts, through the favorable outcome of enforcement actions against the manufacturer. But the advertising had been so widespread that Secretary Flemming found it expedient in November of 1958 to issue a specific warning to the public about claims still being made. "For bees," he said, "royal jelly is indeed a miracle food, but it has no practical value for humans as a food, drug or cosmetic. The claims made for it are groundless."

A fraud far crueler in its implication was an attempt made in New York State to market another "miracle of science"—a "brain food" designed to improve mental functioning in backward children. The entrepreneur behind this scheme had packaged for sale a vitamin dietary supplement rich in wheat gluten. The supplement is undeniably nutritious. It can be bought from reputable drug or vitamin sales outlets at about $1 per hundred tablets. As his self-appointed reward, perhaps, for claiming it would cure sick minds, this operator hiked the price up to $5.

Mercifully, he was caught at an early stage of his operations. New York State's Bureau of Consumer Frauds and Protection put him out of business (by a civil agreement) in December 1958—thereby furnishing one more argument for the usefulness of organizations like it.

The Genial Society's pursuit of personal happiness is not after all limited to inner physical well-being. No red-blooded citizen can long be content with mere "tranquility and blessed relief." Hence the wide and fertile market for cosmetic improvements and body-building and beautifying devices.

Leading any list of what the experts call "cosmetic frauds" are those perennial life partners, the hair restorer and the bust developer. Exponents of the former, working through their local "salons" or heavily advertised special shampoos or solvents, like to pose as "one of America's foremost professional authorities on hair and scalp disorders." Their ads hold forth the possibilities not only of preventing baldness, but—as one merchant put it—of causing new hair to grow in 95 to 97 per cent of all cases. Almost invariably, the advertiser claims that his preparation is "an amazing revolutionary treatment for the scalp and hair . . . now possible through a modern miracle of science."

The Federal Trade Commission and local Better Business Bureaus shout themselves hoarse each year warning about the dubiousness of such claims, but the warnings do little good. In fact the hair-restoring merchants are almost unfailingly able to get honest testimonials from their more nearsighted customers that hair veritably sprouted after the first steady applications. What hair can be grown is only a fuzzlike growth called "baby hair," which soon washes out, leaving the pate as bald as ever. Dermatologists testify that hereditary or male pattern baldness is impossible to cure by any known means. Where falling hair is the specific result of a medical condition, it may be helped, but only by specific medical treatment.

The most damning testimony against the hair restorers, however, explains why so much of their work is done through the mails. FTC and Post Office Department inspectors have long chuckled over the fact that most of these people are themselves quite bald.

Concurrently with the hair-restoring propaganda, a stream of ads and circulars continues to tell American womanhood that even the dowdiest can hope to have what the Chrysler Corporation used to call the Forward Look. Some of the advertised bust developers, after the plain wrapping is removed, turn out to be nothing more than a pair of dumbbells, tied with pink ribbon, with perfunctory directions for their use. Others are more ingenious. One firm offered its customers a glass tube, to be held in the lady's mouth while she performed various exercises, thereby arousing chest circulation and developing the pectoral muscles.

There is no scientific basis, needless to say, for the claim that devices of this sort can produce larger busts through exercise. They are at least relatively harmless—unlike many of the tablets or estrogenic creams which are also packaged for this purpose. Estrogenic (hormone) preparations should not be

used except under a doctor's supervision. Whatever development this method may produce can be more than canceled out
by the possibility of dangerous aftereffects.

The makers of such articles are very often the same people
who deal in the painless "weight-reducing" schemes, or the
glossy cure-alls for more serious physical disorders. Living as
they do on the margins of legitimate business activity, they have
developed a Protean ability for changing their corporate shape
to suit the market—and the current state of federal or local
enforcement drives. Take the career of one John T. Andreadis,
sometimes known as Timolean T. Andreadis or John T. Andre,
as it crops up in the files of federal regulatory agencies and
the Better Business Bureau.* In October 1946 Mr. Andreadis
first broke into notoriety as the subject of a Postal Fraud Order
enjoining the sale of his "Glamour Mold Self Massage Kit" designed to reapportion ladies' weights in the most flattering
way possible. In February of 1948 a second enterprise, Hollywood Beauty Consultants, ran afoul of the Post Office through
its handy "Hollywood Body Toner" scheme for reducing.

In May 1955 Andreadis agreed, at the Post Office Department's further insistence, to discontinue claims made for a
product called Sustamin, which purported to cure arthritis and
rheumatism. While Andreadis' lawyers were settling matters
with the Post Office Department, his Wonder Drug Corporation
was getting further government complaints with its advertising
for Regimen tablets.

Another busy enterpriser named David L. Ratke was arrested in New York City in August of 1959 for a variety of
"false and misleading advertisements." Among his present
and past promotions was Livigen, a "skin food" that claimed to
remove wrinkles, the superwonder "7-Day Reducer," and a

* And also specifically noted in the Blatnik testimony.

"golden liquid" called Favinol, "nature's tissue-growing secret," that encourages "a clear, new skin to grow in overnight." A man of far-ranging, eclectic interests, he had also gone outside of the cosmetic line, through the years, with such lively products as the Borg-Johnson Pocket Radio (already mentioned in Chapter II), a falsely touted battery additive, a car cloth named Roll-A-Shine which conspicuously did not "end car waxing, washing, polishing forever," "Powdered Heat" pellets which were equally ineffective in their claim to "end snow shoveling forever," a phony lawn beautifier and a misleading mail-order tree-nursery business.

It is not too difficult to establish the true nature of the Andreadis and Ratke concern in the field of self-improvement. The files of both federal and state law-enforcement agencies are rich in similar case histories. Yet the problem of regulating these Operators' activities is very often a matter of degree, which makes it a peculiarly difficult one for the law to handle. A fake arthritis cure, an illusory bust developer or a speciously worded ad promising "airline careers" with "free nationwide job placement" can be exposed—on occasion—and isolated for the frauds they are. What about the overzealous copy writer who cleverly gives the impression that a reputable chewing gum company's products can bring weight down the easy way—with "diets" mentioned in a brisk undertone?

Or tooth paste ads? There are few appeals more familiar than the exhortations to brush your teeth with the *new* dentrifice "with the scientific ingredient 77-B2, banishing tooth decay, and eliminating harmful germs forever." We forgive their hyperbole, confident that their message is essentially hygienic and trustworthy. Yet representatives of the American Dental Association have testified that the major manufacturers of tooth pastes lull Americans into bad dental habits with their assurances of secret ingredients and the need for minimal brushings. False advertising, the dentists say.

Or take the large and hence presumably reputable dancing school that brings the customers in for a "free lesson," only to bludgeon them, if they are unwary, into accepting a long and highly expensive instruction contract, an unending treadmill of cha-chas, mambos and Viennese waltzes, done at a far faster financial tempo than the customer can afford.

The latter device is only the latest fashion in the sort of enticement that rubs shoulders with outright fraud. Far too many dance studios have begun to get their customers with promises of jolly parties, glamorous teaching partners and adroit compliments about the neophyte's rhythmic potential. Some now offer life memberships to the unwary. But once his checkbook is bound to the dance floor, the customer notes that the quality of instruction often falls off. The vivacious creature who mamboed with him last week is now working on a new prospect in the adjoining studio; the parties are something less than lonely-heart meccas; but the installment due dates keep coming up.

In October 1959 three major dance studios in New York City, Arthur Murray Dance Studios, Dale Dance Studios and Fred Astaire, Inc., were among the first to sign a code of ethics after some conferences with the state Attorney General's office. Among other clauses the code provided for plainly marked contracts, the use of competent instructors and refunds of money paid, if the student were forced to discontinue his course.

A similarly interesting tale can be told of the numerous health and body-building emporia which have lately sprung up over the country. Like the dancing schools, some of the reputable gyms merely hook the customer into a long, long com-

mitment. If he wishes, he can come in to flex his muscles every
week of his life—although the exact pleasures to be found in
so doing seldom live up to the prospectus. But among the gyms
he is also likely to find outright frauds. In 1959, for instance,
New York State's consumer frauds bureau was getting a heavy
volume of complaints from people who had signed up for long
months or even years of body-building sessions, only to find
the gymnasiums inexplicably closed for "alterations." One lady
in New York City found herself thus locked out after only two
weeks of instruction. (She had signed up for a year's course.)
She wrote a plaintive letter to the frauds bureau, asking *a*)
whether she was required to keep up payments, and *b*) how
she could get her sneakers back. Such dodges reached proportions where a state law was passed, giving the state injunctive
powers against firms abusing the long-term contract plan.

Crookedness of a far more obvious nature is found in the
"degree mills" still grinding out their ration of phony diplomas
in various states of the Union, ranging from A.B. or B.S. degrees
to high-flown articles like the D.D.M. (for Doctor of Divinity
in Metaphysics). A 1959 publication of the American Council
of Education noted that "more than two hundred such colleges
and universities were discovered, with operating addresses in
at least thirty-seven states. . . . One association that represents
many of these phony colleges and universities, and maintains
a seal of approval for their use, states that their annual business
amounts to $75,000,000 and that their enrollment in one recent
year was 750,000 students."*

Such figures represent only a fraction of the total amount of
fake or borderline institutions offering on-the-spot or corre-
spondence-school training for trades, crafts or specific jobs—
like certain notorious airline-hostess training courses which
purport to furnish not only training but guaranteed employment

* *American Degree Mills*, by Robert H. Reid.

if the student pays her money. But some institutions granting college or graduate-level "degrees" are obviously the most egregious frauds of them all. They are hardly a new phenomenon. Diploma mills were well known as far back as the 1880's and 90's, when some particularly nasty scandals involving the sale of bogus medical degrees were uncovered in the Midwest. After World War II, the Veterans Administration turned up many of them, in the course of investigating institutions qualified to give instruction under the G.I. Bill of Rights law. But they have never so proliferated as at present.

The reasons for this are simple. First, the college degree has been enshrined as the most necessary of all status symbols in our world. The higher the degree the better. When a degree means an increase both in earning power and community position, the incentive increases to get one, by hook or by crook. The second reason is the emergence of new countries and new technological opportunities throughout the postwar world. In the technological sense, all of the new countries look up to the United States (if not, with sadly increased frequency, to the Soviet Union) as the fountainhead of modern efficiency. "An American degree" in Burma or Indonesia—or for that matter in Italy—may mean an even greater rise in status for its owner than for an American at home.

For these degrees, or many of them, are legal. The institution may offer the sketchiest kind of brush-up courses in its curriculum. It may consist of nothing more than a promoter and a few secretaries, mailing out their certifications after the student has done no more than send his money order and fill out a lengthy application blank. But the loopholes in many state laws governing the granting of degrees are big enough to accommodate a regular college campus. Actual accreditation of a school by competent educational authority is often a long and difficult process; state examining boards which grant licenses in the professions are often notoriously strict. But in many states an institution can legally grant degrees merely by paying a nominal fee for incorporation.

It was this way in California before 1957 (the incorporation fee was $25). In that year a subcommittee of the state legislature began an investigation of this abuse. The subcommittee found between 50 and 100 "diploma mills" operating in the state, most of them in the Los Angeles area. As in other states, their activities were bringing down complaints from foreign countries as well as their own. A native of Samoa, for instance, had paid $1,000 to a Honolulu doctor to secure a Ph.D. degree from an unaccredited California "university." He was delighted to find that the Californians threw in a Bachelor of Science degree for good measure.

The California investigation resulted in a stiff 1958 state law which sets forth specific conditions under which an institution may grant degrees. To grant "a diploma of any nature," the institution must get the approval of the state Superintendent of Public Instruction. The evidence suggests that the diploma traffic in California is no longer a serious factor.

However laudable the premise of strong local government, the fact remains that "diploma factories" and hundreds of other frauds thrive on the existence of separate standards for educational certification and law enforcement in each state. For want of a uniform federal norm, the 1958 action of the California legislators must be repeated, state by state, wherever the degree factories thrive. Ultimately, the Council of State Governments may negotiate some degree of co-ordination.

Divided authority, however, is only part of the problem. Relatively few definite ground rules can be laid for such fraud's detection. In the last analysis, every plan or clinic or preparation must be investigated and tested on its own merits. There are obviously many legitimate diets, good health foods, beneficial medicines and well-run correspondence schools serving this country. The job of uprooting the fraudulent minority is made tougher since the Operators strive always to adopt the protective coloration of honest enterprises. And the size of the enforcement staffs which must separate the good from the dishonest is distressingly small.

At least until recently, for example, the entire Division of Scientific Opinions in the FTC's Bureau of Investigation has operated on a budget of well under $100,000. Only a fraction of this amount is allocated for medical testing. The Food and Drug Administration devotes a larger amount of time and money to medical frauds, but its jurisdiction over them is sharply restricted. Local agencies in some states and cities do additional police work in this field, of course, but *their* effectiveness is necessarily limited not only by their own resources, but by the fact that the cleverest of the medical fraud or borderline operations are interstate.

So the Federal Trade Commission and, within its jurisdiction, the Post Office Department, work with Better Business Bureaus and, sometimes, local Chambers of Commerce to restrict this kind of large-scale chicanery. They are handicapped by the legal constrictions prevailing in consumer protective work. It always has been the agency which must prove that the advertiser has intentionally misrepresented his product, or worse. Action against a cure-all promoter may be resisted through months of tortuous legal argument. It is all too rarely that the Federal Trade Commission uses the injunctive power given to it.

Meanwhile, back at the factory, the arthritis "remedy" or the "no-diet" reducer is rolling off its small assembly line and roping in the suckers through heavy advertising campaigns. Often, by the time the undermanned agencies get around to taking action, the operators have so thoroughly exploited their particular product that they are only too happy to sign an affidavit of discontinuance or accept a consent order abandoning a particular practice. This done, they can then move on to the next product. As we have seen, some entrepreneurs make a career of switching businesses, always just a few months ahead of government action.

The public health, as well as the public pocketbook, would profit greatly from the same increase in regulatory power already advocated to protect the consumer in general. Representative Blatnik said after his House subcommittee's investigation of some FTC operations: "Generally we have to have economy. But I am asking: can the American citizen support this most lucrative racket of any criminal activity, running into hundreds of millions of dollars? It is not a question whether we can afford it. We are already paying for it."

Some precedent has already been set in Congress toward putting more teeth in the health laws. In March 1959, after nine years of legislative haggling, a new amendment to the Food, Drug, and Cosmetic Act became effective. It ordered manufacturers to pretest food additives and submit data proving their safety to the Pure Food and Drug Administration before going on the market with them. In itself, this is not specifically directed against medical fraud; but it sets a powerful precedent in putting the burden of proof on the producer, not the inspecting agency. As John L. Harvey, Deputy FDA Commissioner, noted, "This is the first law anywhere on the globe that requires a food to be proved safe before it can be marketed." Extended to the field of health advertising, other laws like this could drive much dangerous quackery out of business.

But the enforcement agencies by themselves, if they grew tenfold, could not eliminate such operators. In medical frauds, even more than in simple consumer frauds, the Operator finds his greatest ally in the make-up of the Genial Society. Its members are so used to being protected by government or other organizations that individual suspicions are eroded far beyond the danger point. Because so many things in their life—the water they drink, the food they eat, the cars they drive in, even the books they read—are tested by some "big organization," they have a pathetic faith in the indefinite extension of the testing process. Because they see so many medical advances, their suspicions for the most extravagant claims are completely disarmed. What Senator Warren G. Magnuson, Chairman of the Senate Commerce Committee, angrily denounces as indiscriminate "white coat" advertising has a fatal fascination for the modern American.

Witness the ads of the modern cure-all promoters. Slogans like "government-approved," "medically tested," "doctors say" run through them almost without fail. They are the tested ingredients for producing the proper Pavlovian salivations in the consumer. The modern American cannot easily be excused when he accepts the Operators' unsupported testimony that he can be cured, improved or beautified without lifting a finger. Why take so many bland assumptions on blind faith? Many social critics have already made the point that faith in technical progress can degenerate into a semireligious superstition, as real and as unshakable as medieval excesses in relic-hunting or the Puritan belief in witchcraft. There are not many Americans, of whatever religious faith, who actually believe that God can work concrete miracles for them. There are a great many who believe that doctors can. And if doctors, why not the "magic wonder drug" of the TV commercial?

No civilization in the world's history has ever so hated and feared death—if only because death has been proved so often to have been accidental, unnecessary or easily prevented by "prompt medical precautions." Take a sample appeal of a respected and very useful fund-raising organization, the American Cancer Society, as it appeared not long ago, sandwiched between the brassière and beauty ads in *Glamour*, the popular magazine for young ladies. "You know those rare days," the message begins, "when *everything* checks? Air smells good. Food tastes terrific. Even the old face looks good in the mirror. *Today* can be that kind of day. Just do two things. Call your doctor for a thorough medical check-up for cancer. Then write out a check—a nice fat one—to the American Cancer Society. . . ."

A poet or a priest in the worst ages of "superstition" might have found some macabre humor in the thought of dedicating the first balmy day to a cancer check-up. But health is the one aspect of life which we moderns take with grim sobriety. He who does not is our closest equivalent to what the Puritans used to call a public blasphemer.

It would help if the Genial Society could season this dedication to medical progress with some intelligent skepticism. We might do a little more checking with real doctors before we take the word of the "medically approved" nostrum in the advertising pages or the white-coated hawker in the TV commercial. Otherwise, however muscular the government policing agencies grow, we shall still be shelling out our money, and often endangering our lives, for the fake reducing tablets, the specious health-diet cure, or the fatally deceptive "cancer clinic."

IV

FULL STEAM IN THE BOILER ROOM

The madness of stock-jobbing is inconceivable.
This wildness was beyond my thought.
> Sir Edward Harley, The Crown's
> Auditor, on the bursting of the
> South Sea Bubble, 1720.

Fondness for investments, the urge to put one's money into profitable securities or bonds, has survived crashes, panics and depressions and has played a major part in keeping American capitalism healthy beyond the dreams of critics or students. There are now more than twelve and one half million citizens who own their own corporate stock. Tack on the millions with indirect interest in stocks through life-insurance policies, savings accounts, pension funds and the like, and the total swells to over 110,000,000.

In 1958 there were $17 billion worth of new corporate securities offered to the American public.* The total value of stocks quoted on the exchanges by 1958 was edging toward the $262 billion mark—almost three times what the figure had been at

---

* This figure includes only those securities which come under the jurisdiction of the SEC.

the beginning of the fifties. Such figures make their own argument for the broad base of American capitalist ownership, and its continuing fondness for venture. To keep the bellow in the most sustained bull market in history, investment houses use every come-on device known to modern persuasion: radio and TV commercials, newspaper ads, more handily placed branch offices—in residential sections, even in railroad stations. The time is virtually upon us when the house-to-house canvasser from a Wall Street brokerage firm will have replaced the Fuller Brush man.

Small wonder, therefore, that this condition has given the Operator a mother lode of opportunities for every type of fraud and artifice. Reputable brokers have been moved to cite the "alarming speculation in questionable stocks" or "the crescendo of inflationary language" in ads and prospectuses. Early in 1959 President G. Keith Funston of the New York Stock Exchange gave some "cautionary" warnings himself. A more consistent witness than denunciations, warnings or newspaper stories is the ever-increasing activity of the Securities and Exchange Commission, the government agency with primary responsibility for securities regulation. In the last ten years its stop-order proceedings, suspensions, injunctions and criminal indictments have doubled, trebled or quadrupled—depending on the type of action taken.

A brief look at some standard SEC prosecutions will suggest how rich is the take in security frauds, as compared with most other types of underhanded economics. The Sweet Grass–Kroy Case, which the SEC publicly investigated in 1957,* demonstrated the ease with which two small and dubious mining

---

* Due to the difficulties of fixing individual responsibility in such actions, and the lack of similar securities laws in Canada—and effective extradition procedures—the prime movers in this manipulation were beyond the reach of any punitive action. The registrations of the stocks involved, however, were withdrawn.

companies, controlled by the same group, were able to fleece American investors of something approaching $6,000,000. A similar enterprise, indicted in December 1958, defrauded its customers of $2,000,000 by grossly inflating the value of another Canadian mining stock. In a properly organized stock fraud, not only is the take a matter of millions, but the enterprise can be nursed along for years of steady dividends before enough suckers achieve the wisdom necessary to raise a hue and cry.

In the last five years state officials, especially in California and New York, have finally started tightening the bolts on protective devices like the blue-sky laws for securities registration. U.S. Attorneys are increasingly likely to go to court with securities prosecutions. Both the SEC and local law-enforcement agencies have drafted their own lists of do's and don't's for prospective investors, e.g., "Be skeptical of any stock issues offered over the telephone," and reputable brokers add their own cautions to their clients. Such cautions are elementary, but an appalling percentage of investors do not heed them.

Just how many is impossible to estimate. Nor is it possible to assess the annual loss to investors from the stock operators' activities, although estimates have ranged as high as $200 million. Nowhere in the business world is the border area between fraud and honest practice wider. Nowhere is it more difficult to distinguish—and prove—the difference between unwise or unlucky risk-taking and an outright intent to rob. Nowhere in the business world is our native optimism so ill-supported by native caution.

The character of modern security frauds, as suggested by recently exposed and convicted cases, at least offers a powerful argument for the variety of the Genial Society's imagination. The more visionary the offering, apparently, the better. In 1957 a California promoter lifted $200,000 from the pockets of assorted investors on the simple prospectus of a wingless air-

plane capable of carrying 4,000 people 25,000 miles nonstop
at an average speed of 400 miles per hour. (He was grounded
for three years in a federal penitentiary.) A Seattle enterpriser
enticed investors to help reactivate an abandoned mining claim
by broadcasting stories of his reported finds: a human skull, a
crumbling wheelbarrow stuffed with pieces of valuable gold-
bearing ore, etc. A Dallas man found temporary prosperity by
selling stock in an organization called Atomotor Manufacturing
Co., Inc., the widely advertised possessor of a self-energizing
engine which ran without fuel. Another promoter made heavy
profits from marketing shares in a "magnetic logger." This
device was guaranteed to tell its user not only where oil fields
were situated, but the precise depth of the oil and the exact
number of barrels which a discovered field would produce.

In New York State alone, in the course of an average year,
the stock operators' work ran from local real-estate development frauds to the Texas "oil corporation" caught writing New
York investors that a $300 investment could "pyramid practi-
cally overnight to $60,000." Some Manhattan investors were
clipped in a fraudulent scheme to produce TV puppet shows;
some fell victim to the operator of a hair-and-scalp-treatment
clinic who offered bargain stock shares to customers at his scalp
salons. Other successful New York bilking operations traded on
new record companies, Aqua-lungs, fashions, a Cape Cod tourist
business, oil prospecting on a Greek island, astrology predictions and a book purporting to tell the secrets of successful
investments.

The better to stimulate the customers' imagination, most
such schemes have elements of novelty and timeliness. A discovery that makes news also makes suckers. Hence the observable chronology of fraudulent stock representations. Although
the legendary oil claim will always be with us, exercising its

almost Biblical appeal to the incautious,* it yields in popularity to progressively newer enticements. The fame of nuclear energy brought on a ten-year boom in phony uranium claims. When uranium prospecting palled in the public imagination, and its difficulties grew more obvious, along came the lure of space. Since 1957 there has been a heavy increase in the promotion of dubious stock issues for exotic rocket fuels, missile manufacture and other components of space or supersonic travel. The words "nuclear" and "electronic" have become "musts" in the stockateer's high-flown prospectuses.

The appeal of such issues is strengthened as the pace of modern discovery grows swifter and the explanations behind the discoveries grow ever more incomprehensible to the lay mind. The average citizen becomes readily complacent in the midst of his wonder. In the era of commercial jets, man-made satellites and electronic guidance systems, what's wrong with the idea of a wingless airplane carrying 4,000 passengers 25,000 miles nonstop?

But even financial credulity has its limits. So, to be successful, securities frauds must observe some basic proprieties. Only a minority of the citizenry will be taken in by the obvious fakeries of the fantastic idea, the crudely printed stock certificate, the salesman with the clear look of a man who has already bought a ticket to the next town. Even Simple Simon gets to know that the "something for nothing" pitch really stands for "nothing for something." This is notably true after he has been cleaned out a few times. The widest danger comes from Operators who offer something for something. These practitioners

---

* Two confidence men from Fort Worth actually used a religious appeal in their literature, which extracted one million dollars from investors in "the world's richest undrilled oil field," a barren tract of Utah land with no mineral potentialities. "Again thanks to Him," ran the climax to their prospectus, "from Whom all the joyful things of the earth flow forth; a Divine Guidance without which this exceedingly great joy could not now be ours . . ."

may be divided arbitrarily into two categories, although in practice they often overlap. They are: the manipulators and the "boiler-room" boys.

Manipulators make their money by artificially raising or lowering the prices of existing stocks. A manipulator may bid up the prices of an existing legitimate stock, by an artful pattern of rumor and strategically placed orders, then sell out himself —very profitably—at the briefly swollen level. Naturally, the price takes a steep nose dive the moment his shares are dumped on the market, and the resultant crash is generally a painful experience for the stock's original holders. This sort of deal can best be worked where issues of the stock concerned are in short supply on the market. Obviously the slightest spate of organized buying or selling will have immediate results.*

A crooked stock trader can help the cause along with overblown advertising, sudden flurries of trading to catch the eye of the ticker-tape watcher, and judiciously placed rumor. In a situation as sensitive as a boom stock market, rumor alone can exert a powerful influence. There is not too much exaggeration involved in the scene from an old Hollywood movie in which the Wall Street tycoon's new secretary, asked about her boss's mood, innocently replies, "Oh, he's just like an old bear today" —thus producing a stampede of brokers posting down the corridors screaming, "Sell, sell, sell."

Many manipulators are out-and-out crooks, but the charge of manipulation is often raised against reputable brokerage firms. In August 1959, for example, the SEC suspended a large public offering of 240,000 shares of securities by a New England clothing firm. The SEC contended that the underwriter in the

---

* The relatively small amount of trading done in the exchanges in proportion to the total stock held—most shareholders do not trade at all—is another factor which can work in the manipulator's favor. As Burton Crane notes in his book *The Sophisticated Investor:* "Sales of fewer and fewer shares of stock, relatively, set the prices for all shares of stock."

transaction, a New York firm, had artificially pumped up the price of the stock with an eye on the new offering. By a sustained campaign of buying, the charges ran, New Yorkers had raised the price from ⅝ to 1³⁄₁₆.

This rise was undoubtedly facilitated by a dividend declared to stockholders shortly after real buying began. The SEC charged that the company lacked the earnings to justify the dividend. The Commission argued further that the dividend was inspired by several partners, who also were connected with the New York brokers. The report concluded: "The declaration of a dividend not warranted by the business condition of an issuer contemplating public financing is characteristic of manipulative schemes."

The brokerage firm appealed the SEC ruling and denied that there was any manipulation of the stock, which by this time had reached an almost irreducible low.

If there is room for any argument in such cases about who is a "manipulator," there is no mistaking the larcenous intent of Category #2, the "boiler-room" operator. He takes his name both from the high-pressure nature of his work and the barren, scarcely furnished *décor* of the loft offices which are his favorite headquarters. In every respect, he is a criminal caricature of a reputable broker.

To their telephone and mail customers, the boiler-room operators make scrupulous effort to pose as "big firms" which are models of probity. In so doing they show themselves far more clever than their lineal ancestors, the "bucket-shop" proprietors who infested Wall Street in the twenties. The bucket shops were outright places of thievery. They would promise a gullible investor to buy him a certain number of shares, generally blue chips like Standard Oil or General Motors, take his money, then disappear. There were naturally many variations on this theme. Some bucket shops led the investor on by making initial profits for him. But the end was always the same.

The boiler-room specialists grew to business maturity in a less heady atmosphere than this. With the coming of the Securities and Exchange Commission, in 1933, the country's stock exchanges received what amounts to a night watchman, if not quite a police force. The widest-eyed investor has a faint understanding that securities must now be registered and that brokers are under some sort of elemental surveillance. More importantly, the sharp promotor knows that a straight bucketing of customers' orders would very likely get him into trouble in a hurry. He therefore studies the law with care and sets up an organization which is at least superficially within its bounds. He makes sure that the stock he sells has some market value. Naturally, in disposing of his stock issues, he continues to select the type of investor who asks of a security salesman not "How much income can I derive from this investment?" but "Are you sure it's going up?"

Intensive planning is often required to turn the customer's hoped-for escalator into the promoter's toboggan. Operators at this level frequently possess a form of business genius, which might have taken them far in legitimate financial maneuvering, had they been gifted with more patience and conscience as well. For their specialty, and their "business" existence, is predicated first on their ability to exploit a honeycomb of federal, state and foreign securities regulations—which often conflict—so that the act of issuing their securities will appear both legal and plausible. With this foundation, they are ready to proceed with their ancient sales routine.

The first essential is to have some kind of asset, the value of which is subject to dispute—say, a tract of frozen land in western Canada which happens to be within fifty miles of some rich iron and uranium deposits and which a geologist was once heard

to praise (at a Toronto dinner table) as an area with possibilities. ("Sub-Zero Tundra," the prospectus will later relate, "is
located in the very heart of the fabulously wealthy iron and
uranium deposits in Remote County. Geologists have authorita-
tively stated it to contain one of the greatest ore potentials on
the North American continent. Note, in the enclosed geological
sketch, the favorable position of the monoclinal fold . . .")
Until every inch of the property has been explored, no one will
ever be able to say with certainty that it is worthless. Nor will
anyone be able to say with certainty that the land, given the
wealth of know-how contained in Sub-Zero's Board of Directors,
may not some day be worth even more than the $1,000,000 at
which Sub-Zero is capitalized. The actual property may have
cost no more than $50,000 in actual land prices.

Once incorporated, the next problem is to avoid registering
Sub-Zero's forthcoming security issue with the SEC, or anybody
else who might ask embarrassing questions. This can be done
by funneling the shares through a small corporation or two,
and possibly transferring the property to the subsidiary (which
is of course also owned by the promoters). Rule 133 of the
SEC's regulations states that if one corporation absorbs another
one—*i.e.*, exchanges its shares for those of the merged corporation—this is not regarded as a sale. It therefore needs no registration.

After thus increasing the distance between themselves and
the public eye, the promoters may go to the trouble of "washing" the stock on some loosely supervised exchange. They will
sell some shares to themselves, to give Sub-Zero a market value.
Jack Sly, the promoter, may have bought only 500 shares of
Sub-Zero from his own corporation, at $1 a share. But his sales-
men can later tell customers confidently that Sub-Zero is now
quoted at $1 on the Edmonton Exchange, and going up fast.

To further decrease the danger of prosecution, some Operators favor a sort of puck-passing game between Canada and the U.S., whereby ownership can be shifted back and forth to take full advantage of extradition barriers, local laws on corporate records, etc. The gentry who physically transport the shares across the border are known fittingly as "bag men."

Some Operators eliminate most of this footwork by acquiring the husk of a company which has seen better days and retains a certain respected position in the minds of traders, if not the public. As we shall see, this dodge is particularly valuable if the company has retained its listing on the exchanges.

The next step is to start manipulating the stock itself. Acting through dummies or subsidiary "corporations"* by aggressive buying, wash-selling, tape-painting† and other manipulated devices, the promoters work the price of their stock up or down. In this practice their operations are limited only by their own ingenuity and resources, the vigilance of the local exchange government, and the sucker market. But to reinforce their own selling and buying, they must also work fast to simulate popular interest in their issues.

Now enter the boiler-room specialist. He is the man who takes over from the promoter at a fat and fast fee (generally 15 per cent over the counter and 15 per cent under) to dispose of the stock to the public. Sometimes promoter and boiler-room operator are the same man, or at least partners. But they need some specialized knowledge between them to run a good boiler-room brokerage business. An ambulance-chasing lawyer, after all, has to go to law school first.

Although the boiler room's address is recognizably in a big city's financial district—an important factor in a mail and tele-

---

* It must be remembered that a corporation can legally be called such even though it consists of nothing more than a file cabinet, a desk and an empty hatrack. In this field, this extreme abounds.

† Painting the ticker tape is an old dodge in which large purchases by one person or a group are separated and staggered, in order to give an appearance of general market activity.

phone operation—the interior is crudely functional. Visitors are not encouraged. In the outer room of the loft office a long line of girls address envelopes. An inner sanctum is manned by as many as 40 salesmen, sitting behind batteries of telephones. The salesmen's principal equipment, aside from a glib line of conversation, is a larded description of the issue the "firm" is currently pushing, plus a long list of prospects. These will be drawn from the stockholder or specialty lists which are marketed freely in Wall Street and other financial centers for the benefit of reputable brokerage houses.

The ritual in most boiler-room operations is standardized. The prospect is located, possibly by his answering a return form ad inserted in the papers about some "promising new securities." Then he is "papered" for several weeks with tout literature detailing the rewards of ground-floor participation in the new stock—generally an issue which few decent brokers have yet heard of. After this softening-up process, the first real overture is made by an apprentice salesman known as a "coxey" or an "opener."

"Mr. Eager," one typical opening spiel ran, "this is Mr. Blank of the G. F. Rothschild Co.,* the brokers in New York City—you know, the House of Rothschild. Mr. Eager, we've been sending you our market letters, as you know. I'm calling you now in reference to Great Sweet Grass Oil Company, which is listed on the American Stock Exchange. Have you done anything about this stock? No? Well, it's now selling in the market around $4 per share and, Mr. Eager, as surely as I am talking to you on this telephone, the stock will reach $10 to $12 in the next 60 to 90 days. In fact, I'm being conservative when I say

---

* This example was taken from a typical pitch given by the now defunct firm, G. F. Rothschild Co., which stoked the boiler-room operations on the Great Sweet Grass Oil swindle. Needless to say, it had no connection either with the fabled transatlantic house of Rothschild or with the eminently respectable brokerage firm of L. F. Rothschild in New York.

this. Brokers here on the Street are talking $10 to $20 before the first of the year and many of them are buying stock for their own accounts. Mr. Eager, if I were instrumental in you making a nice profit on my recommendation, I certainly feel I could come back to you in the future when we have another issue to recommend to our clients. Isn't that so, Mr. Eager? Now, as a businessman you can appreciate that the growth of our business is based on making money for the customers. . . . I am sure you realize I wouldn't risk my business with my other clients or with you by recommending something I knew nothing about. Mr. Eager, if I am fortunate enough to get you to come along . . ."

His instinct for easy money whetted by this persuasion, Eager may order a small bit of stock or seem disposed to do so. Now a "dynamiter" or a veteran stock "loader" takes over. His job is to step up the tempo and get the subject feeling as tense as a sorority candidate the day she is pledged. "It's now or never . . . only a limited amount still available . . . I've bought it myself . . ."—so goes the persuasion. Up and up the loader raises the ante ("A man in your position should buy at least 1,000 shares") and no mercy is shown. "They drive not for conservative, but for distress sales," a veteran SEC man once observed. "If they find that a man has $20,000 loose, they'll go not for $18,000, but the full $20,000. The more desperate type of salesman will steer his man to the bank to get his earnings, or suggest that he borrow money."

If he finds out that the prospect has present stockholdings, the loader does his best to get him to sell and restock his portfolio with the new issue. The old lures of greed and vanity are skillfully mixed with that manifest failing of people in the Genial Society: the thirst for "inside" information. "This is something special, Mr. Eager," says the loader, "and I can tell you right now we're only letting you in on this issue because we'd like you for a permanent customer. Not even the rest of the firms on the street know about *this* one." (The last remark is usually correct.) Conditioned by a steady diet of securities dope sheets, the customer prepares to buy.

Once the sucker is hooked, the salesman goes on to the next telephone number, piling up his commissions as fast as he can lift a receiver. The calls are invariably long-distance. To take proper advantage of the discrepancy between various state securities regulations, and the difficulties of long-range prosecution, a good boiler-room man likes to keep his prospects at an arm's length of from 500 to 1,000 miles from his office telephone. When a boiler room is working at full steam, it is not unusual for the talkers to run up a telephone bill of $40,000 a month. In the more cost-conscious lofts, egg timers are supplied to the loaders in an effort to keep calls within the three-minute limit.

The art of the boiler-room operator is to stimulate the sucker's hopes of soaring prices, string him along as lengthy a trail as possible, encouraging him to buy still more—while he can. When the game has been played through and the investor comes to grips with reality, he discovers that his losses have been catastrophic, but not total. The average loss to a boiler-room investor is 50 per cent of what he put in.

The files of the SEC are packed with classic examples, almost all of them discovered too late to forfend the loss. There is the Arizona doctor who lost $3,500 on a $7,000 purchase of Canadian oil stock; the Sioux City businessman who bought two Canadian and one American oil stocks for $94,500 and lost $37,000 of it; the citizen of West Point, Miss., who dropped $7,730 out of $13,790 in five months of steady purchasing. Most ironic of all are the cases where investors unloaded perfectly valid stocks, on the advice of fast-talking stockateers, and bought semiworthless issues with the proceeds. Another doctor in Decatur, Ill., sold off his shares of excellent insurance company stock, added $5,000 in cash and sank it all into purchases of Canadian oil issues. He dropped $28,000 on a total investment of $56,000.

When the day of reckoning comes, the boiler-room operator enjoys an ancient advantage: no sucker likes to admit that he has been taken. Where the duped investor elects to make a stand for his rights, if not his money (which has probably been spent), he finds that the boiler-room man may have a strong line of perfectly legal defense. The sucker, to begin with, may not have read the fine print on the back of those nice green brochures about Baffin Depths, Ltd., which states that the property has not yet been surveyed. Even if no such obvious trickery was present, the operator can fall back on the old question of *intent,* which proves such a stumbling block in the prosecution of securities cases. How was he to know that those 1,000 acres of frozen plain in northern Ontario have thus far proved to be good for nothing except moose pasture? He had honestly thought that the land was a treasure house of untapped mineral wealth. Who is to prove that his thoughts were otherwise? After all, the stock still has a market value of something like a third of the original. And explorations are in progress . . .

At root, the type of man who runs this sort of activity is little different from what society calls the "common criminal," *i.e.,* the crook who works with his hands. Crime patterns in recent years throughout the world have shown a steady shift to the more lucrative and less detectable areas of white-collar crime by men who once might have turned more naturally to safe-cracking, hijacking or more violent forms of stealing. As the Swiss criminologist Paul Reiwald put it: "In our view the influence of civilization on criminal law is: the curve for crimes of violence falls, the curve for crimes committed by cunning rises."

Within the field of nonviolent crime, the Operators display a great facility for switching their specialties. And recently no area has proved so attractive to numbers of shady bookmakers, retired race-track touts, and crooked con men of all descriptions as downtown Manhattan. "When the suede-shoe boys got through with the housing racket in California," one SEC official noted, "they went on to the tables at Las Vegas. When Las Vegas got hot, they ended up selling stock in the boiler rooms on Wall Street."

The dynamiters, bag men and other pillars of the boiler room often conceal hefty criminal records. In February 1958, to cite a not-untypical case, New York State authorities barred one James Carlton Graye, head of the downtown Manhattan "brokerage" firm of J. C. Graye Co., from the further sale of securities in the state. An affidavit filed with the order noted that Graye, alias James Webb, had a criminal record which went back to 1927. His past convictions included counts of automobile theft, possession of burglars' tools, robbery and escape. His current activities, far more profitable, centered on a high-pressure boiler-room campaign which sold hundreds of thousands of shares in something known as Atlas Gypsum Corp., a cleverly named but almost completely worthless mining enterprise.

No finer examples of this gray art can be found than two gentlemen named Lowell Birrell and Walter Tellier. Formerly brokers and, in Birrell's case, a financier of some consequence, they are now temporarily out of action, following the collapse of bubbles too obvious to be overlooked. Tellier has taken up residence for a four-and-one-half-year term in a federal penitentiary. Birrell is at the moment rusticating in Brazil, having thus far fought off all attempts to extradite him to the United States for trial. The stories of both men are instructive.

Through most of the fifties Walter F. Tellier was the uncrowned king of the boiler-room business. In little more than ten years of operating, he made himself, by his own admission, "a couple million." Just how much he made or how he spent it no one has yet been able to peg. A veteran of shady securities deals, he started work, after a limited business-school education, as a salesman for a Hartford, Conn., securities company in the late twenties. The firm failed in the 1929 crash, an event which permanently decided Tellier against honest securities marketing, and in 1931 he began activities with his own concern. His selling operations were of a modest nature throughout the thirties, when the newly organized SEC, heavily staffed and firmly mandated, was on the lookout for any vestige of old-time sharp practices. It was only after World War II that Tellier shifted into high gear.

In the late 1940's investments were sprouting on American exchanges, with new products and scientific discoveries at last within reach of the civilian population. Tellier started up with the boom, although his luck was not good at first. He first drummed up investments in a new type of car; but the project grew so palpably risky that he was forced to make full restitution on the shares he had already sold when the car firm went under. His next venture was oil. He paid his first visit to a federal court in the aftermath of a collapsed scheme for selling phony oil stock. Tellier was only working for the oil brokers, however—he was not a principal in the operation— and his lawyer was able to get his case dismissed.

In 1950, however, he found his true *métier* in the relatively unexplored art of uranium-pushing. He reopened his long-inactive firm of Tellier and Co. at 1 Exchange Place, Jersey City, because the New York State tax made it expensive to activate his penny stocks* and set out to circularize the pub-

---

* In October 1959, Governor Robert B. Meyner of New Jersey proposed new securities regulations to head off "the unscrupulous operator" of this sort.

lic on an unending sequence of stock issues. He concentrated
on the newer possibilities in minerals. Tungsten, oil, electronic
schemes passed through his customer files, but it was in ura-
nium-mining prospects that he excelled. By 1955, the period of
his peak operation, a carefully built-up sucker list of 110,000
people had come to depend on Walter F. Tellier for bold,
forward-looking investments in virgin minerals or unexplored
territory, virtually guaranteed to make a dramatic profit far
above the timid gains of ordinary securities. Between 1953 and
1955 Tellier underwrote forty issues of stock. This would have
been a heavy burden even for an honest securities broker, and
it strained the ingenuity and the vocal cords of the 30 salesmen
whom Tellier kept busy at the telephones.

His method of doing business seldom varied. He would first
have his lawyers set up a mining company, e.g., Mesa Uranium
Co., incorporated under the handily lax corporation laws of the
state of Delaware. Mesa and others like it (Tellier's lawyers
liked to set up several at a time, for convenience' sake) would
limit their capitalization to $300,000 a year. In this way Tellier
could take advantage of Regulation A in the SEC codes, allowing firms with less than $300,000 capitalization to file only a
brief account of their origins and holdings, without any need for
audited disclosure papers.

Mesa would then send out an "offering circular" to the public.
This evangel stated that prospects of a very high order were
almost in sight. Although the offering was legally labeled as "a
speculation," the accompanying pitch made it plain that pre-
cious minerals were about to spill out of the ground, just given a
little more capital for exploration. Some 2,000,000 shares would
be offered to the public, at 15 cents a share. Another 2,000,000,
the circular noted, had been issued to management in return
for the "wealth of experience," "know-how" and land rights
which management was putting into the enterprise—and a cash
outlay amounting to a token $5,000.

What the circular did not point out was that 1,000,000 shares were actually in Tellier's pocket and that "management" consisted of a few Tellier stooges. In all such operations Tellier posed as merely the underwriter, carefully disguising his ownership.

The first issue was generally an expensive one for Tellier. The underwriter's commission he extracted from the deal came to $75,000 in the case of the Mesa issue. But of this he had already run up expenses totaling $47,000—printing and mailing costs, advertising, legal fees, etc. Nor was it possible immediately to take out the stock money which landed in Mesa's treasury. There were salaries and costs here to take care of, also, as well as a small investment in perfunctory exploration of the land's real possibilities.

But on the second stock issue and all subsequent, he made money fast. After waiting a few months, he started leaking the word that Mesa was jumping off its plateau with half-revealed possibilities. The dynamiters pounded away at Tellier customers. They alluded to a forthcoming dividend, and Mesa's speedy listing on a stock exchange thereafter. As soon as this happened, the pitch went, the stock would be worth ten, possibly twenty times the current going price. Ads were placed on the financial pages of the *New York Times*, the *Wall Street Journal* and lesser organs, hinting at big things ahead and announcing the offering of a few more shares, at twice the original price. The "few more shares," of course, were the 1,000,000 which Tellier had reserved to himself at the beginning of the transaction.

With sales going well on the second issue, Tellier further stimulated interest by having the issuing company send out a progress report to shareholders. This was the actual basis for his raising the "market" price for future offerings. All such progress reports would give a rosy account of Mesa's potentialities, as confirmed by recent engineering studies, and hint, again, that the company's powerful new machines were just about in position to get that almost limitless store of uranium out of the ground.

By this time the customers were virtually scrambling in their eagerness to get in. Tellier helped the stampede by purchasing shares from original buyers at twice what they paid for them (whereupon he sold them to new buyers at still higher rates). Not that the original customers could get away with any hard cash from the operation. After making their paper profits, Tellier's salesmen easily talked them into buying shares of yet another underwriting, this time practically guaranteed to make *really* fabulous profits. Meanwhile Mesa Uranium continued on its festive way, with money pouring into Tellier's pockets from two sources: the inflated commissions he got for disposing of the stock and the profit from the sales of his own shares.

All of the companies Tellier sponsored had some substance to them, if it were nothing more than an abandoned Nevada mining claim. One, curiously enough, turned out to contain some valuable property. This company disentangled itself from Tellier and survived the crash of his paper corporate empire. Most of the others fell apart the moment Tellier stopped juggling their successive issues, brought down to earth by the pull of financial gravity.

The longest-lived of Tellier's money-makers, and the one for which he was finally convicted, was the Alaska Telephone Corp. swindle. Alaska Telephone, when Tellier chanced upon it, was a small and notoriously unprofitable concern operating a few widely scattered telephone and electric-power facilities in Alaska. Its yearly losses steadily increased, rising from $4,248 in 1948 to $52,678 for the first six months of 1955. At no time in this period did its assets come close to covering its liabilities.

In 1951, with the collusion of two of Alaska's executive officers, Tellier mapped out a plan for selling off a series of

Alaska Telephone debentures. He was to receive a handsome piece of brokerage incentive: 20 per cent sales commission, $20,-000 expense allowance and a five-year preferential right to all future Alaska Telephone financings. The initial outcome more than justified Tellier's expectations. He and his salesmen, working through ads and phone calls, flushed enough eager customers for a handsome $299,500 worth of sales. Of this Tellier netted an immediate $80,000 in commissions. The rest of the money, as the salesmen advertised, was to go into just the right amount of plant improvements to put Alaska Telephone over the top. Needless to say, very little of it ever found its way to the isolated exchanges and power stations in Seward, Wrangel or Skagway.

In January 1953, with Alaska Telephone going deeper into the financial snowdrifts, Tellier marketed a second series of debentures. There was a similarly profitable scale of allowances and broker's commissions. To get this issue air-borne, Tellier and his salesmen told prospects that the company had just about reached "the break-even point," with *really* big and profitable operations just around the corner. In 1954 they marketed a third series. This time they assured the clientele that Alaska Telephone was actually operating at a profit. Its bonds had become a "gilt-edge" investment.

In reality, by January 1955, Alaska Telephone was barely a step ahead of bankruptcy proceedings. Its cumulative deficit totaled $320,986 and there were tax liens of $94,000 against it. Through all this deterioration, however, Tellier had continued to pay interest to the bondholders out of a corporation set up for the purpose, to avoid arousing suspicions. The income from Series B would be used to pay interest and charges on Series A, Series C to pay the freight on Series B, etc. Round and round they went on this ancient swindler's wheel. Yet Alaska Telephone's sucker trade, as the payments kept coming, remained

secure in the belief that it was on the receiving end of a proud
and steady investment.

Tellier had barely wound up a fourth bond issue, in mid-
1955, when the SEC made up its case against him. After months
of preparation, the government indicted him on December 1,
1955, on charges of violating the antifraud provisions of the Securities Act of 1933—plus the old, reliable Mail Fraud Statute.
The following April, he was indicted again, this time for fraud
in connection with the sale of various other stock issues. These
included Mesa Uranium, Yellowstone Uranium Mining Corp.
and, fittingly enough named, Paradox Uranium Mining Corp.

Tellier was sentenced to four and one half years in prison in
April 1957, on the 1955 indictment. He appealed his conviction
all the way up to the Supreme Court, being well-equipped to
spend large sums for legal fees. This process took an additional
year. It was not until 1958 that Walter Tellier finally took the
train to the Federal Penitentiary at Atlanta. His career was
aptly summarized by New York's SEC Regional Administrator
Paul Windels, Jr. (who had convicted Tellier as an assistant
U.S. Attorney) as that of an Operator "completely and utterly
unscrupulous—as hard-bitten a criminal as anyone could find."

The record of Lowell McAfee Birrell, who has continued to
fight extradition from his Brazilian hideaway, makes Tellier
look like a street-corner confidence man. Where Tellier contented himself with manipulating the shares of half-real companies, Birrell bored right inside a succession of very real and
once-profitable corporations. With various partners he held
dominion over a large but chronically shifting industrial kingdom. His take was considerably larger than Tellier's. The most
informed guess has it that Birrell sucked something approaching
$50,000,000 out of corporations under his control in twenty
years of "active business life." Although several United States

district courts, the SEC, insurance officials in four states and any number of anguished receivers have spent long months trying to retrace his corporate evolutions, no one yet knows exactly where Birrell and his partners began and where their depredations stopped. He could extract corporate assets with the delicacy of a man who can make a hole in an egg and suck out the yolk.

A child prodigy who had graduated from Syracuse University at the age of 18, Birrell studied law at the University of Michigan. Like Tellier, he began his career as a respectable member of society—in his case a highly regarded young lawyer working for the formidable New York firm of Cadwallader, Wickersham and Taft. He left the firm in 1933 and shortly after started buying into his first company, a drug-supply house in New York. Within a year or two he had acquired another one, and bought into the Fidelio brewery. He did this on borrowed money, which he repaid satisfactorily—making his initial backers the luckiest of men by comparison with those who came later.

During the 1940's Birrell expanded his interests to cover Brooklyn real estate, an export business, an industrial sirup concern and considerable stockholdings in a concern called Claude Neon. This offered vast possibilities for unobtrusive buying and selling. Although Claude Neon, as the name implies, was in the lighting business, its principal advantage for Birrell was its stock's respected trading position on the American Stock Exchange (then still called the Curb Exchange).

By the end of World War II, Birrell had grouped most of his interests under a holding company, Greater New York Industries, which stayed in business (if we can use the word) until the collapse of Birrell's kingdom in 1957. In 1946, Greater New York acquired control of William Penn Fire Insurance. It speedily sold to its new affiliate (which still had some ready cash on hand) two recently acquired drug companies. In that

same year, Greater New York's balance sheet showed a rise in
short- and long-term debt to $2,155,000 from $822,567 in 1945.
There was in addition an item of some $2,000,000 labeled
"investment in and advances to affiliates."

Such items were to become frequent in the ledgers of the
companies Birrell infiltrated. His basic strategy never varied.
It was to palm off badly watered securities on companies he
controlled, in exchange for good value-bearing issues. The
profits from such one-sided trades inevitably found their way
into Birrell's pockets. But the precise tactics of his transactions
varied brilliantly, with the money's real destination masked
behind a welter of holding companies, newly acquired affiliates
and bewildering intercorporation transactions. Birrell pulled out
of Claude Neon, for example, in 1949. In the same year the
other stockholders, in the manner of men who did not quite
understand what had hit them, began legal proceedings against
him. A federal court awarded them a judgment of $3,256,639.40
—but only after almost nine years of legal argument. Needless
to say, the Claude Neon stockholders have yet to see any of this
money. Other stockholders, notably some in Greater New York
Industries, were even less fortunate. They *lost* their suits against
Birrell, a very capable lawyer. It took years before they could
even get access to the books, to record the ruin of their investment.

Birrell concluded a temporary but profitable alliance late
in the forties with a shrewd Californian. Stewart B. Hopps is a
San Francisco man of affairs who has long specialized in insurance properties. Hopps later asserted that Birrell caused him
much financial pain, but fortunately his current housing establishments in Palm Springs and San Francisco show few signs
of poverty. In the words of a *Fortune* article in November 1959:
"Hopps has maintained, to the satisfaction of the courts, that
if any dirty work was done, it was Birrell who did it."

It was not long afterward that Birrell seized control of the San-Nap-Pak Manufacturing Co., Inc., makers of facial tissues and other household paper products, whose name was later changed to Doeskin. Birrell's manner of operating here showed gifted simplicity. Having insinuated himself into Doeskin's management decisions, he caused the company to exchange its own valid assets for worthless shares of various Birrell-controlled organizations—American Druggists Syndicate, Inc.; Anemostat Corp. of America; Securities Corp. General, etc. Hard cash was paid to Birrell and his friends for these paper stock certificates by the gentlemen who then held the controlling interest in Doeskin. Birrell then paid back the hard cash, with something extra, to the Doeskin stockholders in return for their own valuable interest in Doeskin. The result of this day's share-shifting, in which little money actually changed hands, was to install Lowell Birrell in the driver's seat of a respectable corporation, which he could then plunder at will, while using its paper assets to bore into yet other enterprises. The management of Doeskin continued to make money after the change in ownership. Its products continue to be respected. But as other Doeskin stockholders later charged, Birrell was attempting behind management's back to convert a business asset to a holding company of "practically worthless" securities.*

Possibly the most thoroughgoing of Birrell's plunderings was the acquisition of the Inland Empire Insurance Co., a profitable and growing organization with headquarters in Salt Lake City. In 1952, Inland's management went out to seek more capital to handle its increasing potentialities. Unfortunately, their search went no further than the Leadenhall Corporation, an outfit directly linked with Birrell. He and his friends had ac-

* In this as in some other elements of the Birrell story I am indebted to a series of articles by David Steinberg in the New York *Herald Tribune* in October 1957.

cumulated the sort of experience in insurance financing that would surely have given pause to Inland's earnest executives. There was, for example, the Rhode Island Insurance Co., of Providence, which atomized itself in 1950. Birrell and his friends were authorized to select Rhode Island's investments. Given this charter, they milked Rhode Island, its stockholders and policyholders of most of their assets, by their clever juggling of stock with other paper holdings. In a petition for damages in the California Superior Court, the Rhode Island receiver later charged: "The failure of Rhode Island was brought about and produced by a history of spoliation, mismanagement and faithless stewardship of the business and affairs . . ."

Simultaneously with his Rhode Island dealings, Birrell was working through the pockets of another corporate victim, Louisville Fire and Marine Insurance Co. He first took most of Rhode Island's profits and diverted them to Louisville, in a series of intercompany deals, then made his way through Louisville's own assets. In 1954 Louisville at last seemed irrevocably headed for the mortuary. Just before it collapsed, Birrell arranged to recover over one million dollars' worth of stock belonging to his own Greater New York holding company. This was just about the last bit of corporate blood left in Louisville's carcass.

For three years Birrell and his associates used Inland the way they had used their other insurance properties. In fact Inland ended up by assuming various liabilities of the expiring Louisville concern. Throughout 1954, when he assumed virtual control through Leadenhall, Birrell kept Inland busy with his game of financial shuffleboard. The original blue-chip stocks vanished from Inland's portfolio, to be replaced by a galaxy of new and generally worthless certificates in various Birrell companies. The Insurance Commissioner of Idaho, who finally put an end to the Inland scandal, listed the melancholy progress: ". . . cash funds at Dec. 31, 1954, were $539,666.61. They had dropped to $22,179.03 at Aug. 31, 1955, and showed an overdraft of $25,221.43 at September 30, 1955. Stocks and bonds held at Dec. 31, 1954, were at a total of $2,406,488.14 and had dropped to $1,181,131.71 at Sept. 30, 1955 . . ."

As their game grew more desperate, Birrell and his friends dropped any pretense of board meetings for their captured company, whose president (before they fired him) was still unsuccessfully trying to pierce his way through the screen of financial chicanery surrounding Birrell's operations. One week end, to avoid insurance examiners, they quickly moved Inland's headquarters from Salt Lake City to Phoenix, Ariz. Before this, whenever Inland, or any other Birrell company, faced an audit, the proprietors always arranged for a quick transfer of legitimate securities to their books, in place of the rickety hold-ing-company stocks. A certain number of legitimate investments were held by the combine for this purpose, more or less as impoverished fraternity brothers might share one dress suit between them, assigning it as occasion demands. Late in 1955 two honest executives of Inland got the books away from Birrell and gave them to the insurance examiners, marking an end to the story.

Birrell frequently used boiler-room operators, including his long-time associate Walter Tellier, to do jobs for him—since no amount of stock-switching would do him any good, unless he could find some cash market for his shares. He could not sell stock in large blocks on the exchanges. This would have meant SEC registration and automatic investigation. So he got rid of his issues in small blocks, through layers of intermediaries, to hide his own interest. In this he relied heavily on Canadian brokers.

He was also able to take rich advantage of two unavoidable loopholes in the SEC regulations. The first of these, necessary to legitimate businesses, permits stock to be transferred without registration, if the transfer is part of a corporate merger and does not represent a controlling interest. Thus Birrell could, for example, stick Inland Empire with a large block of shares in Greater New York Industries, without fear of an SEC examiner looking over his shoulder. He believed in attaining his controlling interests gradually.

The second loophole allows security used as collateral for a loan to be sold off without registration. Birrell used this dodge handsomely. He repeatedly borrowed cash which he never intended to repay, thus forcing the lender to sell off his stock issues for him, as the only way of recovering its money. Thus, in a sense, the lenders became Birrell's "fences."

Behind these major operating devices were a hundred small tricks and dodges, the products of Birrell's long experience. He rarely, if ever, used a personal checking account, clearing all business through his attorney, members of his family, or his own legal account. (As an attorney, he claimed many of his gains as simple legal fees.) He kept his books moving—always just one step ahead of the auditors. Still the greatest stumbling block to an adequate investigation of his enterprises is the disappearance of almost all the significant balance sheets.

In the end his own appetite betrayed him. It led him to swallow prematurely, in 1954, the corporate body of the Swan-Finch company, a modest and originally successful manufacturer of oils and greases. Swan-Finch represented a most tempting prize. A small family company, it had unlisted trading privileges on the American Stock Exchange, a privilege given to those companies which had enjoyed it prior to the SEC act of 1934. This meant that Swan-Finch stock could be quoted on the exchange, and traded, without the necessity for any financial statements, either to the Exchange or to the SEC.

In May 1954, using his prestige and stock control of Doeskin

Products (where he was then Chairman of the Board) and Greater New York Industries (where he was president), Birrell took over Swan-Finch. Immediately, he started printing new stock certificates. The number of shares soared from some 94,000 as of Dec. 31, 1954, to a grotesque 2,800,000 at the beginning of 1957. The new shares were issued in exchange for various of Birrell's other corporate "assets," although as of this writing investigators have still been unable to discover what all of them were. And Birrell also bought into several more concerns with the proceeds. As before, he marketed his Swan-Finch holdings to the public through boiler-room "brokers," or as loan collateral. He stimulated a demand for the stock by skillful publicity and an actual expansion program. But by this time the pace necessary to keep all these balls in the air had grown too fast to avoid public attention. After Swan-Finch stock had dropped from $7 a share in late 1956 to practically nothing in 1957, the American Exchange suspended trading. By this time the SEC had worked up a good case against Birrell, although cruelly handicapped by the fact that so many of his operations were just barely inside the law—at least as long as he kept the stock moving and the books away from the auditors. Although SEC officials recognized him as one of the worst stock-ateers in history, it was only on a technicality (*i.e.*, that his maneuvers amounted to an unregistered new issue) that they got a consent order against him, in April 1956.

Birrell signed the consent order, under protest, and agreed to stop all Swan-Finch trading. Once his momentum was thus slowed, his position deteriorated fast. He was forced to sell off his lavish gentleman's farm in Bucks County, Pa., in the same year. Investigators and reporters who visited Bucks County thereafter uncovered some details of a private life which rivaled Birrell's business practices. He was famed in his neighborhood as a giver of Lucullan entertainments, whether at home or taking groups of friends out feasting at nearby inns. A social Alpinist, he instituted an annual charity horse show at his place, Echo Farm, in an effort to meet the horses in the area and their socially prominent owners. It was at one of his horse shows, in fact, that he received the subpoena to attend court hearings on the state of Swan-Finch stock.

For all this high living Echo Farm enjoyed the same shaky capitalization as Birrell's other business enterprises. It was always mortgaged to the breaking point. Local tradesmen soon demanded cash for their supplies.

One year, when he had declared heavy business losses from operating his herd of Black Angus cattle, Birrell learned that Internal Revenue Service inspectors were on their way to check over his livestock. He had to import some cattle for the occasion, which he did with the same alacrity used in switching a valid stock holding from one corporation to another. He was said to have given his cattle special injections to make them look sleeker, before putting them up for sale—not akin to the maneuver originated by Uncle Daniel Drew in the early nineteenth century.*

Late in 1957, while still protesting his innocence, Birrell said adieu to Bucks County and most of his corporations. He decamped to Havana with an as-yet-undetermined amount of assets and an attractive girl friend. From there he went to Rio de Janeiro, to observe in precarious safety the gradual exposé of his past transactions. Questioned by reporters there, he deprecated the press comment. "It's just a complicated business problem," he said.

As of this writing, the claims against Birrell multiply in vari-

---

* Drew was in the cattle business before he discovered the possibilities of stock manipulation. He was wont to keep his cattle thirsty on their way to be sold, stopping at a water hole to fill them up just before arriving at the drover's market, where the bloated beasts brought exceptionally good prices. This was the origin of the famous phrase "watered stock."

ous federal and state courts. The biggest and best-prepared case against him is a New York County indictment for grand larceny prompted by his Swan-Finch dealings. He is charged with stealing $14,000,000 from this one company's stockholders. Of Swan-Finch itself, all that remains is its petro-chemical division, now operating under Illinois receivership. The last traces of Birrell's personal direction of the company were a few filing cabinets and some empty desks, standing alone in a deserted Fifth Avenue office.

The cases of Tellier and Birrell illustrate the difficulties that lie in the way of successfully prosecuting the operator in securities. The problem of collecting adequate evidence is immense. In making their case for Lowell Birrell's indictment, the New York District Attorney's office talked to some 400 people with knowledge of the case. Even after such spadework, the trial of a securities offender demands a huge investment in time and energy.

SEC Administrator Windels, who has prepared and prosecuted an impressive number of securities cases, analyzes it this way: "There's an old case in the common law of a man who sold a one-eyed horse. He didn't say it had two eyes, but he led the horse around in such a manner that the buyer thought he had seen both sides, although he'd actually seen only the one with the eye. No outright lie had been spoken, but there had been a deception.

"Similar deceptions created from half truths, are perhaps the principal device of stock frauds. But selling stock isn't like selling a concrete object that you can see and check for yourself. You have only a piece of paper, the value of which depends on the value of the inaccessible things it represents.

"Thus, activities that would be relatively harmless in the sale of a *tangible* asset can be harsh fraud in the case of a security.

The decision in the case of the one-eyed horse—against the purchaser—asserted the doctrine of 'Let the buyer beware.' But the law in the case of securities is not 'buyer beware,' but 'seller beware.' The prosecutor must get this proposition across at the very outset, if he wants to have any chance of winning a case based upon the often-nebulous, and always complicated, deceits of a securities fraud."

District Attorneys shy at trying securities cases, not only because they are tremendously technical, but because of the high-priced, specialized legal talent available to the defense. Juries are notably hard to convince, unless enough pitiable victims are hauled into court to present the case against the securities criminal in its most concrete terms. Judges tend to give these operators light sentences, even when they are convicted. Judges themselves are by no means immune to the widespread popular feeling that condemning a common safecracker is one thing, but it is a horse of a different color to criminalize a seemingly reputable "businessman," whose sensitive fingers may never have actually felt the cold, hard metal inside the till.

As we have noted, the Genial Society today is itself "overprotected" by its profusion of laws and regulations—or, more exactly, by its corollary trust that there must be an enforceable law or regulation to cover everything. Letting someone like Lowell Birrell loose among people of this mentality is tantamount to dropping a man with a bad common cold in the midst of some superscientized society of the future, where colds have been so long banished that they are unknown. The result in either case would be a huge toll of unexpected casualties.

The answer to the credulity of the overprotected is obviously not an automatic cry for "more government regulation." No government agency can ever coerce an investor to invest his money wisely, nor should it attempt to do so. Crooked speculators will exist on the stock market's fringes, as long as the market exists—just as people will try to tout implausible horses as long as a single track stays open. What *is* wanting is the oiled and willing judicial machinery which will apply existing laws strictly and treat the operator in securities as a criminal, not just a dashing privateersman gone a little wrong. The depredations of such men will be cut down to size only if they are treated as crimes by the courts and in the public mind.

The securities market has gone a long way since the fearful day of the first modern crash, the bursting of the South Sea Bubble, in 1720, and the successive financial panics of early industrial history. The United States, the greatest stock-market country in history, has itself survived a decade (1919 to 1929) when half of the $50 billion of securities sold proved ultimately worthless. But the beast of rash speculation still lurks under the counter. Only a steady effort will keep him there—to say nothing of sweeping him out.

V

THE CON MAN IN THE

GRAY FLANNEL SUIT

"Dear me, you don't think of doing any business with me, do you? In my official capacity I have not been authenticated to you. This transfer book, now [holding it up as to bring the lettering in sight], how do you know that it may not be a bogus one? And I, being personally a stranger to you, how can you have confidence in me?"

"Because," knowingly smiled the good merchant, "if you were other than I have confidence that you are, hardly would you challenge distrust that way"...

...."Your logic I will not criticize, but your con-fidence I admire, and earnestly, too, jocose as was the method I took to draw it out. Enough, we will go to yonder table, and if there be any business..."

This dialogue is from Herman Melville's book, *The Con-fidence Man*, written in 1857. Making allowances for the archaic language, it remains a valid description of the principle on which tens of thousands of Americans make their dishonest

living. In the United States, the native con man came to prominence with the rise of the frontier, when labor was hard, money
or the chance for gain plentiful and the law either lax or nonexistent. His kind has continued to profit and to multiply. The
upholstered world of the Genial Society would represent a
Mecca rich beyond dreams of plucking to the river-boat operators of Melville's day.

Unlike the amateur or semipro majority of Operators, the
confidence man is no borderline case. He is by profession a
crook. He is dedicated to fleecing his fellow citizens, and he
works as quickly and as painlessly as his professional skill and
their gullibility will allow.

Most confidence men in their prime have already seen the
insides of various jails, and are likely to see more. Even in jail
they represent a Brahmin caste among criminals. They display
an intellectual and a social contempt for the duller-witted and
more poorly paid men in the "heavy" rackets, e.g., safecrackers,
heisters, robbers. Intelligent and quick-witted, wardens depend
on them for their supply of librarians and similar prisoner office
help; at the same time the con men are conspicuously un-
regenerate. Law-enforcement officers usually count on seeing
them again after they are released.

In the old days their very vocabulary was a tribute to the
intricacies of their calling. The term "con man," in fact, for a
long time referred only to the kind of swindler who could first
allow his "mark" to make some money in a dishonest scheme,
then "take" him for a larger sum. The scene of his racket was
called "the big store." His accomplices were variously known as
"shills," "inside men," "lookouts," etc.,* and he ran their work
according to a stern protocol.

---

* A shill is an accomplice who seems to win at the con "game," thus lulling
the mark into a sense of false security. An inside man is the receptionist who
ushers the mark into the con man's rented premises. A lookout acts as the
doorman at such an enterprise. For these and other definitions I am indebted
to David W. Maurer's *The Big Con*.

In recent years, however, the multiplicity of opportunity for making a fast buck has blurred such old-fashioned distinctions. "Con man," as the expression is commonly used, now covers all kinds of grifters or swindlers. There are still traditionalists among the fraternity. As late as 1958 federal officers in the Southwest were investigating a swindle that sold fake gold bricks to suckers, in the ancient tradition.* But their number decreases. The modern confidence man works in the most unexpected places—in 1958 New York City police turned up a bingo rackets ring whose members used counterfeit cards to infiltrate church bingo games. The modern confidence man advertises, and uses new promotion methods. Whether his game is fraudulent insurance claims, fake cemetery lots or shady real-estate transactions, he plays it cool and mechanized.

The advance-fee real-estate racket, a scandalous deviation from a respectable method of advertising properties, exemplifies the scale of the modern con man's operations. It involves the wholesale extortion of advance "commission fees" on the sale of property which is never—or almost never—sold.

This play works with appalling ease. A firm of bogus "real-estate brokers" seeks out prospective sellers of homes or businesses, often through high-pressure advertising. ("Do YOU have something to sell?") First by telephone, then by personal visit, a "salesman" from the firm makes contact with the prospect. He paints a picture of buyers who can barely be restrained from showering money on the property owner—often far in excess of the modest price he may have named. His firm stands ready to handle the whole transaction for an agent's fee, payable in advance. The fee is usually one per cent of the property's value. The prospective seller is led to believe that it will be refunded in the unlikely event of no sale.

In all too many cases the seller consents, pays his money, and

* Equally ancient was the origin of the swindlers, who happened to be a bunch of fast-talking Yaqui Indians.

starts the family packing, in the expectation that they will soon be off to Florida. But the sale almost never happens. On investigation the property owner finds that what he actually signed was merely a contract stating that the firm would perform certain advertising services for him in connection with *his* attempts to get rid of his property. Sometimes, to keep the promoters within the strict letter of the contract, the advertising is done, but never on a wide scale. In general the high-pressure salesman and his firm make close to a 100 per cent profit on the deal.

The racket in advance fees got its start in Chicago some years ago, then spread through the Midwest and on to the Pacific coast. (In the last three years 662 cases were cited in California alone.) More than 70 firms are now involved in the business, with an annual take, the Federal Trade Commission has calculated, of close to $50,000,000 yearly. Since 1954, the date of the first FTC action, complaints have been piling up against them in geometrical progression. The biggest and the worst of the advance-fee sharpers has been clearing $2,000,000 a year, with branches established all over the country. Its proprietors have grown bold enough to fight a recent FTC action against them, still pending in the courts.

Tragically, these high-pressurizers concentrate on old people anxious to retire, small businessmen with little cash, *et al.* The poorer and more helpless a prospect, the better. Quite a few blind men have been cited among the victims. Some salesmen extract preliminary commissions from eager sellers on the basis of a phone call. (When the check is received, the deal is regarded as closed.) The average take is about $250 per customer, split roughly on a two-to-one basis between the company and the salesman. Although the FTC can undertake and has undertaken cease-and-desist actions against some of the real-estate operators, there are as yet no federal statutes to punish their brand of misrepresentation. Most of them move too quickly across state lines to be within the reach of local prosecutors.

In the summer of 1958 one Williams Parker, an ex-convict who had just left the advance-fee racket, told a Senate sub-committee some of the tricks of his former trade. Speed, said Parker, was essential to success. Storming the prospect quickly —in the old tradition—the con man would induce him to believe, for example, that the "big" prospective buyer was interested in acquiring only a certain number of like businesses in the area. Therefore, seller and salesman had to work fast. "You had to find out how much money he had," Parker explained. "That was the most important question to ask him. You arrived at that by going slowly into whether he owned cars, how much his present cash balance was in the bank, etc. There was no use in going for a $1,000 or $200 or $400 fee unless he had the ready cash."

Curiously enough, Parker was often able to make sales from property owners who had already been victimized, a fact which makes its own comment on the Genial Society's consumer sense. "Some of those people loved it," he told the senators. "It is a fact that they did love it. It is like the crooked roulette wheel if it is the only one in town. They would continue to go. In fact, I think a lot of them would simply give you money who did not want their business sold. But they would dream about it. All the people I sold to had sick backs or wanted to go to Florida. These were the two excuses we had."

The exasperating thing about the advance-fee racket is the difficulty of successfully prosecuting the con men who run it. As Senator Henry M. Jackson noted in the course of the Senate's investigation: "The misrepresentations of the salesman, upon which the businessman relies, and the wording of the contract are not in the least related." As always, the smooth talker working the con relies on a combination of need and greed in his victim—just the way the old-timers used to sell gold bricks or the Brooklyn Bridge.

When the salesman finally appears on the scene, after whetting his prospect's appetite by a series of intriguing mail circulars, telephone calls and delayed appointments, he talks too fast and interestingly to encourage any reading of the contract. The "client," giving his check to the salesman, does so with words like "nationally advertised," "immediate sales," "money back if the deal doesn't go through" ringing in his ears. If he ever attempts to go to the law about his defrauding, he finds that his signed contract reads differently.

Most of the contracts bind such advance-fee "firms" only to advertise a listing in newspapers or a stated periodical. They make no mention of *what* newspapers (most salesmen cite the *New York Times* or the Chicago *Tribune* or the Los Angeles *Times*) or the circulation of the glossy bulletin, which is generally sent to a few real-estate brokers. As for "money back," a common clause in such agreements notes that all the client's money will be refunded "in the event this agreement is not accepted" by Fraudulent Turnover, Ltd., or whatever outfit has printed the contract. Needless to say, they seldom turn an agreement down. Finally, there is the stipulation, tucked away in the finest of fine print, which occasioned Senator Jackson's comment: "This agreement contains the entire understanding between us and no other representative or inducement has been made that is not set forth herein." So the victim has little more to show a jury than his own pained countenance.

The advance-fee con men find it useful to pose as models of probity. One outfit based its operations on a booklet called *How to Sell Your Business and Beat the Con-men*. Another California group took its payment in the form of promises to pay, and never hesitated to sue on the strength of the commitments made in the fine-print contracts.

To keep their franchise as business enterprises, also, the advance-fee racketeers are careful to make a few actual sales of property on their lists. The Federal Trade Commission has pegged this amount as less than one per cent of the total offered. But the very fact that they do sell something makes it even more difficult to distinguish them from the *legitimate* advance-fee real-estate brokers, whose wide advertising outlets can indeed give value received to their clients.

A bill was recently introduced in the Senate setting up penalties of fine and imprisonment for anyone who uses false representation in getting a contract for services. On a local level, some states and real-estate boards are fighting the racket —although in at least one case, California, where the advance-fee sharpers abound, the constitutionality of a new law was challenged as "discriminatory." In New York State, where one of these advance-fee merchants has been doing as much as $35,000 a month of advertising business in his bulletin, a bill has been passed requiring a detailed registration of fees, forms of contracts, etc., with complete information about the names, addresses and criminal records of the entrepreneurs.

A complex operation like the advance-fee swindle requires a certain amount of resource and at least a patina of business experience. But there are new varieties of the con game to fit almost every purse and imagination. The puzzle-fixing racket, at least until it was broken up, was a fine example of the return a one-shot essay in fraud could yield to its proprietors.

The ring, led by an ambitious young man from Detroit, was formed early in 1958 with the object of cashing in on the cash-prize puzzles which so many American newspapers use as therapy for their circulation problems. Two New York companies have long been supplying both puzzles and answers to any newspaper willing to subscribe. The contests are about scrambled words or meanings, and they generally drag on for weeks in a series. Answers are mailed out by the puzzle companies, preferably to banks in the subscriber's home town—to avoid any possibility of tipping the answers along the line. The Detroit man and his friends had the inspired idea of setting up a nonexistent Canadian newspaper, through two Canadian accomplices, as well as a nonexistent bank. They could then subscribe to the puzzle feature service, get the answers in advance, and win contest after contest in the papers back home.

The modest "syndicate" found accomplices in various American cities where the newspaper puzzles were running. Regularly, they would telephone them the prize-winning solutions in advance. The accomplices were to split their take with headquarters after extracting a small commission for themselves.

This puzzle swindle worked especially well with papers on the West Coast, since the time difference practically guaranteed that their fictitious Canadian paper, located in Ontario, would get even last-minute answers well ahead of them.

The puzzle ring finally cracked because its leaders depended too much on amateurs, who were jittery about their fraudulent puzzle premiums. The two large Portland, Ore., papers, the *Journal* and the *Oregonian*, got wind of the fraud, put their reporters on the story and unearthed one crooked contestant, who had fled to Seattle after making $950 on a contest. (He had turned $2,000 over to the syndicate. Another contestant, a woman, was discovered to have kept only $300 of her $2,600 prize.) The Portland papers asked the FBI to investigate, after first making an embarrassed front-page admission that their own puzzle had been fixed. In March 1959, after a short investigation, FBI agents arrested 12 persons.

Other con men have had more success in holding out the promise of eventual instead of immediate gain. Various Midwestern farmers are still rubbing their jeans after the 1950 exposure of an "inheritance" swindle which netted its proprietors some $200,000 in a few years' time. The outline was simple. Henry Ford, the sharpers said, was about to divide his estate among loyal stockholders, in a desperate effort to fend off inheritance taxes. A person had only to put up a certain amount of money—since Ford "needed ready cash"—to receive vast quantities of Ford stock (at least the certificates said it was Ford stock) which would greatly increase in value. One man, for instance, bought $7,140,000 in bogus certificates for a trifling $81,000. The acuteness of the stock-buyers can be gathered from the fact that the scheme continued in full flower for three years after Ford's death in 1947.

More recently, organized tourism has proved a popular magnet for sucker money. In 1958 a New Yorker, nominally a laundryman, extracted well over $200,000 from well-meaning acquaintances who had invested in his alleged project for placing company tours with large steamship lines. A few years before, another operator had worked out a scheme for selling "cut-rate" cruise tickets from his headquarters in Guatemala. Although he netted hundreds of orders, the tickets never arrived for their purchasers. The nearest they got to overseas travel was the vicarious satisfaction of seeing the entrepreneur journey to federal court in Columbus, Ohio, where he was arraigned and convicted.

Side by side with such up-to-date dodges stand a few remaining staples of the old-time con man's art. This year, last year and next year a certain number of Americans are sure to be taken in by the venerable Spanish-prisoner racket. This device for extortion is literally almost as old as the Spanish Armada, having been originated by 16th-century sharpers who posed as survivors of the Armada, ready to pay huge sums of money to anyone who could engineer their return home. Currently, it is most often based in Mexico. Each year, as regularly as the *World Almanac*, letters appear in the mailboxes of various Americans, allegedly from a prisoner suffering for some fancied wrong in a Mexican jail, or elsewhere south of the border. He has been directed to the particular addressee, the letter invariably goes on, because of his known feelings for the downtrodden and the oppressed, courtesy of an intermediary who is tactfully not mentioned.

The prisoner, by his own admission, has large sums of U. S. currency hidden away. If the money is found, it can be used to bribe his way out of jail. Naturally, it can only be recovered by someone above suspicion, with no ostensible reason to interest himself in the case—an American tourist, say. The recipient of the letter need only go to a prearranged point to pick up the money, deliver it to an intermediary and take a huge commission for his humanitarian pains. Of course, he must also bring some money *of his own,* for necessary running expenses or, incredibly enough, "evidence of good faith."

The Post Office Department, the agency most intimately concerned with mail-order robbery, annually fishes up about $100,000 worth of marks swindled in this tested game. No one knows what the actual take is. Traditionally, the people who complain about it represent a tiny percentage of the actual losers.

The pocketbook drop, known familiarly as the "poke," is far more widespread than the Spanish-prisoner swindle, although probably just as soundly based in antiquity. In this beginner's con game, one of a two-person team will drop a pocketbook, wallet or fat-looking letter, in apparent innocence, as he or she is walking down the street. His accomplice will watch closely the behavior of the passers-by. If a man picks up the wallet, and calls after the owner, he is presumably honest and no prospect for a con game. If the next man picks up the wallet, says nothing and furtively starts to pocket it, the crooks have found themselves a target.

Looking his helpful best, the second con man then walks over to the "finder" and assists him to count the contents—let us say $3,000 in fake securities. As the mark's eyes are popping over his discovery, the con man suggests a quick deal. "Give me $750 cash," he will suggest, "and I'll forget I ever saw you pick that up." In an unbelievable number of cases, the finder agrees.

Every day a certain amount of money changes hands in this way or in variants of the "poke" in which one of the con men "finds" the cash bundle. In March 1959, for instance, the following news item appeared in the Boston *Herald*, under the heading "Woman Loses $2800 in Confidence Game":

Mrs. —— reported to police yesterday that she had been robbed of $2800 by two women in a confidence deal. She said that a woman of about 25 met her in a Malden store Thursday and told her she had found $3600. A red-haired woman of about 35 joined the conversation and scolded the younger woman for disclosing the secret. The two women then decided they would permit Mrs. —— to share in their find if she obtained $2800 from her bank account and let them hold it as a token of confidence. Mrs. —— complied.

Mrs. —— said she later returned to the store to meet the women and receive her share of the money. The women did not keep the appointment.

There was, unfortunately, nothing in the least unusual about Mrs. ——'s willingness to show her "good faith" by turning her own money over to a stranger. Stories like it can be found every day in the newspapers, the reports of local precinct detectives or the informal complaints of suckers who are too ashamed of their own greed and gullibility to admit their losses to the police. Mrs. ——, in fact, was a shining exception to the general reluctance of victims to testify against their defrauders.

Often the reluctance bases itself on more serious grounds

than wounded pride. In preying on the avarice of their marks, con men can involve them in enterprises which are on their face illegal. The "wire" game, for instance, one of the old stand-bys, involves getting race results ahead of time by allegedly tapping Western Union wires, and placing bets accordingly. Few suckers are likely to admit their participation in such a scheme. Yet the police, if they wish to act against a con man, must have a signed complaint from the victim before they can make an arrest stick.

As deftly as they size up a potential victim, con men can scent winds of police drives against them, the fact that a town's law-enforcement authorities can no longer be "fixed," or worst of all a dwindling supply of suckers. Trimming their sails, they move with predictable rapidity. If temporarily driven out of one area, they compensate by increased exactions elsewhere. Between 1954 and 1958, for example, the incidence of pocket-book drops fell by 70 per cent in New York City. This was due to a heavy police drive against them. But at the same time, there was a 50 per cent increase in pocketbook-drop cases reported to New York from elsewhere. In most cases the drops turned out to be run by the same operators who had been arrested in New York.

When they do light in a locality, experienced con men have a knack for making themselves at home, knowing that affluence and seeming stability are almost essential props. The late Serge Rubenstein, the still-mysterious financier whose instincts and operating methods were those of a high-level grifter, used a typical device for impressing suckers who visited his rented Fifth Avenue mansion. There was one huge baronial hall, the Oak Room, furnished like a palace. The rest of the house, in the words of an investigating detective, "was a fleabag." But the clientele never got beyond the Oak Room, where they could gape at the tapestries and listen to the soothing sounds of Rubenstein's expensive long-distance telephone calls.

Probably the greatest front man in the history of the confidence game was one Joseph R. Weil, known to several generations of fellow grifters, district attorneys and newspaper readers as the "Yellow Kid." In a career that lasted from the beginning of the century to his last arrest in 1940, the Yellow Kid did his fellow citizens out of something between three and ten million dollars. Weil was a master actor. He worked the "big con" against bankers, farmers or salesmen indiscriminately, through an ingenious series of disguises. He took a Missouri banker for $125,000 worth of fake stock issues, posing as a representative of the Imperial German government. He defrauded three Maryland spinsters of $280,000 in the guise of an Englishman representing a London oil trust. He stole gamblers' money on the outcome of rigged prize fights and once sold a huge slice of nonexistent timber rights in northwest Canada to an American businessman for $60,000.

Many of Weil's games used dozens of temporarily hired accomplices. (He once set up a bogus bank for a day, in temporarily rented premises.) Yet he based his success on the facility with which one man could acquire the "confidence" of a mark, and a mark carefully selected for his wealth and acquisitiveness.

The very individualism of their approach explains why Weil and old-time swindlers like him have been replaced by mechanized team play. Although the small-time pocketbook drops persist, they are by their nature limited to the egregiously gullible—old ladies or recently arrived immigrants. And they are small pickings. The modern con man anxious for a big killing or a steady (and heavy) source of income has to change his tactics and, in a sense, incorporate.

In the first place, rapid communications and the availability of investment information have sharply cut down the number of five- and six-figure suckers in the United States—to say nothing of increased income taxes. Gone, too, is the type of old-fashioned businessman, accustomed to making decisions by him-self, who was the best kind of mark for an individual con man with the right brand of persuasion. Modern businessmen are largely calculators, not plungers. They tend to make their decisions jointly, keeping both business associates and their families well informed about their plans. What would happen now to traditionalists like the Yellow Kid or Melville's riverboat sharper, who depended so heavily on creating watertight per-sonal "confidence" between the individual con man and his mark? Suppose, for example, that the mark takes the con man's proposal to his friends in his investment club—or decides to try it for size by running it through the office computer?

Veterans like the Yellow Kid were right when they said that "there isn't a good con man left working in the U. S. today."

His successor, the con man in the gray flannel suit, has all too easily adjusted his crime to changing conditions. If he has less chance for a "play" on the lone, tremendously rich sucker, he has a whole new field for his operations due to the spectacu-larly wide distribution of the country's wealth. The democratiza-tion of plenty and the carelessness of the Genial Society, in fact, make the spectacular "big con" unnecessary. It is easy enough for the larcenous like the sharpers in the advance-fee racket to take money from a wide sampling of their neighbors, without long weeks of searching for the miserly but gullible Missouri banker.

Take the welfare state: its concern for organized charity and insurance. In both these fields crooks have proliferated. The more emergency relief payments became standardized, the more they were taken for granted and regarded by some as a legitimate part of their income. In New York City, probably the world center of this kind of fraud, scarcely six months passes without some investigation into people fraudulently getting and/or staying on the relief rolls. Only a few of these cases represented people who had temporarily falsified relief claims for emergency reasons. With most it was a virtual way of life.

The area of private charity is equally rich in possibilities, and more professionally exploited. Consider the number of charitable appeals reaching a moderately prosperous city-dweller in the northeastern United States: Cancer Fund, Heart Fund, Cerebral Palsy, Community Chest, Multiple Sclerosis, Red Feather, hospital funds, Boy Scouts, National Tuberculosis Foundation, Lighthouse for the Blind, Warm Springs Foundation. On the number goes—to say nothing of individual churches and hospitals, church welfare agencies and other specific local worthy causes. Now most of these (certainly all those named above) are reputable, worthy and well-run causes. But their very proliferation makes it impossible for an individual citizen to do much checking before he contributes. He may be approached by mail, even by telephone. He may be solicited as part of a local drive in his neighborhood, office or apartment building. If he is reasonably prosperous, his reaction is to give something to almost all of them—and he makes little distinction about his gifts, other than occasionally examining the list of prominent sponsors gathered on the sides of the letterheads.

This attitude is made to order for modern con men. It is not too difficult to insinuate oneself into the fund-raising activities of some worthy cause, or to institute such fund-raising. Nor is it hard to get a covey of prominent names for window dressing. In many cases, the operators remain within the law by contributing a portion of the money collected to the charity. They disguise their own take under the heading of collection expenses.

A not untypical example of a good motive gone wrong was the fate of the W. C. Handy Foundation for the Negro Blind, which was haled into court in New York State in March 1959

to answer charges that a substantial sum had been mulcted by
one of its organizers. The foundation started out in 1949 with
the best of intentions. Suitable names were gathered for the
letterhead. Its founder, the late composer of the "St. Louis
Blues," kicked it off himself at a fund-raising drive in 1951.

After eight years of existence, however, the Handy Foundation made the mistake of hiring one David A. Ulrey, a former
Washington, D. C., "advertising executive" to supervise its
collections. Ulrey took advantage of the foundation's officers
to run the drives and the ledgers by himself, with the most
liberal deductions for fund-raising expenses. When his accounts
were finally audited, they showed a total of $35,216 collected
in 17 months during 1957 and 1958. Of this, Ulrey had turned
back only $3,583.61.

Fortunately there has been a decrease in this peculiar type
of "charity." An estimate of three per cent waste in charitable
donations due to fraud, in 1950, had decreased to something
under one per cent in 1958, according to the National Association of Better Business Bureaus. This would put the amount
tossed down the drain to charity con men in 1958 at $70,000,000
—the total donations for all philanthropic causes in the U. S.
(including education) being the sum of $7.1 billions. Other
sources estimate the fraud deductions as more like $150,000,000
—and this does not include the untraceable amount wasted in
nonlegitimate "overhead" charges. Twenty-one states now require fund-raisers to register annual statements. Legitimate
charity workers in the American Association of Fund-Raising
Counsel have also set up their own policing code, to keep the
con men out.

Yet the charity fraudsters can scarcely hold a candle to their
distant cousins, the multiplying race of con men who specialize
in fake insurance claims. These rubber-boned, agile-witted
swindlers represent a profitable re-creation of the old Greek

legend about Antaeus, the giant who bounced back twice as strong every time he was hurled to the ground. In their crudest form they are known as "floppers." "Floppers" fall down on "slippery" floors in large department stores or supermarkets, tumble deftly in front of slow-moving automobiles, collide fortuitously with rocks at the sites of building excavations. Then they submit their claims to the stores or the insurance companies. Although they often forge their medical reports they can occasionally enlist the help of a crooked physician.

For some professionals, "flopping" is a way of life. One family in an Eastern city has already compiled a colossal group record. The head of the house submitted 28 claims for personal injury to insurance companies between 1941 and 1954; his wife had 15; their 12-year-old son and his five-year-old sister, three apiece. A mother-and-daughter team, operating out of Cincinnati, Ohio, were arrested in 1955 after a 15-year career of false insurance claims.

The more skilled among them are often able to fool the average examining physician, especially in tried-and-true areas of medical complaint like slipped discs, sacroiliac cases and the currently popular "whiplash" injuries from automobile crashes. A lady named Grace Walker, known generally as "Rimrock Annie," boasted that she had been treated in 50 hospitals in her career before she was finally brought to book recently in Denver, Colo. Only one doctor had tumbled to her fraud, in all these visits.

Rimrock Annie's specialty happened to be head injuries. Her left pupil was dilated, after a childhood operation for mastoid. This always helped establish one symptom. She would bite her lips to draw blood, which she would then place in her ear. ("I made it appear to squirt from my ear by shaking my head.") Vomiting came easy to her, as did double vision, which had developed in the course of her hard-working career.

Maxwell Riffkind, sentenced in Chicago in 1954 for fraudulent claims against insurance companies, was as agile a planner as Rimrock Annie was a flopper. Riffkind was spotted by chance, when an insurance adjuster grew suspicious about the same rare rifle being lost twice in two months. It developed that Riffkind, under two aliases, had filed both applications. In the course of investigating him, the adjusters uncovered a long history of similar fraud, including his most famous coup, the one-man automobile accident. Without even bothering to set up a fake wreck, Riffkind, with a lawyer accomplice, would sue himself—again working behind two separate aliases—for an accident which never happened. He collected seven times on this dodge from various insurance companies.

Other craftsmen in this field insisted on realism. Jerome A. Rader, who was sentenced to jail in Los Angeles on February 13, 1959, for his intricately staged "accident," had arranged to have his own arm, leg and shoulder fractured by a chiropractor. The plan was to have the owner of a heavily insured car knock Rader's car over a cliff in Coliseum Park, Los Angeles. The Raders, drugged, would then be put in the wreckage. Injured and apparently unconscious, they were ideally set for lucrative action against the insurance company.

Unwilling to ride so far down the garden path, the driver of the heavily insured car tipped off the Los Angeles sheriff's office and the plot was foiled. In the course of checking Rader's past, the district attorney found that he had made at least 34 successful claims for injury or damage money in recent years, most of them for small amounts, and collected at least $19,438.

Although the folklore of insurance companies is rich in stories of gifted "floppers,"* these old pros cause only a dwindling pro-

* Still popular is the story of the man who had won a huge settlement from a sympathetic jury for an accident which the insurance investigators knew to be faked. "We'll be watching you," the adjuster said to him after the trial,

portion of the investigator's worries. The Association of Casualty and Surety Companies, which has been tracking down injury rackets since its claims bureau started up in 1937, finds that the number of veteran lone-wolf con men in this racket—as with other departments of the craft—has dwindled. But replacements have more than made up for this loss. On one hand, there is the new team operation, equipped with floppers, chasers and crooked lawyers, which makes a business out of accident-fixing. At the same time, the number of amateur chiselers has risen astronomically. The multitudinous $75 frauds are impossible to investigate individually, but their prevalence is another clue to the slackening of ethical and moral standards among the U.S. population.

Organized accident frauds which are brought to book emphasize new mechanization. It is no idle matter, these days, for a district attorney to start proceedings against a gang of insurance operators. In the famous case in New York City (mentioned in Chapter I), which was finally settled in 1958, indictments were returned against 43 men and women. All of them were heavily implicated. The case took two and a half years to try, in which time most of the small fry involved, after co-operating with the prosecutor, received suspended sentences. The ringleader, a lawyer, received a suspended sentence in turn, despite the fact that he had been found guilty on four counts of grand larceny and three counts of conspir-

---

"and the minute you get out of that wheel chair, we'll have you." "I'll save you the trouble of investigating," the "victim" replied, "by telling you exactly what I'm going to do. I'm spending a week here at the Waldorf, then I'm taking the biggest suite on the *Queen Elizabeth* for an ocean voyage—still in my wheel chair. I'm going to hole up at the George V in Paris, after further medical check-ups, of course. After that I'm going to Lourdes, and you're going to see the most amazing miracle in history." What the U.S. jokesters who told this story did not realize was that a Frenchman actually carried out this plan in 1952, after receiving 10 million francs for permanent spinal injuries suffered in an auto accident. When he arrived in Lourdes, he announced himself "miraculously" cured.

acy. The judge who sentenced him thought he might be "rehabilitated."

The extent of the gang's depredations should have been enough to convince any judge that he was dealing with hardened professionals. The ringleaders included an insurance appraiser, an insurance adjuster and a former garage owner. The front organization they operated was disguised as an "automotive service." In less than two years, the ring staged some 35 accidents and took several insurance companies for what the prosecution calculated might run as high as $1,000,000.

The ring began modestly with simple one-car accidents. If a man brought in a car with a crumpled fender, the proprietors would give him a fast sales talk. "Look," their argument ran, "you have a $100 deductible policy. This fender won't cost more than that to repair, so where does that leave you? You foot the whole bill. Now if you want to leave everything to us, we can fix your car, give it a new paint job, and it won't cost you a cent. Let the insurance company pay for it."

This would have appealed to most members of the Genial Society, more or less conditioned from birth to regard insurance companies as living cornucopias. If the car owner agreed the technicians went to work. They took a selection of smashed parts from their large stock, substituted them for the good fender, hood, grille, etc., then telephoned the insurance appraiser. By this time, the claimed damage was more like $800 than $100. After the appraiser had approved the disbursement, skilled mechanics restored the original parts, fixed the slight actual damage the car had sustained, and split the take. In this stage of their evolution, the gang generally contended that the car had hit a pillar on Manhattan's West Side Highway. "They hit it so often," an assistant district attorney observed, "that it's a wonder it's still standing."

Later our "automotive service" experts devised more ingenious methods, like the multicar accident. The customer with the dented fender now turned out to have "lost control" of his car, most often in the predawn hours on some little-traveled avenue. He claimed to have hit two or three parked cars in the process. A few personal injury claims were thrown in for added realism. (One woman was paid for a household accident. A man received a settlement on a doctor's bill actually tendered him for his wife's prenatal care.) Separate claims were filed for all of the cars involved, thus materially increasing the profits. Once the same car appeared in six different accident reports. Each time it collected.

Such easy-money claims are constantly increasing. They elicit such widespread co-operation partly because of the popular feeling that an insurance company is fair game, partly because legitimate claims often take so long to process. Where the "injured" parties threaten legal action, they take advantage of the well-known tendency among insurance company lawyers to "settle" at the drop of a deposition. For with the heavy claims now being made, court action can be very risky. No insurance lawyer can count on a jury's sympathy.*

Public unconcern over the prevalence of such accident frauds is hardly logical. There is a direct connection between the amount insurance companies pay out in claims and the rates they assess for their product. Consider Miami. There in 1959 the average driver was paying about $71.80 a year for his automobile insurance. Against this, residents of Palm Beach paid an average of $42.80, people in Tampa only $33.60. The discrepancy was not the result of a bad safety record. It was a

---

* Commenting on the drop in profits of Lloyd's of London in the late fifties, the *Financial Times* pointed its finger across the Atlantic: "People in America have taken increasingly to suing their doctors, their nursing homes and even their lawyers for malpractice. In addition, American lawyers, sometimes operating on a percentage basis, have grown increasingly skillful at gaining the last legal cent for personal injury."

reflection of jury verdicts and accident settlements in Miami's Dade County.

In January 1959 a series of indignant articles in the Miami *News* and its sister paper, the *Herald,* put together the horrible accident-settlement record of what insurance companies delicately call a "claims conscious" area. In Dade County's last three-year rating period, there was an average of three injury claims for every 100 cars insured. The average rate of settlement was $1,189 per case. The average for the rest of the state was only 1.8 cases and $825 respectively.

The wounds cited in most cases are interestingly similar. They run to back or neck injuries, with complications like nervousness, impairment of vision, dizzy spells, etc. Some "whiplash" injuries to the neck are of course legitimate, and they may necessitate a victim's long and painful treatment. But the bounds of coincidence are surely strained in cases like the recent bus crash in which all 13 passengers claimed "whiplash" injuries, each working through a different lawyer.

Mysteriously, a great number of these accident "victims" never improved under treatment—that is, until the case was over, when recovery was swift. Medical bills in many cases were inflated to tumescent proportions, swollen by expensive "diagnostic evaluations," consultation fees and physiotherapy treatments. The Miami *News* recalled a legal brief on the theme of miraculous recovery prepared some years before by a firm which represented some insurance companies. The brief cited some interesting cases. A painting foreman whose back injury had allegedly prevented him from working again was found back at his brush (although his $55,000 settlement enabled him to drive to work in a new Cadillac). A dump-truck driver received $100,000 in 1949 after a neurosurgeon declared: "There is nothing known to medical science that will restore a permanently damaged brain such as [he] has." Three years later he was found engaged in the business of hauling oranges to New York City. He had also taken over a local market, in which he worked when not on the road.

The *News'* findings also exposed for Miami the indispensable partner to this fraud, the ambulance chaser. There was necessarily a lawyer involved in each case, less often as a mere accomplice than as the man who had set up the entire scheme. One Miami attorney was so careless as to submit the same claim, with not only the exact medical symptoms but even the same typographical errors, to two insurance companies for two different accidents. ("Clerical error," the attorney pleaded.) "Ambulance chasing," the papers editorialized, "has apparently become a fairly common practice among certain elements in Dade County's legal profession. So has the practice of padding medical bills to justify huge damage claims for relatively minor injuries."

Although the charge of "soliciting" (the legal term for ambulance chasing) warrants automatic disbarment proceedings, if proven, it is often more comfortable for local bar associations to pretend that it seldom turns up. Yet in other places than Dade County, the rise of suspicious injury claims has impelled strong action. Just before his retirement at the end of 1958, New York State Supreme Court Justice George A. Arkwright concluded a two-year investigation of unethical legal practices with strong recommendations for prosecution. As a result of his findings, some 64 Brooklyn lawyers were put under investigation. He found, the judge admitted, "a sordid picture of unethical, unlawful and sometimes criminal practices by certain attorneys and persons acting in concert with them."

From the insurance investigators' standpoint, ambulance chasing is a major problem. They divide its practitioners into four general categories:

1. "Soliciting" lawyers who drum up trade themselves. Some

of the attorneys under scrutiny in New York City had amassed the total of 900 negligence cases in one year. Most such lawyers have their own "chasers" out finding business at hospitals or at the scenes of accidents.

2. Free-lance chasers, who auction off their "cases" to the highest bidder. An efficient free-lance chaser can rack up as much as $50,000 a year.

3. Police and tow-truck operators, working together in various localities, can easily steer an accident victim to their legal collaborators. The tow-truck men can help make a convincing wreck out of a lightly damaged car, once they get it into the garage.

4. Crooked doctors. There are some who refer all accident patients to lawyers as a matter of course.

The punishment for chasing is not severe—in most states not more than 30 to 60 days in jail. Few states have any specific laws on the books against the practice, and most of these are inadequate. Yet there is no question that the chaser and other operators in the fraudulent-claims racket are among the most persistent and successful professional swindlers in the country.

Forgers and passers of bad checks were once at the low end of the con man's caste-conscious totem pole. Now they have advanced formidably. Commonly known as "paper hangers," they are viewed with disfavor by all imaginative swindlers as pedestrian types barely worthy of the swindler's name. Yet they pose a more widespread threat than all the machinations of the orthodox con man. Since there are no national tabulations of bad-check totals, it is impossible to estimate how much the Genial Society loses annually from "paper hanging." Some authorities peg the figure as high as one billion. In January 1959 the FBI estimated that one year's cost of bad-check passing ran to $535,000,000 (for 1957). Said J. Edgar Hoover, ever ready with a ringing phrase, "The plague of fraudulent check-passers is assuming the proportions of a national pestilence."

We can say with assurance that the cost of this pestilence for 1958 and 1959 has risen. Since 1955 it has jumped by 30 per cent each year. The FBI bases its increase estimates on the number of bad checks actually sent to its offices for examination —inevitably only a small fraction of the total. In the fiscal year 1957 the Bureau looked over 30,093 checks with a face value of $5,053,846. For fiscal 1958 the figure was 33,027 bad checks, totaling $7,944,827.

Americans now do roughly 90 per cent of the country's financial business by checks. The check totals continue to increase, aided by the high-pressure selling campaigns of banks who virtually give away free dishes to entice more checking-account customers. It can be imagined how the vistas for fraud multiply.

In his crudest manifestation the paper hanger will steal a single check and forge it, or alter a check which has somehow come into his possession. He takes it to a neighborhood store (preferably in somebody else's neighborhood) and palms it off on the storekeeper, generally over a week end or during a bank holiday. He may have altered the signature only slightly, or invented a wholly new one to go with some piece of identification with which he has equipped himself. Or he may indulge in the sort of crude fancy which only proves that the man who cashed it *a*) is a half-wit, *b*) never learned to read or *c*) is possessed of subconscious charitable impulses. Each year thousands of checks bounce on bank cashiers' desks signed by witty noms de plume like "U. R. Stuck," or—in the case of blank checks—made out to that incredibly long-lived paper-hanging institution, "The East Bank of the Mississippi."

Banks, businesses, police and district attorneys' offices conduct their regular campaigns against the bouncing of checks. Shopkeepers are exhorted to demand complete identification, check signatures, etc. Some businesses take photographs of all check cashers. One manufacturer, getting at the source of forgery, has worked out a check which produces the word "void" the minute ink eradicator is applied to the paper.

Most bad checks take a relatively low bounce ($10 or $20), and will hardly send the receiving firm into bankruptcy. Countless times, the person who bounces a check is a law-abiding citizen of good intentions and bad arithmetic (or so the merchant must assume). If his check bounces, it is made good with all the exchanges mandatory in this situation.

"Good heavens, no," says Trusted Customer. "Well, I'll speak to my wife about that . . . You say it was *my* account? I have no idea how . . . the bank assured me and I'll get on the phone right away to the cashier. Of course, put it right through again and it will be all right."

The merchant generally upholds his part in the dialogue with equal politeness: "I'm awfully sorry to bother you . . . there probably was some mistake . . . Of course, I'll send it right through . . . and while we're talking, we have some of those specially priced . . . shall I save one for you, then?"

A customer who is once refused check-cashing privileges is apt to become a noncustomer for a good long time. He will prefer the more accommodating establishment on the other side of the street.

There is no sure answer to the merchant's dilemma in this relatively innocent situation, although a few ameliorations may be suggested. British banks have long extended overdrafts to their depositors, thus obviating a near crisis whenever a checkbook owner falters in his arithmetic. The British banking system does not seem to have suffered from this practice. The overdrafts are paid and there is a far more solid tradition of loyalty to the local branch among its customers.

Perhaps permission of overdrafts would fail among the mass

of Americans and be no more successful here than the British custom of unarmed police officers. But it can be argued that the U.S. banking principle of "if a check isn't covered, send it back," as practiced by the big-city banking colossi, undermines many depositors' sense of personal moral responsibility as truly as it simplifies life for the bank's bookkeepers. An attitude of "beat the bank" grows up in the Genial Society, side by side with the mentality of "beat the government" or "beat the corporation." Ingenious dodges of check bouncing, check kiting—or, as it is more politely termed, check "switching"— multiply.

Of course, businessmen who accept checks should be more vigilant. Yet, paradoxically, the clever crooks sometimes profit by the very vigilance of storekeepers and small businessmen who demand identification before they will cash a check. If some elementary alertness will freeze out the crude signer of checks drawn on the "East Bank of the Mississippi," not so with the experienced paper hanger. Some women in the field take children along on their check-passing expeditions, as an index of reliability. One man used to purchase fishing licenses in the names of the individuals whose checks he had stolen, then use the licenses as identification. Another professional once enrolled at a university in order to use his student identification card as surety for his operations.

One of the great artists among the paper hangers, who deserved his newspaper designation as "king of the con men," was an operator named Joseph Levy. Levy was last apprehended in August 1958 for breaking parole less than a year after his conditional release from Atlanta Federal Penitentiary. But he had been at the business of check passing since 1914, the year his first conviction was recorded. Through a long life of luxury punctuated by occasional unpleasantnesses—26 arrests and eight convictions—Levy developed a facility for name-dropping which went well with his look of respectability.

His usual tactic was to drop in on some merchant and order an impressive gift for an impressive person. The gift he would pay for by check, a large check made out for considerably more than the article's purchase price. Yet who could deny extra cash to a man so obviously friendly to the great and prominent? Witness the plight of the sporting-goods store where Levy once bought an expensive set of golf clubs. The address he sent them to was the Vice President's Office, Washington, D. C. The card he enclosed was friendly: "Dick, beat the boss, Leon." Pity the manager of the perfume counter where Levy ordered an expensive assortment to be sent to Mrs. Mamie Doud Eisenhower, 1600 Pennsylvania Avenue, Washington 25, D. C. Invariably the imposing addressees sent their "gifts" back and Leon, or whatever alias he was using, had disappeared.

Often Levy would pose as a man of prestige himself. In June 1958, just a few months after his last release on parole, Levy marched into the office of the Governor of Utah and introduced himself as the administrative assistant to the Governor of Illinois. After lunch with Governor Clyde and an extended tour of the Utah state capital with Clyde's administrative assistant, Levy asked if he could cash a small check. The check, for $150, bounced.

An "artist" like Joseph Levy, fortunately, is not born every day. Currently, check bouncing is practiced either by multitudes of desperate or professionally larcenous individuals, with little pretense at *savoir-faire,* or by close-working and efficient gangs of check passers and forgers. These latter have adapted new organizational techniques to the practice of phony cash signatures. Their requisites are few. They need only a car, a certain amount of daring and some ability at forging checks and instilling confidence when cashing them. The first step in their operations may be simple theft. Having cased an area thoroughly, the gang will make off with a batch of checks from some company's offices. Its members will then scatter, preferably over a week end, and pass the resultant forgeries in various sections of a city. The look of authenticity on such checks is undeniable, and if the gang is reasonably cautious they will be passed.

The cruelty and refinements of most modern con games, *and the ease with which they are accomplished,* illustrate the changes which have come over the art of the grifter. In his heyday, the Yellow Kid could look scornfully on his dupes, and with some justice. "Those sorrowful suckers over whose wrongs prosecuting attorneys cry to high heaven," he once said, "are nothing but thieves at heart. In selecting a sucker I had only to establish first that he was a sucker and second, that his covetousness and greed were as great as my own. Then I knew I had him."

The modern mass-production con man has no such pretensions. The very nature of his impersonal advertising techniques results in the innocent and honest being trapped with the greedy. The rather poor and the barely solvent are in fact more susceptible to his methods than the dwindling number of the very rich. Almost everybody in the Genial Society has some money, and is hence within reach of his blandishments. And it is sad fact that our level of intelligence has not made any soaring movements commensurate with the spectacular rises in our standard of living.

Many of the old-time con men have retired in protest against the gray-flannel syndicates—to say nothing of the widespread competition from amateurs. "In all my life," as one of the Yellow Kid's associates was heard to say, "I never heard of a real racket man padding an expense account."

VI

GOOD MEN GONE WRONG

Woe to them that are at ease in Zion.
—Amos 6:1

At 3:00 P.M. on the afternoon of January 12, 1959, the Honorable George A. Brenner, former Surrogate of Westchester County, a one-time county judge and twice candidate for Congress, successful New York and Westchester lawyer, Democratic Party leader, teacher, bank director and pillar of the community, crashed a borrowed car into an abutment of the Major Deegan Expressway in New York City. Both of his legs were broken and he suffered multiple internal injuries, which caused doctors at Misericordia Hospital to worry about his chances of survival. He was to remain a stretcher case for six months.

The first reaction of shocked condolence which followed this news was muffled in the headlines which appeared barely a week after the judge's odd accident. He had been indicted by the New York County District Attorney's office on charges of forgery and larceny, accused of milking various creditors—banks, corporations and individuals—of something like $1,300,-000. The real amount of his pilferage, as developed in further investigations, went higher. He had stolen from friends and

business associates. Totaled one by one, the charges against
him would have made him liable to a penalty of 650 years in
jail.

There is no more typical comment on a big fraud or embezzlement exposure than that of many New Yorkers on hearing of it:
"Too bad in a way it had to happen. Just think, if he'd got away
with all those deals, he'd have been in the big time. It just goes
to show you . . ."

As an illustration of just how close the inflated "big time"
is to the busted "big deal," the sad case of Judge Brenner is
most instructive. For a great deal of his life, George Brenner
worked out an urban version of the American success story. He
was born in New York City in modest circumstances, but he
began to attract attention early in the game with his quick
mind and an affinity for hard work. He was first in his class at
Fordham and he supported himself through law school
by working as a high-school teacher. Even before he passed his
bar exams, he had interested himself in problems of labor and
management. He was among the pioneers of the formal instruction courses designed for rank-and-file union members to further
union democracy as well as make the unions more effective
bargaining instruments. He taught at the respected Xavier
Labor School, an organization founded by the Jesuits for this
purpose.

Through these connections Brenner gradually developed
a large and increasingly lucrative practice as a labor lawyer. He
was at one time counsel to the International Longshoremen's
Association and also represented John J. O'Rourke, who ran
the New York area for the Teamsters. It is doubtful if he had
any hand in the corruption later uncovered in these bodies. He
was a force of good among the unions he represented, which
included many besides these. He handled other types of law
as well, and his downtown Manhattan offices had the prosperous
air of a business with plenty of briefs on the table and plenty

of clients' checks going into the bank.

His private life was a model of probity. He married early and his wife bore him three sons. They moved to Westchester, where Brenner kept a branch of his New York office. Like many ambitious lawyers, he was an inveterate joiner in civic organizations. He became active, also, in laymen's groups of the New York Catholic archdiocese. He was in demand as a speaker at Communion breakfasts. At one time he was elected president of the Fordham University Alumni Association.

By the fifties, Brenner had also plunged hip-deep into local politics. In two successive elections he ran for Congress as a Democrat. To do this in Westchester County, most of whose denizens regard Republicanism as synonymous with social respectability, generally indicates more courage than sense. But Brenner was popular, and he rolled up impressive votes even while losing. In 1955 a Democratic governor appointed him a county judge in Yonkers and in 1957 the county surrogate. He tried to win the later elections for both these offices, but failed. Again, however, the votes were unusually large for a Westchester Democrat. Brenner's friends kept telling him that he would ultimately be the man to crack the Republican strangle hold on the county. After that, the field was clear for state office. Meanwhile, his speaking engagements multiplied and he had transferred his offices to an expensive location in midtown Manhattan. In Westchester, he moved his family from their old Yonkers dwelling to a new house in Bronxville, a more fashionable district. He acquired an extra car, and a small cabin cruiser.

In a word, Brenner was the model of a respected citizen, the sort of man whom associates consulted when a problem wanted solving or a friend got himself into trouble. He was kind and genuinely hospitable. If he seemed pompous on occasion, or in dubious taste in having his photograph, resplendent in judicial robes, decorating the reception room of his law offices, this is the kind of license recognized as harmless, and readily granted to the prominent.

Yet in the offices behind the judicial photograph, Brenner came to conduct a weird double life, in which desperation produced a half-fraudulent resourcefulness which in turn bred a brazen criminal confidence. This inner life had its origins in the failure of his campaigns for Congress. Lulled by the frequent applause of dinner meetings and Communion breakfasts, Brenner had put all his faith and more than all his money into these losing battles. When the election returns were counted, he had spent his savings, and he was badly in the hole. His friends had not put up the money he had hoped for during the campaign. He began to borrow heavily.

In the course of the next few years Brenner managed to pay off these original debts and others by herculean efforts in his law business. Meanwhile, he kept casting about for shiny new business possibilities and further advancement in politics, thereby canceling the ground he had gained. His much-prized judgeship appointment in 1955 paid little, and left him less time to make money in his private law practice. By 1956, when he was defeated trying to win another term, he was badly behind once more. His only assets were several hundred thousand dollars owed him as a fee by the International Longshoreman's Association, which he had served as counsel until 1955.

The ILA had trouble settling the debt, but its president, Captain William Bradley, agreed to give the judge a number of promissory notes, which he in turn discounted for cash. Some of the people who accepted the notes, or who gave him loans on the basis of other security, were less than reputable, and their terms were harsh. But Brenner continued to need money. He moved his law offices at much expense and continued to devote great energy to his political plans. When his term as surrogate expired at the end of 1957, he ran again for re-election. Once more he proved that Westchester Country was strongly Republican, even for a popular Democrat. His debts were reaching critical proportions, although—interestingly enough —his standard of living kept ascending. He had long since cashed his last legitimate promissory note from the ILA.

By early 1958 some of Brenner's creditors were growing importunate. It was at this point that an old acquaintance named William Singer, a man of sharp wits and past criminal convictions (for swindling) to his credit, suggested that the judge might ease his way out of his difficulties with the purchase and resale of lucrative Manhattan real-estate property. The property was the Shelton Towers Hotel in mid-town and it looked good. Brenner decided to strike out and buy it. He hoped to refurbish it in a hurry, then sell the property and the lease to one of the larger hotel chains, at a heavy profit. He concluded a 14-year lease for the hotel in July 1958, raising money for it on the basis of short-term loans. By this time Brenner was all too well acquainted with the type of loan that demanded quick payment (generally in 90 days) and heavy interest. Ironically, a few more such obligations seemed the only way in which he could pay off those he had.

In the negotiations leading up to the Shelton Towers lease, the only collateral left to Brenner was 7,500 shares of stock in the First National Bank of Yonkers, N. Y., of which he had been for some years a director. He used this stock in raising money for a preliminary deposit on the hotel and for clearing up some of his high-interest debts. Hard-pressed to meet the full down payment, Brenner thought he could make his shares do double duty. Up to this time there was nothing wrong with Brenner's financial position that a quick killing in real estate could not have rectified. Now, assisted by Singer and other unsavory new associates, he went decisively over the line.

On July 1 he got a $190,000 personal loan from an investment firm on the basis of duplicate stock certificates of the First National Bank of Yonkers. Singer used his expertise to forge them. Methodically, his certificates were reproduced with the same numbers, so that the holder of the forged certificates, if he checked at the bank, would discover that the numbered shares in question had indeed been issued to the judge. And who would think of questioning the judge?

But the situation at the Shelton Towers proved no solution. Refurbishing took far longer than expected, and no large hotel chain seemed eager to take the lease off Brenner's hands. The holders of the steep 90-day notes (the $190,000 loan involved a $225,000 repayment) demanded their money. So Brenner and his associates went back to the printing press. Eleven times the same 7,500 First National shares were pledged as collateral, to various banks and individual creditors. No one suspected.

Brenner continued to live well while conducting these manipulations. He had bought a new $100,000 house, which promptly acquired first and second mortgages. He forged outright more of the ILA promissory notes, without bothering to get any accomplices in on the deal. He mortgaged possessions which he no longer possessed. (When indicted, he owned two large cars, but he was making payments on six.) At the height of his hotel troubles, Brenner visited the Motor Boat Show in New York and after some impressive financial sleight of hand came out with an expensive new cabin cruiser.

The house of cards began to collapse, fittingly, one evening in the Casa Cugat, the night club in the Shelton Towers, when one of Brenner's creditors, casually discussing the judge's difficulties with an acquaintance, heard that the judge had pledged his Yonkers bank stock to the Federation Bank and Trust Company in New York. This seemed strange, since the creditor himself was holding as collateral what he thought was the total of

Brenner's interest in the Yonkers bank. A few telephone calls established the astonishing fact that he and Federation were holding shares with identical numbers.

It took weeks before the full impact of Brenner's transactions was felt. He turned out to have mortgaged his law firm's offices in New York, among other things, beside extracting large amounts of the firm's profits for his personal ventures. By the time of his first indictment, phones were ringing all over New York City and Westchester, as various bankers, lawyers and plain creditors discussed the vain possibility of making good their losses.

Until the very end the judge was unperturbed. He had narrowly missed getting the Democratic nomination for Attorney General in the 1958 election. The day after his accident he had been scheduled to introduce Vice President Nixon at a formal New York dinner.

To this day George Brenner's many friends cannot understand what made him do it. He was not addicted to high living or purposeless spending. The old syndrome of "bookies, babes, booze," beloved by veteran surety-company investigators, would have no relevance in his case. Yet he represents a classic motive for white-collar crime: the desire for power and prestige. Politics was Brenner's specific weakness. But with his hopes for political success went all the demands of front and display which the Genial Society engenders.

Another searcher for recognition, on a less ambitious level, got his comeuppance for much the same reason. In 1958 John J. Tobin, Jr., a 30-year-old civic booster from Youngstown, Ohio, pleaded guilty to the embezzlement of more than $200,-000, after an exposé which rocked his community to its foundations. Tobin was also interested in politics. When he was elected to public office in November 1957, he was the youngest councilman in town. People were already talking about him in connection with the next mayoralty race.

Tobin's position and salary were far less than Brenner's, but he demonstrated convincingly how a man can do a lot with a little. He never earned more than $100 a week, as an adjuster for the American Associated Insurance Companies. For two years he swindled this firm grandly, by submitting false accident claims and collecting them. His claims were well documented with faked newspaper reports and the testimony of bribed lawyers and doctors. He had two close associates, one Paul Shade and an attorney named Allen J. Swaim, who took care of his legal work.

Their bubble burst only one month after his triumphant $10,000 City Council campaign, when someone from the main office finally began to ask questions. All three blew town in a hurry, leaving the normal afterbirth of bad checks, deserted families and less fortunate accomplices. Tobin himself was picked up in February 1958 at a hotel in Houston, where he was living under the name of "Donald Lucky." He had already joined several prominent Houston bottle clubs, so that he could meet "the right people." He and Shade were well on their way into an out-and-out swindle, based on a fake "engineering" company.

Why? In the first place, Tobin was quick to point out, he had kept certain rigid business standards. He never cheated on his salary or his expense account. All he touched was the $200,000 worth of claims. About that he was notably unrepentant. "I'm just like everybody else," he told police in Houston. "Nobody cares about defrauding an insurance company."

Through his swindles he had continued to be a model husband and father, doing odd chores around the house when he was not out fixing claims or slapping political backs. Admitting that he spent the $10,000 on his Council campaign, he told about his plans. "With money, I could have been mayor, too."

Jack Donald Hubbard, who at 35 received the Fort Worth Junior Chamber of Commerce award as the "outstanding young man of 1955," concealed a different sort of talent behind his civic position. In August 1957 he and several accomplices were indicted by a federal grand jury for their complicity in a state-wide check-kiting ring. Almost until the moment of his indictment, Hubbard had been president of the River Oaks State Bank. He was district chairman of the Boy Scouts, first vice-president of the Ridgelea Civic League and an elder of the Ridgelea Christian Church. Starting out as a bank runner just after high-school graduation, he had worked his way up the ladder in the best Texas tradition, quickly and nimbly. He had been president of the River Oaks bank less than a year when his particular bubble burst.

Check kiting, as we have seen,* is a different and more complex process than simple forging. With the urge to credit as strong as it is, there are few up-and-coming businessmen who can claim to have resisted the temptation to write a pressing check just a day or two before some money is due, in the prayerful expectation that their deposit will get into the bank's ledgers before the check they have cashed comes home to roost.

A deft operator, with banking connections, can turn this emergency device into a paying business. He cashes a check at one bank based on inadequate or nonexistent funds at a second out-of-town institution. By the time the check is presented for payment at Bank No. 2, he has covered it with another phony check drawn on a third bank. This process can go on indefinitely as long as there are checks coming in and fleet-footed people to cash them—preferably at widely separated points. The cash gained can be used for working capital, as it were, between checks.

The risk is obvious. Since the check kiter is in the position

---

* See Chapter V.

of a man juggling a dozen balls in the air at the same time, he can never stop. The only breathing space available to him, outside of the time involved in clearing the checks, is the presence of an accomplice in one of the banks, who can hold bad checks when something goes wrong with the system.

When Hubbard and his ring dropped their juggling act, after a 10-month investigation by the FBI, they left a sum of $986,-203.14 unaccounted for. The losses were divided among 12 banks throughout the state of Texas, with one bank in Kansas City involved. Among them the defendants had 21 checking accounts in various names at the River Oaks bank alone. Thousands of checks had been passed over an 18-month period.

In Hubbard's case, the supposition was that he was drawn into the act through bad companions, a disbarred attorney and a real-estate man. Other than that the people of suburban Ridgelea could find no reasons why Fort Worth's "outstanding young man" had gone sour. Again the refrain went up: "What made him do it?"

Two qualities distinguish all such white-collar criminals, immoderation and self-delusion. The first is the same flaw which scars the villains in the fairy tales of the brothers Grimm. It is the wolf who eats too much that gets his comeuppance, and woe betide the greedy goldsmith who goes back for a second bag of gold. Generations of children have privately wondered why the wolf or the goldsmith could not have been content with his first stroke of good fortune, without trying to crowd his luck. Recent generations of criminologists (we have been warned by our psychologists to keep children away from Grimm) can ponder afresh the same phenomenon.

Many men have a jump-off point where the infrequent dishonest practice turns into a way of life. A lie-detector expert who has made a career of ferreting out embezzlers, reckons for his professional purposes that the theft of $1,000 is a good dividing line. But most cases are matters of a man forsaking normal prudential mechanisms, as ever-richer illegal prizes come within his ken. In the end, he is most often caught in the manner of the Grimm brothers' greedy wolf, who ate so much of the farmer's produce that he was unable to squeeze out of the escape hole in the cellar.

A sure candidate for a graduate degree in immoderation was one Roscoe David Coon, Sr., who made off with $678,000 during a six-year stewardship as vice-president and cashier of the Joshua Monument National Bank of Twenty-nine Palms, Cal. When he went to work for the bank, as the story was told in *Fortune,* his worldly wealth consisted of a small house and two 1937 cars. By the time he was arrested, he had bought a stable of 36 horses, which he raced at various tracks. He had built seven houses in the area, invested in a finance company, a lumber company and a night club and made easy personal loans to fellow citizens, including two bank directors and the bank president.*

Immoderation is a blood brother to the second characteristic of these operators: self-delusion. A fine expression of this tendency was one given in a California federal court. A contracting engineer had claimed that the $50,000 paid him in the space of three years by a company receiving large fees from his employer was simply remuneration for special engineering services, which he had done in his off hours. "It is one of the oddities of human character," Judge Yankwich commented, "that by sheer process of telling oneself or being told a situation is other than it actually is, one can come to believe in the fiction rather than the fact."

* It is time, incidentally, that people got over the illusion that bank presidents are extravagantly paid. In August 1958 the U.S. Comptroller of the Currency reported to Congress that almost 50 per cent of the nation's bank presidents earn less than $10,000 annually.

It was doubtless some form of fiction-over-fact that sustained the activities of Miss Minnie Mangum, the assistant secretary-treasurer of the now-defunct Commonwealth Building and Loan Assn. of Norfolk, Va., whose trial in June 1956 unearthed a total embezzlement of $2,885,000 over her 28 years of service there. (She lived modestly and gave most of her gains to charities, relatives and friends.) A comparatively tiny but equally extreme form of self-delusion was displayed by the trusted department-store employee about to be given a testimonial dinner for 25 years of faithful service. On the eve of the dinner, he was discovered to have stolen a $200 dress from the store—so his wife could have something nice to wear to the dinner.

All of these examples of fraud or embezzlement involve people of respectability and stature in their communities. Stories of the office underling having an illicit fling more readily get into the newspapers—like the Canadian bank teller who fled the Royal Bank of Ottawa with $290,000 in his black bag and was finally nabbed in the men's room of the Chez Paree night club in Denver, his new de luxe convertible waiting at the curb. But such defalcators are not nearly so dangerous to the society around them as what we might call the responsible business defector.

One of the foremost authorities on white-collar crime in the country is Norman Jaspan, who discovered so much uneconomic peculation in his management engineering work with various firms that he founded an adjunct to his management consultant business, called Investigations, Inc., specifically to check up on employee dishonesty, bribes, kick-backs, manipulations and other forms of embezzlement or larceny. In 1959 Investigations, Inc., uncovered dishonesties of some $60,000,000 in management cases. Of these losses, 62 per cent were attributable to executives or supervisory personnel.

Executives and supervisors [Jaspan explains] don't come into a company to be dishonest. They are influenced and pressured into cheating in a variety of ways. They may have to make themselves look good for an executive meeting, or for a chance at promotion. Or, their ego may be at stake. All too often an executive is reduced to a choice between failure and dishonesty. He has so much pressure put upon him either by choice or by the nature of the business that he simply cannot accomplish what he has to do.

Their own rationalization, in turn, protects such people from looking on themselves as thieves. It is carried to such lengths that they are often quite genuinely shocked to be labeled as crooks, when they are caught.

This rationalization is of course helped by mismanagement. Often people turn to crime when they feel they are not treated with dignity. But it is helped also by the vagueness of modern morality. The borderline is so badly defined. The bottle of liquor becomes a case, the basket of fruit leads to the color TV set. The supervisor or executive doesn't have to hide his loot under his shirt when he leaves for the day. He can manipulate, falsify and steal, and make it all look perfectly legitimate, and because he is in a position of trust, he is not likely to be questioned.

To illustrate how vague morality can get, Jaspan has often cited the case of the manager of a large New England retail store, whose firm authorized him to give damaged goods to charity, as a deterrent to employee pilferage. The manager gave away the damaged goods. He also gave away $85,000 worth of *un*damaged goods, over a three-year period. He took nothing for himself. Everything was turned over to his local church. Each year the manager's fellow church members gave him a testimonial dinner, as a monument to such powerful Christian giving.

Since only one out of 10 cases ever sees the light of day and barely 20 per cent of U.S. companies are bonded, the national statistics are sketchy on embezzlement—to say nothing of in-

dividual open-field running like the Brenner frauds. But every
count made by insurance and bonding companies and independent experts indicates steady, often startling yearly rises
in the amount of "taking." Roughly one bank in every five has
sustained an embezzlement in the last three years. The amount
insurance companies have paid out on fidelity losses has jumped
130 per cent in the last 10 years—more than twice the normal
cost-of-living rise. Jaspan calculates that total losses* of this
sort to American businesses rose from a half billion dollars at
the end of the postwar period to more than one billion in
1959.

The annual sales volume of American department stores is
now roughly $16 billion. Shortages come to $200 million annually—more than half the amount of the net profits. In 1959
the country's supermarkets sustained $100 million loss from
employee thefts, which canceled out profits on $5 billion worth
of sales.

Authorities in the field agree that their statistical embezzler
archetype is a respected employee in his late thirties, married
and the father of two children. He is well liked and enjoys the
respect of his community. He started to work in his particular
place of employment seven years ago. He has been whittling
down the profits for three.

The embezzler may be a loner, a man with unusually easy
access to other people's money. Such was the assistant manager of a building concern in New York City, picked up in
August 1959 after four years of padding the pay roll with
fictitious names. It had been in his exclusive charge. Similarly,
there was the office worker at a Midwestern newspaper known
for its crusades against political bribery and corruption. This
man was arrested in October 1959 for squandering the funds

* This total does not include losses arising from kick-backs, unnecessary over-
time, diversion of customers, etc.

of the paper's Employee Credit Union, of which he had been the treasurer. (The editors, loyal to their quest, noted the fact on the front page.)

More often the embezzler is able to spread his crime over a widening area—as he attracts the notice of friends or co-workers and makes them accomplices. In the summer of 1959 a classic case of collusion was turned up in Rock Island, Ill., among the tolltakers on the Centennial Bridge between Rock Island and Davenport, Ia. A few of the tolltakers had developed a cavalier attitude toward the money entrusted to them shortly after the bridge was opened in 1940. The attitude was contagious. At certain hours they would turn off the treadle that recorded a truck's or a car's weight, thereby canceling any record of tolls thus collected. On a good day a man's take at the treadle might go as high as $40.

The racket collapsed when one tolltaker refused to participate and told his story to the local state's attorney. Investigation suggested that the total shortage would exceed $750,000.

If a person has been "taking" on his own, he understandably turns a blind eye to the peculations of others. When fraud losses, both direct and indirect, run deep inside a company's blood stream, they can seldom be eliminated even by tight screening of new employees, or wide uses of automation techniques. (The mind boggles at the geometrically ascending rate of damage which can be done by a dishonest human being feeding doctored figures into a mechanical brain.) The Jaspan firm contends that it can add some 20 per cent to the profits of a business by an over-all survey embracing everything from accounting methods to office morale. Jaspan chafes at the fact that so many businesses spurn the chance to make such savings. "Not only is management missing an unparalleled opportunity to increase profits," he says, "it also stands indicted for failing to preserve important moral standards in business."

The kick-back is a more fashionable, single-breasted version of open embezzlement. Most givers and receivers of kick-backs would be quick to denounce the embezzler as a crook who deserves immediate prosecution. If a man getting his first kick-back has a slight twinge of conscience, the passage of time readily convinces him that the money or goods he accepts are not bribes but perquisites of office, sanctioned by custom.

The kick-back, probably for this reason, is the most contagious form of business dishonesty. It appears in an almost infinite variety of forms: direct money bribes, "loans," property gifts, shares of businesses, the use of cars, apartments, etc. Some "givers" go to the lengths of putting influential "takers" or their relatives on their company pay rolls.

Although the total take in kick-backs is estimated as high as $5 billion annually, any accurate statistical picture is, once again, impossible to obtain. But the rise in the incidence of kick-backs is unquestioned. Here are a few straws in the wind. A 1958 poll published in *Sales Management* magazine noted that more than *one third* of 200 sales executives questioned had lost business when they refused to participate in a pay-off. The February 1959 issue of *Textile Industries* reported, on the basis of various executives' informal appraisals, that "from ten per cent to several times that of total sales in various chemical specialty fields are made on the basis of kick-backs, excessive entertainment, and similar shady goings-on."

Kick-backs naturally proliferate in businesses where the competition is heavy, like clothing, food or entertainment. (See Chapter X.) Intense competition generally results in greater weight placed on the personal element in business. Companies rely increasingly on the good will of buyers and purchasing agents, paid to pick and choose in fields where the differences between competing products may actually be slight. The next step is obvious.

Bad times also spur the kick-back system. The recent recession of 1956-1958 drove businessmen to the wall in a wide variety of industries. Often the price of survival was a crooked deal with suppliers or retail outlets. From this few shrank.

Once a kick-back system is installed, in good times or bad, it is very difficult to get rid of it. Witness the sad experience of American companies involved in that prelude to the kick-back, the lavish Christmas gift. Some estimates hold that no less than $2 billion annually are burnt up by American businessmen for such tangible good will, principally in the holiday season. The gifts, starting out with humble lighters or pen-and-pencil sets, have reached extravagant proportions in some industries. They include stock shares, Cadillacs, winter cruises, cases of whiskey, TV sets.

When a company tries to cut down on its giving, it runs into the problem of one bad apple corrupting the barrel. For if only one or two purchasing agents crassly demand their gift tribute, everyone must be taken care of.

A 1958 survey by Ohio State University's School of Journalism polled a number of companies on the issue of Christmas giving. Nearly half of the responding executives—representing a large sampling of the country's big business—admitted that their companies gave until it hurt. Yet a majority, as noted in a *Reporter* magazine article, said they disliked the whole idea. This discrepancy between taste and behavior was of course accounted for by their fear of losing business.

The more unscrupulous sort of executive has worked out a variant on the Christmas gift, to his personal profit. This is to purchase, say, $10,000 worth of gift certificates at a department store for distribution to clients, customers, *et al.* The $10,000 is charged off as a business expense. But somehow a good $5,000 worth of the total finds its way into the hands of the executive's family or friends. Especially in New York City department stores, salesgirls have grown used to the post-holiday spectacle of executives' families loading up the larder and the clothes closet with the firm's gift certificates.

The worst thing about the kick-back is the readiness with which it is institutionalized. After a few years kick-back money becomes a vital part of a family's economy, on which its very standard of living depends. Veterans of the Federal Trade Commission in Washington remember the man who wrote to the FTC some years ago, asking if there were some way in which its local office could enforce payment of his monthly kick-back, which was in arrears.

Nor are such cases restricted to people in the buying field. Purchasing agents and buyers, it must be emphasized, are as honest as anyone else—probably more honest, considering the relatively low percentage of them who give in to such obvious temptations of their jobs. Shipping offers vast possibilities for criminal collusion. A company traffic manager, for example, draws kick-backs averaging $1,000 a month from a trucker who handles most of the shipping between his firm's mills. Duplicate invoices, padded "waiting time," and various other excess charges represent the trucker's sizable reward.*

Beyond doubt, the dress industry in New York City, one of the most brutally competitive in economic history, acts as virtually a pilot project for every variety of kick-back. Not long ago a Manhattan dress manufacturer bared his soul to Herbert Robinson, a highly able New York lawyer who has brought more than 100 bribery cases to the courts through the last five years. The manufacturer told Robinson how the process operates with buyers whose favor he competes for.

"A young buyer comes in new to me," he explained, "and maybe the first time he's in—we're all rushed—I give him a

* For this and several of the foregoing anonymous case histories, I am indebted to Norman Jaspan's recent book, *The Thief in the White Collar*, which gives much detail on these and similar examples.

sandwich in my office. Later we'll have lunch a few times, until one evening I take him and his wife out to a very good dinner. The wife sees the nice things around her—she gets discontented. She wants something like them. I take them to the theater. Next thing that happens he takes a gift certificate or a bond from me. After that I own him."

No record of the kick-back business would be complete without mention of the most egregious taker of recent time, a New York dress buyer, Stanley Sternberg, who worked for a branch of the Sears, Roebuck company until his enforced retirement in 1952. In the course of his many years of service, he bought millions of dollars' worth of clothing for Sears and took, by reliable estimates, a cool quarter of a million from the clothing manufacturers.

Sternberg, a pathologically acquisitive man, drove the manufacturers to despair with his levies. In return for giving them advance information on the type of clothing Sears wanted (and buying it thereafter), he received regular payments in bonds and cash. At his arrest, he had on hand $137,000, distributed in 27 banks. He insisted on regular daily lunches and had his and his family's clothes purchased from manufacturers' charge accounts. When he bought a new house on Long Island, he was given, after some broad hinting, a $475 dryer, a custom-built TV set, gas range, refrigerator and thousand of dollars' worth of household improvements, down to a Barcalounger chair.

One manufacturer was detailed to take Sternberg's aged parents to dinner almost nightly. Another manufacturer's wife, famed for the quality of her cuisine, was called upon to supply a home-cooked turkey whenever the Sternbergs craved fowl. He once suggested that a manufacturer supply an employee to push his father's wheel chair. He chiseled stamps, stationery, newspapers and cigarettes. "Nothing," the dress manufacturers recall, "was too small for Sternberg."

Most honest Americans will shake their heads at the grossness of the kick-back artists, or wonder sadly how the trusted Westchester judge could "go wrong," or what could turn Fort Worth's Junior Chamber of Commerce "man of the year" into a check kiter. When crime appears in the bosom of respectability, there is an involvement far different from routine shock and disapproval.

Newspaper readers in New England were startled not very long ago by the trial of a respected former state official on charges of embezzling more than $200,000 from an estate for which he was trustee and executor. The trial ruined his reputation. Yet he had done nothing worse, according to the standards of both law and ethics, than the New York lawyer, also a trustee of an estate, who illegally borrowed funds from his trust to build himself a big house in the country, then repaid the money—with no one the wiser. In the New Yorker's own mind, he had committed no crime. He had paid the money back—*i.e.*, he had got away with it.

The criterion of "getting away with it" grows increasingly popular in the Genial Society. It is part and parcel of a half-conscious dissociation of civil or white-collar crime from an individual's public morality. The more important the person is who gets away with it, the less people want to believe in his guilt.

A painful lesson of this sort was given to the stockholders of the H. L. Green Co., the variety-store chain, in the spring of 1959. Their hastily retired president, Maurice E. Olen, of Mobile, Ala., had been hailed as a merchandising genius at 34. In the postwar years he had built up a small business of his father's into a chain of 123 low-cost variety stores operating in the South. In November 1958 his firm merged with the larger Green concern, and Olen was elected president of the com-

bined company. In March of the following year two of the
Green directors held an emergency press conference in the
New York offices of the Securities and Exchange Commission
and made the painful announcement: "The auditors informed
H. L. Green Co. that their investigation of the Olen division
to date had disclosed an apparent deficiency approaching
$3,000,000 in the net assets of such division, the principal items
being an overstatement of merchandise inventories and a failure to record accounts payable."

The sad avowal was a far cry from the confident mood in
which the Green Co. executives had announced the acquisition
of their young president less than half a year before. In 1958
H. L. Green, established and respected in the industry, was
searching both for new management blood and a chance to ex-
pand in the South. Olen looked like an answer to any firm's
prayer. He had a reputation for a keen sense of merchandising,
which seemed to be amply borne out by the way in which he
made his family firm the fastest-growing soft-goods chain in
the U.S. "It's refreshing," wrote one New York business column-
ist at the time, "to see youth assuring our nation its future
growth." If Maurice Olen's company had not been exactly distinguished for its sound financial base, it was conspicuously
aggressive and successful in that all-important division: sales.
Manufacturers were happy to give the Olen Company goods
on consignment and southern banks were eager to advance
credit. For the young president was known as a man who could
keep goods moving. The more goods he moved, the more he
expanded, the more he borrowed—but he kept them moving.

Not long before his merger with the Green Co., Olen decided
to offer a $1 million issue of stock in his company. The invest-
ing public gobbled it up, its zeal kindled by the figures of net
worth which Olen supplied. As a New York SEC official put it
later, "The stock went out the window in a few hours."

H. L. Green's directors were as impressed by this marketing

success as anyone else. When they met Olen, they were equally impressed by his drive and determination. A merger was approved and Olen chosen to direct the combined enterprise. With the merger went an exchange of stock. Olen received the lion's share of $5.5 million worth of Green stock, in return for giving Green control of his own company's assets. He then drew $6 million from Green as working capital for his newly merged Olen division.

An indictment later handed down by a New York federal grand jury told this corporate success story in strikingly different terms. In chilly legal language Olen was charged with failing "to record in the ledgers of the Olen Company, Inc. all of the outstanding accounts payable to vendors of merchandise," although he did not neglect "to record on the books of the Olen Company, Inc. as operating expenses a substantial portion of the expenditures for capital improvements." Olen and other defendants were charged with a successful scheme to "arbitrarily record on the books of the Olen Company, Inc. a warehouse inventory figure of $112,210, when in fact said warehouse inventory was approximately $1,000,000." "Financial statements and related schedules," the indictment continued, "did not fairly present the position of the Olen Co., Inc. and its subsidiaries. . . ." As for the stock issue, it was based on "a registration statement including prospectuses which contained false and misleading statements" of some material facts and omissions of others. So the indictment lumbered on.

Not long after the events which the grand jury thus memorialized, the Green Co. executives and directors had begun to worry about their new president. When the company sent its own accountants to investigate the status of the Olen Company, Inc., their worries deepened to alarm. By March the bubble had burst. Olen returned $2,000,000 worth of stock and other assets to the Green Co., but it was too late.

On December 3, 1959, the grand jury indicted him on charges

of conspiracy and violation of the Securities Act of 1933 and the Securities Exchange Act of 1934.

As with other big-time operators, there was no hint of personal irregularity in Olen's life. He, too, was a victim of what might be called "the illusion of abundance," a by-product of the ordinary consumer urge to possess more and more and more.

The pressures that force persons into fraud are admittedly strong. Faced with their variety—the propaganda of abundance, poor supervision, gullible businessmen, excessive government regulation, high taxes, bad example, social strivings or even cultural aspirations*—how does a member of the Genial Society keep on the straight and narrow without the aid of some moral gyroscope yet to be invented? Or does he more often fall in with the theme of the hit song from *My Fair Lady*:†

> With a little bit of luck
> With a little bit of luck
> When temptation comes, you'll give right in . . .

One answer to this is Clarence Darrow's observation: "Some boilers are safe at 20 pounds pressure to the square inch, but will break at 40. The boiler is neither honest nor dishonest. It stands a certain pressure and no more. Man cannot be classified as honest or dishonest. He goes along with the game of life and can stand a certain pressure for the sake of his ideals, but at a certain point he can stand no more."

This might have been a saving, if not essential, philosophy for a veteran criminal lawyer; but it would be disastrous to

---

* A quiet-mannered clerk, D. Omer Tobias, who worked 30 years for a manufacturer at Troy, Ohio, looted the company for $375,000 in that period. Most of this he invested in a huge private art collection.

† Copyright © 1956 by Alan Jay Lerner and Frederick Loewe. Chappell & Co. Inc., New York, N.Y., publisher and owner of allied rights.

accept it as a valid comment on the individual's susceptibility to crime. The boiler philosophy of crime is just as rigidly determinist in its way as the Marxist theory of economics. Like the latter, it overlooks the element of free choice in every human being, a choice which can be and has been exercised despite accumulations of pressures. There was no pressure on the lady Eve to eat the apple—she lived in the midst of plenty —other than her freely chosen whim. There was every pressure on the Prisoner of Chillon to recant and get out of jail, but his free choice resisted it. So on through an infinity of examples.

We might well forget about Darrow's pressure theory and start thinking about man's God-given gift of moral choice. A morally well-instructed child will grow up with a greater likelihood of making the right choices between fraud and decent business, even when it hurts. And part of any moral instruction is a respect for the sanctity of other people's property, firmly inculcated.

The word "moral" may be disputed here. The richness of psychiatric discovery and psychological prediction has obscured for many the underlying fact of man's free moral choice (which few good psychiatrists, incidentally, would deny). At the other end of the stick is the fondness of so many national spokesmen and disguised political editorialists for wrapping themselves in a righteous armor of "morality" every time they comment about the weather.

Neither the public morality's detractors nor its self-appointed defenders should make us forget the importance of personal moral choice. For if Darrow's boiler theory is correct, not only the framework of the American business contract, but the foundations of our democracy lose all their meaning. Both are based on a belief in the impermeability and the necessity of man's individual moral choice.

As we have seen, the Operator can be any American. The horrifying thing is that he so often is.

VII
EUPHORIA ON THE TAB

"By Hercules," he used to say, "I don't wonder
That some eat up their substance,
Since there is nothing really sweeter than a fat
*   thrush,*
Nothing finer than a large sow's womb. . . ."
                        —HORACE, Epistles (I, 15)

It was late in the evening, the day after the first of any month. Henry Harried sat undisturbed at his cellar desk, alone with his bills, his checkbook, credit cards, installment-loan coupons, office desk pad and a sheaf of printed forms marked "Expenses: Travel and Entertainment." Like hundreds of thousands of other executives he was about to count up facts and figures that might, if he were lucky, form a rickety bridge between two columns of a double economic life. He pondered with Pilate the ageless question: What is Truth?

Henry's problem was not difficult to describe. He was a $15,000-a-year man who spent about $18,000 and received the difference in one or more kinds of expense allowances. At home he tried to save, fixed the roof himself, viewed with approval the President's TV warnings against excessive spending and wondered what drastic economies could be made to finance his children's later schooling. At his job, in a competitive business where "contacts" were deemed crucial, he was encouraged to spend. As he advanced, he came to spend more lavishly. Headwaiters and ticket brokers were devoted to him. One side of his wallet listed heavily from the weight of cards —hotels, restaurants, clubs and various pay-after-you've-gone organizations—attesting to his easy credit facilities. He was not by nature a glad-hander and he had frequent moral and social qualms about the extent of his commercial hospitality. To be *overly* ostentatious, in certain quarters, was as bad as to be niggardly. However he managed his "front" relationships, they were invariably expensive, and expected to be so.

He found it increasingly difficult to separate the standards and budgets of his office and home life. In fact, as more and more of his friends turned out to come from his special business world, he had about given up the effort. Here at his monthly time of reckoning, he would attempt to reconcile the roles of harried ranch-house owner in the suburbs and part-time Lucullus in town. The expense account offered his only hope of making his finances break even, yet at the same time its very existence assured him that they never really would.

Such was a typical member of the Expense-Account Aristocracy. How much company he had in this group is uncertain —a detailed survey of the membership is impossible. But there is no doubt of its extent and its increase. Each year in this country between $5 and $10 billion are totaled up on the "tab," or "swindle sheet," as the record of travel, entertainment and other business expenses is familiarly called. Restaurants like "21" or the newer Four Seasons in New York, or the Pump Room in Chicago, or hundreds of less well-known hostelries where a shrimp cocktail costs $2.50 or more, would be, to say the least, dim of spirit without the expense account's ruddy, steady glow. In a marginal business like the New York theater, a show may rely on the expense-account trade for at least 30 per cent of its tickets. From this generally decisive percentage the effect of the tab on dramatic culture can be deduced. Because of expense accounts the newest and most indirect of all American industries, the credit-card business, has assumed a prominence that past generations would have thought fantastic.

The regional prevalence of expense-accountism is a matter of debate. Like the medieval Europeans who called social diseases by the names of unfriendly nations,* the Los Angeles businessman will protest concern at the terrific amount of Scotch consumed in San Francisco, the Chicagoan will recoil at the thought of New York's three-Martini lunch and the Detroiter will hold himself shocked by the number of stingers shaken up in Chicago.

It is probably true, however, that New York is ahead in this department. There is no more conclusive argument for this than the profusion of cheerless but expensive "French" restaurants which thrive there, the mediocre insisting as strongly as the few good ones on shrewdly rich prices and unintelligently rich food, served behind a barricade of French phrases which their headwaiters have mastered since leaving Palermo.

To the really big-time operators, of course, the excesses of lunch, dinner and theater-ticket spending are small potatoes. Big game safaris in Africa have been successfully charged off to the company tab—on grounds of the resultant corporate publicity given the firm's huntin', shootin' president. Lodges are built, European vacations are taken, new yachts slide into the water on the strength of the almighty tab. (A long-time resident of Fort Lauderdale, Fla., recently estimated that fully

---

* Syphilis, for example, was known, in various languages, as the French Sickness, the Spanish Sickness, the English Sickness, the Italian Sickness, etc.

80 per cent of the private boats tied up in the basin there were being charged off to some form of corporate activity.) The big spenders have also managed to raise vastly the levels of most entertainment tariffs. Scalpers' prices on tickets to theaters and major sporting events are by now settled at tropospheric altitudes. In its heyday of 1957, it was nothing at all for a scalper to get $75 a seat for *My Fair Lady*. The U.S. government has grown ever less happy—and well it might, since expense-accountism costs the government something approaching two billions a year.*

In the fall of 1957 the Treasury Department made its first formal attempt to sluice back some of the expense account's placer gold. The Bureau of Internal Revenue ruled that everyone who received expense-account money from an employer would have to make accounting of the sums received and disbursed on his personal income-tax statement.

The attempt caused a flurry of concern among a large section of the business community. In businesses where expense accounts are heaviest and the immediate business return therefrom least provable—advertising, public relations, television, press promotion, etc.—the concern amounted to mass panic; the job of documenting every drink and every taxi ride for the Bureau of Internal Revenue curdled the hearts of the most patriotic. Inevitably, after enough outcry had been raised, the tax collectors revised their order. In March 1958 the Bureau conceded that people who reported their expenses to employers, to those employers' satisfaction, need not duplicate their efforts for the U.S. government.

Later the law was tightened. Taxpayers reporting their 1959 incomes had to list their totals of reimbursed expenses, at least, even if they need not itemize.

* This and some following statistics are derived from an article, "Expense Accounts for Executives," in the *Yale Law Journal* (July 1958), by V. Henry Rothschild and Rodolf Sodernheim.

But the problem remained, and it has grown greater. Commissioner Dana Latham of the Internal Revenue Service epitomized it in December, 1959, in the process of explaining his new set of regulations: "There is an unfortunate tendency to try to live on expense accounts."

Although the living may be gracious, it puts some wearying strains on the national moral fiber, and it is this strain, increased by the new pressures of corporate life and easy credit, that lends such interest to the expense-account story. The extreme abuses are well known and have passed into national folklore, generally with significant stops in the Tax Court on the way. The steel broker who claimed a business-expense deduction of $47,946 for call girls known as "female entertainers" did not get away with his claim.* Neither did the manufacturer who noted a $20,000 party for his son's confirmation as a business expense (because many of his business friends had been invited), the undertaker who charged his grocery bills to the mortuary (because his wife met so many good potential customers on her shopping trips), or the real-estate man who charged his company $700 for his mother's funeral. But far more interesting and more disturbing are the uncounted thousands of relatively honest American businessmen who lean on the expense account as a way of life, whose personal and corporate expenditures are run together so inextricably that with the best will in the world, and the best set of tax accountants, it is hard to separate them.

Few even make the effort to do so, and here the distinction between the real Operators and the honest businessman is foggiest. Where Walpole could say "all men have their price" in politics, and Clarence Darrow could make his point about the human boiler, the motto for the expense-account society might

---

* Even in Japan, where organized female entertainment has long been part of the culture, such expense items began to run afoul of the tax regulations in 1958.

be: "Everyone has his own gray area—and just try to find mine."

Expense-accountism did not happen by itself. It is an acute symptom of how quickly a new concept of morality can take hold of a society which still believes that it is abiding by the old.

Men have, of course, been living off the tab through the centuries. Many of Horace's satires and epistles were directed against the Roman counterpart of our expense-account aristocracy. Official entertaining reached heights of sickening magnificence in Rome and Byzantium, and by the time of England's Elizabeth I, one royal visit to a local baron's castle was enough to put all but the wealthiest host temporarily, if not permanently, in debt. If Maecenas or Lucullus rarely thought of their entertainments as business expenses, the barons who entertained Elizabeth certainly did.

In an earlier day, also, most business products were easily identifiable. The characteristics of competing firms could be set quite sharply against each other. If you wanted speed, use Superior Products. If long-term durability was what you sought, there was nothing like Peerless. As competition widened, these differences were no longer so apparent. (The classic case in point has been the depressing uniformity of the Detroit car.) Accordingly, success often does depend on intangibles like personal influence with people. It may never be admitted or documented that Peerless got its big contract as the result of a cleverly staged evening on the town for several of Acme's executives. But if you don't think that evening was important, just wait and see the saturnalia which Superior is planning for the same men next year.

It was only in recent times, therefore, with the advent of such organized persuasion, that a recognized system was devised for expenses incurred in pursuit of legitimate business objectives. It was more recently still, thanks to the growth of modern taxation systems, that these business expenses became an object in themselves—a source of luxury otherwise unattainable.

With heavy taxes, strong unions, advertising, knife-edged competition and government regulation, it became even more difficult to consider business as an existence rigidly separate from a man's private life. More and more, people took their business problems home with them. They often ended by living these problems 24 hours a day, and in the circumstances it seemed only fair to bring something from the cashbox home for their pains. Modern businessmen in effect moved inside the countinghouse—along with their wives, families, yachts, forks, spoons and golf clubs. Calvin Coolidge might not have admired the almost total scope of today's corporate expense accounts; but, as any tax accountant could tell him, never in our history have so many people tried to give literal restatement of his memorable axiom: "The business of this country is business."

The most pressing reason for the growth of expense accounts is the personal income tax and the heavy tax on corporation profits. The U.S. corporation of any size is taxed a flat 52 per cent of its net income. In the days of the excess-profits tax, it could be assessed an extra 30 per cent on top of that. "Ordinary and necessary" business expenses are clearly not regarded as income. When deducted from the gross income, they bring down the net income of the company—and the heavy tax to be paid on it.

Money for business expenses is not necessarily thrown away. Used by a skilled salesman or executive, these expenses can be like bread cast upon the waters. If the company may not find it again "for many days," it may nonetheless come back to the cash registers sooner or later, in the form of an important customer's good will and further buying, the enhanced sales value of the company's—or the individual executive's—name, favorable publicity, etc. Such an investment, which at best will pay off handsomely someday, has cost the company no more than 48 cents on the dollar. (If the dollar had slipped untouched into the net-income column, the Bureau of Internal Revenue would have taken at least 52 cents of it *instanter*.)

The arithmetic of the "tax dollar" is so engraved on the businessman's operating soul that it would take generations to erase it, even if the Bureau of Internal Revenue suddenly cut its levies on corporate profits. In a 1953 letter to *Life* magazine,* Senator Paul Douglas quoted a story by the Australian economist Colin Clark which assesses the situation accurately. (It is no shame to either of them that the story has had more twists and tellers in the business community than anything since the Franklin-and-Eleanor jokes of the thirties.) Three English businessmen, in this version, had just consumed an expensive lunch. When the time came to pay the check, they argued for the privilege. "Let me pay," said the First Businessman. "I'm in the 80 per cent income-tax bracket and this is deductible, so it will cost me only 20 per cent." The Second Businessman countered: "I'm in a 100 per cent excess-profits tax bracket. Let me pay and it won't cost me anything." "Gentlemen," the Third Businessman argued, conclusively, "let me pay. I'm on a cost-plus contract and I'll make a profit."

The institution of the cost-plus contract, incidentally, is no British phenomenon. It has now become a fixture in American business life, particularly in the case of defense contracts between government and private business contractors. It is easy to see how this system arose. Suppose the U. S. Air Force awards a contract to one or more private business concerns for the development of a new missile system. With little or no prece-

---

* Commenting on an excellent article on expense accounts by Ernest Havemann.

dent for either contractor or government to go on, it is natural
that the contract be awarded on a basis of the cost plus an
agreed-on fee for profit. (There is a statutory ban on cost-plus-
a-percentage-of-costs contracts.) The trouble is that this cost-
plus system has spread from use in the absolutely necessary
instance to the point where it becomes a virtual way of life.

The executives of companies working on cost-plus contracts
often have difficulty resisting temptation. In this case temptation is not merely the question of having lavish executive
lunches discussing their particular government projects, but
whether, say, to have the plant air-conditioned while the contract is running. The possibilities for making money "on the
tab" in cost-plus projects are endless. And most of the expenditures are well within the "gray area." More dangerous, however,
than any specific excesses of any one contractor under this plan
is the loose-spending habit of mind which a profusion of cost-
plus contracts engenders in the business community.

Far more important, in fact, than any business advantage
gained among customers is this effect of a good expense account
on the man who has one. The rigors of the personal income tax
are harder to escape, the more prosperous one becomes. So to
many salesmen or low-ranking executives, an expense account
can be far more attractive than a raise. If the customer eats
on it, you eat too. Frequently, so does your family. If you need
a car for business, there is no law against the family using it
week ends. If you have to go to Florida for the convention, it
can be quite a saving to take the wife along (on the family
plan) and soak up her expenses by a little extra "padding" on
your own.*

---

* As generally happens, the U.S. government, if alert in prosecuting expense-account peccadilloes, has lagged far behind private industry in recog-
nizing how much it actually costs an executive to *subsist* away from his office
on a legitimate business trip—to say nothing of entertaining the family. The

At this point moral fiber is apt to bend and twitch, and the Genial Society offers scant pressure to bolster it. It costs less to give a man an extra $1,000 expense account than an extra $1,000 raise, and the commitment is not so binding in the yearly budget conferences. This reasoning is, of course, never codified and rarely voiced. But it spreads through the often studied policy of management to "look the other way" when the accounts are due on the first of the month.

So far we have mentioned only the perils of the company expense account for the man who earns something less than $25,000 a year. The problem he poses for the tax collector, however, is small compared to the big-league expenditures of two kinds of bosses who direct him: *a*) the salaried executive officer of a large, publicly held corporation, and *b*) the officer of a generally smaller, private company, who shares in his company's ownership—the so-called "stockholder-executive."

The executive officer in a large corporation, by long usage and tradition, is expected to conform to the classic idea of a capitalist. His job is the same job that was done by generations of tycoons before him, his responsibilities equal, his large salary—by earlier standards, at least—commensurate. Yet due to the current system of taxation, he speedily finds that salary raises do little but put him in another and higher tax bracket. Since a great percentage of our corporate executive officers have few resources of their own, this threatens to leave him in the position of a career ambassador in one of the more socially active capitals, with all the prestige and authority but little of

standard fixed allowance of $12 per diem for traveling government employees must cover food, lodging, local travel and sundry expenses, whether the government employee involved is traveling in Trieste, Tanganyika or Trenton. If once considered generous, the $12 a day by present U.S. standards hardly permits even a bare adequacy of travel expenses. "If you want to keep in contact with all your out-of-town friends," the Washington saying goes, "join the government. You'll have to stay with them if you hope to stay within your travel expenses."

the established wealth associated with the entertainment demands of his position.

The obvious solution is to load up his expense account—since the executive is identified with the company, his standard of living is assumed to be a matter of company prestige. The courts have frequently backed up such assumptions. In one memorable case, a New York referee conceded that the president of a motion-picture company was justified in charging his New Year's Eve revels to the company, as well as a chartered yacht and his wife's clothing. "The corporation," the referee concluded, "had a good business purpose in chartering the yacht for Mr. Cohn that summer. For the cost of charter and maintenance they had him available throughout the summer at a time when he otherwise would have gone on vacation."

This kind of tactic is the rule rather than the exception in many large corporations. The president may not own the corporation airplane himself, but who better than he has the right to use it? And who is to say that he is not using it on business every time he calls the pilot into action? In the final analysis, is not the health of the president a large, if intangible, company asset? If he chooses to buttress this health by a fast flight to California, is this bad?

It all adds up to the fact that the companies, especially when dealing with their higher executives, regard the expense account most frankly as a fringe benefit. In some cases these fringe benefits have been institutionalized to a scandalous degree. In 1957 the Commissioner of Internal Revenue ordered his field agents to investigate "the use of alleged branch offices established in resort cities for the sole purpose of sending business executives to such cities for vacations."

The confusion and/or dodges found in the expense accounts of some corporation executives reappear with sharper edges among the second category, of the man at or near the top of a closely held corporation. When this executive is also a leading stockholder, difficulties multiply: there is no front-office accountant to blow the whistle on *his* expense account. Hunting lodges, cars, European trips and family outings may appear charged off as business expenses. To be sure, he has a slightly better claim in these marginal cases. It can easily be argued that the entire conduct of the business depends on the health and humor of its dictatorial boss.

The widespread use and abuse of the expense account were interestingly documented in a survey conducted by the *Harvard Business Review*. It was based on the opinions of the 2,800 executives answering the *Review*'s questionnaire—virtually a record turnout for such a sampling. Of this cross-section polled, for instance, 65.9 per cent of the married men were in the habit of taking their wives with them to business meetings and conventions. As one respondent put it: "With taxes the way they are, many men are setting up meetings to which they can take their wives, so they can afford to give her a vacation. Most of the time she probably does something worth while for the company, like getting to know employees' wives [sic]." Over 70 per cent of those reporting were reimbursed for business entertainment at social clubs and almost 40 per cent for entertainment at home. A majority (60.7 per cent) stated that there was no "yardstick" for determining the legitimacy of an executive's listed expenses—and most quite rightly said any "yardstick" system would be impossible to run. At the same time, interestingly, 65.9 per cent of the respondents believed that "expense accounts are often used by a company to give its executives a hidden, tax-free salary increase." In summing up, 53.5 per cent of the respondents stated that "they don't like the way many businessmen handle their expense accounts"—a notable admission for members of an occupational group traditionally uninterested in critical self-judgments.

It must be emphasized that the faculty of splicing the expense account is by no means restricted to the heads of privately owned companies or the harried salesmen and executives of large corporations. Example, if strong enough, always encourages emulation. So secretaries and messengers add five or ten cents to the actual amount of their cab fares, acting out of an unfortunate but wholly understandable instinct that with so many corporate melons being sliced up before their eyes, they deserve for their services at least a bit of the rind.

The public-relations business is far and away the biggest user of expense accounts. Coming right behind it are advertising, entertainment and then of course the activities of sales personnel in all fields. It is in something like public relations, advertising or entertainment, where the element of personal contact is one of the commodities for sale, that the care and feeding of clients have been taken to tremendous lengths. No big American movie company, for instance, would think of putting a major product on the country's screens without a massive program of previews, selected entertainments and press junkets. The latter are now *de rigueur*. "A great picture," says the press agent to the editor or movie writer, "and a really great director. Look, why don't you go over and see for yourself. He's shooting in Spitzbergen now. Tell you what. We'll fly you over to Spitzbergen, just to talk to him. Take a few days. Really go out and see how he works. And of course, we'll stop in Paris on the way . . ."

This technique of the press junket has been carried to impressive lengths. No airline nowadays would think of putting a new service into commission without ferrying several planeloads of selected "media" people to some attractive or exotic rendezvous, after first equipping them with a "press kit" that handily obviates the necessity of any reporting, and following up with consistent liquid infusions that would make any serious reporting impossible. Automobile makers, brewers, movie producers—almost every consumer-goods industry in business has a weakness for the lavish trip treatment.

Originally viewed as marginal, such by-products of the public-relations era are now engraved in standard operating procedure. A restaurant opens a new kitchen, a cosmetics manufacturer gives birth to a new shade of nail polish, a car company produces a new variety of soft-bellied hard-top—out come waves of press kits and the inescapable cocktail party. One of the most agile public-relations counselors, New York's Ben Sonnenberg, has developed professional entertaining at home to a formidable degree. His house can and does accommodate business entertainees by platoons. An imposing edifice on Gramercy Park, it is furnished so spectacularly that the casual visitor wonders whether anyone really lives there between parties.

Yet, barring the successes of a few veterans like Sonnenberg, the general value of entertainment in business slips as surely as bad money drives out good. Entertainment, originally offered as novelty, is now expected. A good part of any publicist's work lies in dreaming up ever more lavish bits of bread and circuses.

Conversely the effect on the recipients, e.g., members of the working press, has been noticeable. Say what they will about their editorial purity, reporters and editors are made of the same clay as everyone else; it takes a rare spirit to release an article critical of Flying Carpet Airways on the eve of a round-the-world "junket" under Flying Carpet's auspices. Only a few publications—*Life* being almost the sole major example—have had long-standing rules against junkets of any sort for their writers or editors. Some even figure outside junkets as part of their editorial budget. I have heard the editor of a moderately large national magazine urge subordinates to "find so-and-so a junket" in lieu of a pay raise.

A temporary check to the prevalence of junkets, entertainments and lavish gift-giving came in the fall of 1959. The exposure of widespread crookery on TV quiz programs was quickly followed by unusually harsh words about the deceptions current in TV advertising and the outright bribery of disk jockeys to play favored records on their radio programs. This last "payola" from record companies to the disk jockeys, although hardly a significant economic item in itself, showed how pure and simple graft came to dominate a segment of the American entertainment industry. Where money was not paid outright to insure a disk jockey's playing a record, various perquisites were furnished. Alan Freed, a prominent New York TV disk jockey, saying good-by to his network in November 1959, defended the practice of taking noncash gifts from friends in the trade. "This," Freed said, "is the backbone of American business."

The wear and tear of expense-account living, to say nothing of graft or "payola," is enough to erode all but the sternest standard of values. The disbursement of his cheap 48-cent dollars gives the businessman a feeling comparable to that of the American tourists in Italy on hearing for the first time that it takes several hundred lire to make up one single dollar. Cheap money in the mind gets cheaper. A sense of propriety once scandalized by paying three dollars to a headwaiter now slips fives, tens and twenties to waiters, headwaiters and captains, without a thought. The palate that once rejoiced in the occasional luxury of a 20-cent cigar now disdains to insult its guests or itself with anything less than a 75-cent Upmann. The household that once served its friends blended whiskey or beer now spends its last dollar to bring in another bottle of 10-year-old Scotch and imported gin. Tastes and standards do not operate on a nine-to-five basis. Once created, they remain, having lost all conscious connection with their origins—which may have been nothing more than the $300 a month vouchsafed a man for office entertainment.

The social burdens of corporate-entertainment relationships pose their own problems. The man whom you fete at the Fandango Club—as well as the fellow who entertains you— becomes a relative-by-hospitality. This relationship has not been formalized in the Western world since the time of the Greeks, who indeed had a word for it: *xenos,* meaning "guest-friend." While modern Americans have not reactivated this Homeric term, the increasingly tight network of hospitality and counter-hospitality suggests that we recognize the obligations it once implied. Constantly, the expense-accountist forges bonds of obligation which may even extend to members of his family— to say nothing of what they do to his freedom of action, critical faculties and sense of perspective.

Competition has reached the point where people vie to see not how little but how much they can pay for their tickets or tables. There is no reason why any healthy, employed American citizen who has shaved and wears a tie cannot overspend triumphantly with little more than a few five- or 10-dollar bills (for tips) in his pocket, as long as he possesses a ball-point pen for signing and a suitable number of credit cards.* Only rarely does the element of grace or pleasure intrude in such dining establishments. Good fellowship is preserved in acres of superfluous cracked ice, hospitality buttressed by pounds of discarded citrus slices and untasted *canapés.* Generally, and often disastrously, the only good value on the bill of fare is the superchilled Martini.

The same indictment of tastelessness can be leveled against other departments of expense-accountism, from the sodden sight-seeing of publicity junkets to the garish unseaworthiness

* In 1959 a 20-year-old New York City clerk, finding himself the legal possessor of a Hilton Carte Blanche credit card, went on a two-month-long tour of expensive hotels and luxury shops from Montreal to Florida and succeeded in running up $19,000 worth of utterly unpaid bills before some extra-fancy check cashing led to his detection.

of the big-time spender's Florida power boat. In the theater, the expense-account market has put a premium on the big, brassy musical, an art form with less merit than a burlesque show and the spontaneity of an automobile ad. For if the cream of this business is rich, it is also very, very thick.

Even amateur sport has capitulated to expense-accountism. It has done so on the highest levels of competition, where the necessity of continual expense accounts has made a mockery of a player's "amateur" status. It is a waste of time for the U.S. Lawn Tennis Association, and its big-league counterparts in Australia and elsewhere, to discipline a player for allegedly misusing his expense account: the players seldom have outside means, and must live on "expenses." "If I'm guilty," the Australian doubles player Mervyn Rose objected after his suspension in 1958, "some others are, too." This was one of the understatements of the decade.

Everywhere leisure has been marched into the tax-deduction column. J. P. Morgan probably thought he was speaking with finality when he made his famous comment that the man who had to ask how much a yacht costs to run couldn't afford one. Now, two generations after him, a whole race of "sportsmen" has evolved which couldn't care less how much the running expenses are. The company pays the tab.

The founders of the noble game of golf regarded their sport as a relaxation, or at best a refreshing competition. It is interesting to watch how far golf, as practiced in most American country clubs, has strayed from this purpose. Business golf would be a legitimate designation for the new version of the sport. It has become purely a status symbol. It is the ambition of most modern American businessmen to become an elder of the local golf club, just as it once was to become an elder in the church. (Since both are Sunday activities, church attendance has suffered proportionately. Young businessmen who are neo-orthodox Christians often solve the problem by either early church or an early golf game.) The golfer is a direct, if unwitting, descendant of the minor baron who was privileged to hunt the stag on the king's preserve. Often a baron had to intrigue for a lifetime to gain this goal. But he had nothing on the efforts of some to niblick their way into the sometimes tightly trapped greens of country-club membership.

The social prestige of the golfer came down to us from the recent past, where an older generation—or more exactly, a very small portion of it—had the money and the leisure to enjoy golf as a quiet sport. In 1913 the income tax law ended the financial security of most American clubs—golf and otherwise—although we had to wait until 1929 for the more spectacular clubman's downfall. As the new executive works his way up, he is in a spot about paying the fees demanded by his rising social position. The answer is of course the expense account. Do not other members enjoy great prominence and power in the business world? Are not "contacts" all-important? So golf goes on the tab. Every year thousands of good American executives charge off all or part of their club bills to the company. The same *Harvard Business Review* survey previously cited found that 49.9 per cent of executives in small companies, 31.8 per cent of the executives in large corporations, and over 40 per cent of top management across the board could habitually charge off memberships in "social clubs or organizations" as business expenses.

To satisfy the Internal Revenue Service, as well as his own company auditors, the social golfer has to distill some business contacts out of his 19th-hole Scotch. Sunday morning, like the Saturday night before, transforms itself into a pleasure mixed with business and not recognizable as either. "Get at him while he's playing golf" is a maxim too frequently heard nowadays. And people believe in it.

Thus members of the Genial Society, in pursuit of ease and

what they hope is the socially correct type of leisure, find themselves living constantly in a world where no real leisure is ever
permitted. Where a purpose is claimed for everything, some
purpose has to be invented. It is not the dedication of an
earlier day when a man lived, ate and slept business, and had
no recreation whatsoever. With us the problem has grown far
more insidious. We live better and eat better, and in far more
comfortable surroundings. But how much of this time is really
our own?

It is a cliché that "you never make money on an expense
account. For everything you put on in padding, you've probably
forgotten some legitimate expense that should have gone on.
If anything, you lose." In the larger context, this is infallibly
true.

Most large corporations have efficient staffs to keep a close
eye on expense accounts—so close an eye, in fact, that the
company accountant or auditor has come to occupy the traditional role of avenging angel in expense-account folklore. The
folklore itself has become imposing. A typical story concerns
the New York publicist who charged his firm $200 for a lunch
at "21" with only one client present. On being taxed with this
obvious inaccuracy (even "21" would be hard put to run up a
$200 check for two, although it might be an interesting chal-
lenge to the management), he pointed out that the client was
in regrettably shabby condition when they met. "I couldn't
take him out to '21' dressed like that," he explained weakly,
"so I took him down to Brooks and bought him a suit first."

Brushing aside fictitious names and cases, the expense-
accountist has a legitimate problem in the way most accountants regard their trade. The accountant's realm, somewhat
like the lawyer's, must be a squared universe, to fit the dimensions of adding machines and standard rules and practices.

Since the world is round, especially in the expense-account field, the accountist gets into trouble. A man may give a present to a valuable client, with excellent business results; if he is wise he will often write this off as a succession of lunches. Anything which does not fit an accountant's pigeonhole is viewed darkly.

Aside from this erosion on consciences and bank balances, widespread expense-accountism does something to the business conduct of the Genial Society. A man bound up with his organization, depending on it for much of his food, housing, entertainment and leisure, is understandably cautious about severing connections with it. While he works for it—or, more precisely, lives within it—he is devoted to furthering its interests, but cautiously so. As William H. Whyte, Jr., demonstrated in his impressive book of the same name, "The Organization Man" belongs to a "generation of technicians." A technician with so great a stake in remaining within his peculiar corner grows ever more faithful, but increasingly timid in his performance.

His are not the bold decisions, the board-room victories, the farseeing visions of the heroes in current business fiction. The man who makes a bold *wrong* decision may find himself out on the street the next week with an embarrassing expense-account settlement pending. The man who delivers a challenging board-room argument may find, even if he wins his point, that he is no longer wanted among the company's chief officers. In its most concrete terms, this may mean a) turning back the keys to the company-owned Cadillac, b) leaving the membership of two highly prized clubs, c) calling his family back from their long-awaited vacation on a company property in the South. It may even mean giving up his very comfortable house.

How much these substantial feudal perquisites influence individual business decisions is something which no sociologist's calipers can measure. But it would be against human nature for a man with $10,000 or $20,000 worth of annual perquisites to think lightly of losing them as a penalty for overboldness. It is demonstrable fact, also, as Whyte and other chroniclers of U.S. business document, that the businessman in our Genial Society is notably less aggressive than the race of businessmen before him. "Whatever I engage in," Andrew Carnegie once wrote, "I must push inordinately." This kind of statement today would make most executives wince, if they did not start telephoning at once for the company psychiatrist. With few exceptions, they know the limits. With taxes what they are, good jobs scarce and perquisites long abuilding, they are not interested in rocking the boat.

It is here that our latter-day magnates go a different road from their medieval forerunners. The feudalists of old lived with risk. A Manfred of Sicily or Raymond of Antioch could entertain lavishly in his castle, aware that the issue of a single battle could transform him into a hunted fugitive. They fended the dangers off when they could. They took their medicine without surprise, generally, when they failed.

The latter-day feudalists who cluster around their company banners grew up, on the contrary, in a society whose highest goal was neither victory nor charity, but welfare. Far more abundantly endowed with the world's goods, they have been conditioned to believe that there is something for everybody, as long as he plays the game—and the angles—discreetly. "It is the organization man," as Whyte says, ". . . who most urgently wants to belong. . . . Over and above the overt praise for the pleasures of the group, the very ease, the democratic atmosphere in which organization life is now conducted makes it all the harder for the individual to justify *to himself* a departure from its norm."

Expense-accountism may well be only a symptom of the feckless "togetherness" which drags like a sea anchor on imaginative action in American business. But it is a heavy symptom. Like so many, it in turn becomes a cause of further sickness. No influence in the world has a more constricting influence on a man's capacity for vision, action and change than those comfortable old chains of gold.

There is no way to banish completely the ills of expense-accountism. High taxes will be with us for a long time. The Genial Society's ways of doing business have grown up organically and logically, as the result of technological and social factors—however unhealthy they seem to us. We cannot change them overnight. As they exist now, expense-accountism is their inescapable by-product. A massive program of enforcement could do the job, conceivably, of eliminating all abuses; but we already have an Internal Revenue Service inspector, lurking, as it seems, behind every third adding machine. There is a limit beyond which a bureaucracy cannot healthily supervise.

The businessmen answering the Harvard questionnaire tended to blame the expense-account abuses on the tax structure itself. They also suggested that the Internal Revenue Service inform itself more accurately on actual company practices in the expense account field, thus eliminating a great many misunderstandings, not to say inequities.

Admittedly we do need, here as elsewhere in the Operator's territory, more intelligent enforcement, backed up by action on the part of the companies themselves. It should be every firm's burden, as Rothschild and Soberborn suggest in their study, to report all extraordinary facilities made available to individual executives, and the company should be prepared to prove their business necessity. IRS field agents, they go on to say, might be given more power to question expense-account practices in local audits. In the case of the small, closely held companies, where some of the trickiest abuses occur, a healthy enforcement drive is in order.

Over and above enforcement threats, businessmen might profitably reflect on some moral history behind their expense-account temptations. The barons and gentlemen of medieval times *did* have codes of morality and ethics. The medieval ancestor of the organization man did not regard his "corporation" as a pocket-size version of the Welfare State which existed for his personal convenience. On the contrary, he was always highly conscious that he owed at least as much to the "corporation"—whether a guild or a barony—as the corporation owed to him. His conscience reminded him that a definite contract existed and that the right fulfillment of this contract depended essentially on him.

The modern man can object all he wants that his kind of corporation, unlike the medieval vassal relationship, has no soul or conscience of its own. To which it can only be said that the conscience of a corporation, like the moral sense of a modern democracy, is an intangible that can and does exist, but only through the demonstrated individual consciences of its members.

As a second strengthener for the frayed moral fiber of expense-accountists, we might note the obvious admonition that keeping in step with new business times does not necessarily mean that you have to bring your foot down (politely and unobtrusively, of course) on your neighbor's shinbone—whether the neighbor be the company auditor, the U.S. government or a fellow salesman. Probably the best thumbnail example of how, in the long run, *not* to do business, is found in the preachment of that celebrated sly financial manipulator of the mid-19th century, Uncle Daniel Drew*:

* The avuncular title came largely from his sanctimonious mien and a propensity for churchgoing. While he was plundering the Erie Railroad, and a considerable section of the stock-owning public, Drew endowed a famous theological seminary in Princeton, N. J., which once bore his name. His gift was for $250,000. Unfortunately it took the form of a note, which was never redeemed.

With this panic year of which I am now writing [1857] a new state of affairs came about in financial circles. The panic was known as the Western Blizzard. It put old fogeyism out of date forevermore. The men who conducted business in the old-fashioned slowpoke method—the think-of-the-other-fellow method—were swept away by this panic, or at least were so crippled that they didn't figure much in the world of affairs afterwards. A new generation of men came in—a more pushful set. I was one of them. We were men who went ahead. We did things. We didn't split hairs about trifles. Anyhow, men of this skin, with a conscience all the time full of prickles, are out of place in business dickerings. A prickly conscience would be like a white apron for a blacksmith. Sometimes you've got to get your hands dirty, but that doesn't mean that the money you make is also dirty. Black hens can lay white eggs . . . It isn't how you get your money but what you do with it that counts.

As many of us approach our monthly soul-searching with the expense account, it should be a comfort to recall that Drew's nonprickly conscience not only left him with the barest minimum of friends, it also left him a poor man. He died with only a few dollars to his name.

VIII
VIRTUE IS NOT DEDUCTIBLE

No other country leans so heavily on income-tax revenues as the United States. Of the total of $85,175,500,000 collected by the Internal Revenue Service in 1959, $42,832,711,000 was paid by individuals as income tax. Of the estimated $46 billions additional which taxpayers gave to state governments in 1959, seven per cent was realized through further individual income taxes, which are now law in 32 states. Since taxes of all sorts take up one quarter of the gross national product, it is easy to see how critically an epidemic of income-tax dodging can affect the American economy. To justify their own abuses tax dodgers may cite many injustices in the tax laws. Nonetheless a widespread tax delinquency presents a picture of a society gnawing at its own vitals.

"Now about these entertainment deductions—pretty big, wouldn't you say?" The examiner smiled his cat-and-mouse best at the taxpayer seated in front of him.

"Large, perhaps, but as you will see, inevitable in the performance of my business," the taxpayer replied coolly. "On this itemized list, I have labeled each of these entertainment costs, down to the tips for hat-check girls. I have noted the people entertained, their business and my exact commercial connection with them. I've taken the precaution of finding out their present whereabouts, and you can easily check the connections with them."

The examiner looked angrily, but half-admiringly, at the lists given him, which precluded any hint of fraud, forgetfulness or fancy padding. He veered off on another tack: "Let's put the expenses aside for the moment and get after this capital-gains statement. Would you mind telling me by what authority you have so arbitrarily listed the greater part of your business income under this category?"

The taxpayer looked at him pityingly. "I can only refer you," he said, "to section 83947, paragraph *b*, subsections 49 and 102 of the Internal Revenue Code—backed up, as you doubtless recall, by the recent Federal Court decision handed down in the Southern District of New York. The last three items in my capital-gains expenditures are so listed, following a valid precedent set by a Tax Court decision of 1799 in the Northwest Territory—I've included the citation. I believe this decision was recently reinforced here by the Circuit Court of Appeals. Shall we go on?"

Sweat moistened the examiner's palms as he rustled through papers, trying to find another bone of contention. "Now these stock transfers," he snapped. "I don't think you can laugh off this one so easily. To say nothing of that dependency allowance for your third wife's four brothers."

"Really, you should know about that. The clarification of the 1954 revision of the 1939 code, as noted in subsection 4683 of paragraph 902, states that securities traded in Liechtenstein for interest-bearing Bolivian notes which have been converted into U.S. Treasury bonds on the Toronto exchange are *ipso facto* deductible as net-loss debentures. As for the dependency claims, a 1959 decision of the Federal Court, Southern District of Texas, has been interpreted to allow all such relationships. If you wish the exact number of the ruling, I'll tell you. But could we get on to the matter of this additional $4,800 refund, due to the depletion allowance from my muskrat rambles? You know, of course, that there *is* a 26½ per cent depletion allowance for muskrat rambles, and I have nineteen of them."

The foregoing may lack the heroics of Walter Mitty's pocketa-pocketa-queep fantasies, but it is an increasingly popular daydream of the Genial Society. It holds scant resemblance to real-life confrontations of taxpayers with officers of the Internal Revenue Service. If any such confounding of the government tax experts occurs, it would more likely be engineered through a battery of supercharged tax lawyers. Yet most Americans cherish the dream. And few could specify whether it is a dream of illicit corner-cutting or simple insistence on one's rights.

In no other area of American life is there a thinner line between the respectable and the criminal, the honest and the cheating, the moral and the immoral than the nebulous realm of the income tax. As the cases discussed will show, the only safe way to define an income-tax violator is: anyone who thinks he can get away with it. "In the prohibition era," New York's District Attorney Frank Hogan has said, "there was certainly a tendency to believe that anything you get away with is right. This may well be true in the tax area today." The dethroned pre-Hoffa boss of the Teamsters Union, Dave Beck, told reporters at the beginning of his 1957 trial for $240,000 income-tax fraud: "It's happening all over America."

Once more, no accurate estimates can be made of the amount of income tax which is *successfully* evaded. High guessers have put it as high as $10 billion a year, although it is more likely about $5 billion. The amount of unreported income each year—a basic figure in assessing the tax leakage—is about $28 billion. Statisticians have calculated that honest payment by everybody liable to income tax would enable the government *to decrease the general tax burden by 40 per cent.*

Some indication can be provided by the records of the Internal Revenue Service. At the end of 1958 the IRS listed 1,280,642 taxpayers as delinquent in their payments. The amount they owed was $1,375,737,000, and the government was busily engaged in collecting it. (A small percentage of this sum represented Social Security payments and income taxes withheld from employees' pay checks but not yet turned over to the government; the major portion involved individual income-tax delinquency.) The total additional tax, interest and penalties the government derived from its tax-enforcement efforts in the fiscal year 1958 were $1,684,465,000, a handy increase over 1957's efforts.

In the course of digging this extra money out of unwilling pockets the Internal Revenue Service, now something under 52,000 strong, had done a great deal of lint-picking. From more than 60 million individual income-tax returns, the IRS managed to verify mathematically 57,585,000. Some 2,841,000 particularly juicy returns were put to the squeeze in an intensive auditing process. As a result of the audits and mathematical checks there were 4,184 full-dress investigations of individual taxpayers, after over 14,000 preliminary investigations had been made. Yet after investigation, only 918 indictments were returned against individual taxpayers for fraud in fiscal 1958. If we extend the year to December 31, there were a mere 1,170.

There are some obvious discrepancies here. The scant number of income-tax cases actually brought to court—1,170 prosecuted for fraud out of 60,000,000 returns filed—sounds as harmless as the incidence of pickpocketing at a nudist convention. It would seem at variance with the huge figure of one and a half billion dollars for back taxes and penalties.

The explanation lies in the purpose of the Internal Revenue Service, which is not to put people behind bars but to collect as much tax as possible. Although every IRS inspector rejoices in the sight of an egregious tax violator going to jail, the principal reason for prosecuting him is summarized in the tax collector's favorite word: deterrence. Knowing full well the there-but-for-the-grace-of-God avidity with which the members of the Genial Society read newspaper reports of tax cases, Washington counts on a conviction of, say, a crooked dentist, or the indictment of a dishonest supermarket proprietor to bring a wave of astonishing rises in reported income on the next year's tax returns of dentists and supermarket proprietors throughout the land. In this assumption Washington is seldom wrong.

There is, also, the question of *which* statistics apply to the problem of tax dodging. IRS officials lovingly cite the tiny percentage of taxpayers with known fraud in their hearts as an index of the taxpayer's fundamental honesty. One per cent is the favorite statistic used. It is a matter of record, they will assert to any newspaperman in hearing distance, that three out of four returns filed each year are correct. Former Internal Revenue Commissioner Harrington said in a 1958 speech, "I think it is a pretty high compliment to the American taxpayer that three out of four don't even make a small mistake."

In the same speech, however, Commissioner Harrington disclosed the reason for the impressive honesty statistics. Thanks to the employee withholding tax (which subtracts a man's tax whether he likes it or not) and the fact that most American taxpayers are simply wage earners, roughly 70 per cent of the taxpaying total use the standard form 1040 or 1040A and take the standard 10 per cent deduction. They have, therefore, almost no opportunity to cheat, except in crude ways like fabricating nonexistent dependents. "Only in the remaining 30 per cent," said the Commissioner, "do we have to take a closer look."

What this division suggests is that people who can shave something off their taxes, legally or illegally, are likely to do so. The whole weight of the IRS audit program is concentrated on this 30 per cent of the taxpaying public. This conspicuously includes: self-employed businessmen, doctors, lawyers, merchants, prosperous farmers, headwaiters, purchasing agents and gamblers—anyone who receives income which cannot be automatically trapped by a government withholding tax form. Naturally, the higher the bracket, the more searching the investigation. The IRS quite rightly refuses to give out its methods of selecting returns for investigation, to prevent taxpayers from taking advantage of them. (Despite its belief in the essential honesty of the American taxpayer, it prefers putting his virtue to as few tests as possible.) But, unless the local District Director is awfully shorthanded, a man earning $20,000 a year, part of which comes from nonsalaried income, can be sure of spending a session, either this year or next, with the IRS examiner rechecking his return. So can people with predictably high entertainment allowances, e.g., public-relations men. The IRS freely admits that in some of the higher brackets nine out of 10 returns are given a fine-tooth combing.

Pledged to support the law, the Internal Revenue Service inspectors are amply justified in their relentless search for the missing item of income, the overpadded deduction, the missing dependent or the sleight-of-hand capital gain. No one leafing through a list even of those convicted or indicted* could fail to notice what a representative cross section of society they constitute. Here is an occupational sampler of people indicted or convicted for income-tax evasion during a certain period in 1957, the year in which a record number of tax evaders were brought to book. Listed below by geographical area (the city

* The record of government convictions in income-tax fraud cases is roughly 98 per cent.

given corresponding to the headquarters of the local IRS District), they make an odd mixture of the "best" elements in American business society and the worst.

Atlanta: hotel executive, doctor, attorney, lottery operator, electrician, public accountant, bookmaker, textile manufacturer, real-estate man, tax consultant. . .

Boston: bookmaker, wholesale meat dealer, painter, textile executive, bookie. . .

Chicago: corporation executive, politician, mayor of an Illinois city, plumbing dealer, attorney, musical-instrument dealer, funeral director, rooming-house operator and abortionist, attorney, motor-fuel retailer, factory worker, accountant, corporation executive, jeweler. . .

Dallas: trucker, building contractor, barmaid, police officer, oil operator, electrical contractor. . .

New York: headwaiter, salesman, painting contractor, car inspector, bookie, physician, salesman, mechanic, car inspector, construction company official. . .

Omaha: amusement concessionaire, farmer, insurance agent, optometrist, jeweler, tax consultant, car dealer, plumber, veterinarian, prison guard, state senator, carnival operator. . .

Philadelphia: garageman, funeral director, attorney, lay preacher, company purchasing agent, numbers racketeer, dress manufacturer, cement contractor, farmer, corporation executive, doctor. . .

San Francisco: landlord, accountant, war-surplus dealer, carpenter, trailer-park operator, farmer, attorney, janitor, furniture dealer, accountant, housewife. . .*

Almost all of these and similar cases involve either the concealment of income or the fraudulent padding of expenses and

---

* I have compiled these samplers from lists of individual tax evaders, in which occupation is included. The IRS formerly listed evaders in occupational groups. In 1954, after a rising chorus of protests, notably from the American Bar Association, the practice was abandoned.

fabrication of deductions. The government, it must be noted, is not too particular about the source of a person's income or its morality, as long as he pays taxes on it. The man who gives a bribe, for example, is not authorized to deduct it as a legitimate business expense—except in certain fields where the Tax Court has ruled that kick-backs are normal practice. But the man who receives a bribe must duly enter the bribe as taxable income. The abortionist in the list above was not prosecuted for being an abortionist, but for not paying a tax on her abortion income. In federal court in Boston, not long ago, the government tried to make a lady embezzler pay tax on the money she had stolen from her employer. The judge in this case, however, ruled that since the money was not hers, she was not guilty of evasion. (She had previously made restitution.)

To make the government take disapproving cognizance of a taxpayer's source of income, it must be about as flagrantly illegal as printing money. Such a case, in fact, came up before the Tax Court late in 1959. A counterfeiter appealed for a loss deduction against uninsured theft. He had been engaged, he explained, in a project to "make some money" by a friend, who claimed he could transfer ink impressions from big bills onto dollar bills, often "bleaching" them out. But as raw material for this venture, he had been required to put up $15,000 in genuine $100 bills. One day his accomplice vanished, taking all the genuine bills with him. The taxpayer demanded permission to take his loss deduction.

The Tax Court denied his appeal from the adverse IRS ruling. To allow this deduction, it held, was tantamount to opposing the federal statutes which make counterfeiting a crime. But it took a virtual *reductio ad absurdum* like this to make source of income a factor in considering a taxpayer's case.

In accounting for suspicious items or explaining away odd deductions, man's unfettered imagination—even in the Age of Conformity—remains a factor to be reckoned with. Probably an all-time peak in imaginative interpretation of the tax laws was reached by a taxpayer in San Francisco. His huge medical expenses, he told the IRS examiners, were due to his doctor's injunction that sexual intercourse, frequently indulged, was just the therapy he needed to quiet his jumpy nerves. He kept obeying the doctor's orders, with apparent zeal, charging the cost of his "treatments" to medical expenses, as well as his transportation expenses to the clinic of his choice.

Often the tax evader is uncovered in the course of a routine audit. But in addition the officers of the IRS Intelligence Division, an extremely competent body of detectives, dig up many of their cases through independent investigation. A man whose name appears frequently on county records as a buyer of real estate, for example, brings himself under immediate suspicion. Quiet real-estate purchases are an excellent way of utilizing unreported cash income. Some Intelligence Division officers have made their best hauls after a day at the races, when they ran checks on the recent tax returns of a few big bettors. One officer in Richmond, Va., while waiting his turn in a line before a bank teller's window, watched a messenger cashing corporation checks—an odd procedure since most businesses deposit their income and draw on it later. On investigating, he found that the corporation was engaged in a complicated scheme to hide extra income.

Whenever a large theft is reported in the newspapers, the tax Hawkshaws invariably start checking. Often the owner of the stolen furs and jewels proves to have turned in tax returns far out of line with such luxuries. To kill time during slack season one summer, the entire investigative staff in one district headquarters started jotting down the license numbers of every Cadillac they saw. Here again, a satisfying percentage of the *nouveau* Cadillac owners turned out to have reported incomes barely large enough to buy a used Gogomobil.

The Intelligence Division has also staged periodic investigations into certain professions or trades. By shaking the tree, so
to speak, with a few symbolic convictions, it generally brings
down a quantity of previously unreported income on the following year's returns. A memorable example of the occupational-
survey technique was the drive on waiters, headwaiters and
supervisory hotel personnel conducted in 1956-1958 in New
York City and other gastronomical centers. It accounted for
many a long face above the chafing dish before it ran its course.

The problem of assessing the exact amount a waiter receives
in tips is formidable, but Internal Revenue experts had long
realized that a good bit of the government's tax money was
vanishing as deftly as a customer's crumpled five-dollar bill disappears into a captain's pocket. In making some cases against
waiters and headwaiters, the government relied on the tested
principle of net worth, *i.e.*, a $40,000 house with a new con-
vertible in the driveway argues that a taxpayer gets more cash
than his $6,000-a-year reported income indicates. Investigators
were also able to estimate a waiter's take rather closely, in some
cases, by checking the total amount of business in dining room
or banquet hall.

Twenty-five waiters and captains were convicted of tax
evasion in the New York area alone, including 13 out of the 33
banquet captains then at the eminent Waldorf-Astoria. On
October 2, 1958, Claudius Charles Philippe, the Waldorf's vice-
president in charge of catering, was indicted on four counts of
income-tax evasion. Philippe, who presided with aplomb over
the Waldorf's banquet department, was accused of evading
$88,706 in income taxes between 1952 and 1955. The alleged
evasions included both legitimate income and added increment
from "cash, currency or kick-backs" which Philippe purportedly
received from Waldorf suppliers. Philippe, when the charge was

announced, denied it and stood on his record. "My connection with the Waldorf," he told the *New York Times,* "is the ideal marriage between the individual and the institution."

Equipped with excellent lawyers, Philippe succeeded in having one of the original counts in the indictment dismissed (the week before he announced a job with the new Zeckendorf Hotel as its operating director). The other charges remained on the docket as of this writing.

In their investigations Internal Revenue inspectors are assisted by thousands of unsolicited tips, much the same as those given to other law officers by various parties unfriendly to the suspect. But the informer who assists the Internal Revenue Service, unlike the police stool pigeon, benefits from a set policy of rewards. By law a person who informs on another taxpayer is entitled to a percentage of the amount the government gains in back taxes. The percentage is never over 10 per cent, and it is paid only in cases where an informer's data have materially contributed to the government's case.

In 1958 some 4,173 people brought information of this sort to the government's attention and claimed a percentage of the take. Although most of the claims were disallowed, a certain portion were accepted. During that fiscal year almost $500,000 was paid out in this way. It was another indication of the tight net the tax collectors try to weave around real or potential evaders; but it is one not overly publicized by the Service. Washington realizes that the implications of such a system are, to say the least, unsavory.

The greatest amount ever secured from a delinquent taxpayer in back taxes and penalties was the nine millions extracted in 1940 from the Philadelphia publisher Moe Annenberg, who also received a three-year jail sentence. It is not uncommon, however, for taxpayers to be caught out with an arrears-and-penalty bill running to one or two millions.

The published accounts of an evader's liability, incidentally, are invariably lower than the actual amount paid in the accompanying civil action. This is of course due to the fact that a fraud conviction demands ironbound proof. Frequently, a good criminal case can be made only on a part of the money not reported or misreported. "And anyway," as IRS officials say, "a conviction for a $500 tax fraud carries the same legal penalty as one for $50,000." Not long ago a man was convicted on a criminal charge of evading $50,000 in taxes. Actually, he had failed to report some $2,000,000.

For 1958 and 1959 the Internal Revenue Service has knowingly cut down on the number of evaders prosecuted, preferring to concentrate its energies on fewer but more significant cases. Many of these turn into legal marathons, even with the best of evidence marshaled for the prosecution. The "respectable" tax evader is likely to be well heeled—to say nothing of less savory folk like the gambler Frank Costello, who enjoyed the attentions of Internal Revenue agents for some 12 years before enough evidence was gathered to indict him, and then managed through legal maneuvering to secure a four-year hiatus between his original sentencing in 1954 and his final arrival at Leavenworth in 1958. A force of 80 agents was required to sift through the curious business dealings of the Bostonian Bernard Goldfine, after his affairs finally received a Washington airing in 1959.

On March 27, 1958, to cite another classic case, Adolph C. (Andy) Burger, a millionaire St. Louis car dealer, was sentenced in federal court to four years for tax evasion. Burger was first put under investigation in 1941. In 1952 he settled tax claims against him dating from the forties, but not quickly enough to avoid continuing scrutiny of his more-current operations. He was indicted in 1953 on a charge of fraudulent practices in his used-car business. As far back as 1948 he had sold used cars to dealers at 10 to 15 per cent markups. This was ridiculously low at a time when used cars were going for 100 per cent markups in what the car men still recall as the beginning of their great seller's market. He had received further amounts, of course, in the form of under-the-counter rebates. The case against him was strong and clear, but because of legal maneuverings it took fully five years to conclude it.

Other recent tax actions, although mercifully shorter, have been similarly pitched against the "respectable" evader, in an intensified effort to show members of the Genial Society that, hard though the tax bite be, they cannot escape it. There was the Washington, D. C., lawyer, finally brought to book in 1958, officially on the charge of falsifying his 1953 return. He had two Cadillacs, a $14,000 house, a family of five, a mistress and nine bank accounts, while reporting a total income of $20,000 over a ten-year period. A respected district attorney in upper New York State was found guilty of a similar offense, less the Cadillacs and the mistress. On August 27, 1958, a prominent local official in Oklahoma was finally sentenced to one year in jail after failing to report the regular kick-backs he received from contractors.

Time and time again, as squadrons of character witnesses will attest, the respectable tax evader is no Operator at all, but a man, with apologies to Oliver Goldsmith,

> . . . to all the country dear,
> And honest as they make 'em 364 days of the year.

Only on April 15 does he stray, and even then he rarely has any consciousness of doing something "really wrong." Take the Portland, Ore., TV commentator who pleaded guilty to tax evasion for the same years in which he had urged his fellow citizens on TV to pay taxes and had emceed several programs of the local Internal Revenue Service office warning about the pitfalls of evasion.

Sometimes the tax evader goes to bizarre lengths. In February 1959 a Texas oilman received a three-month jail sentence—to say nothing of heavy financial penalties—for failure to report his gambling winnings. Over a long period, the oilman had kept the core of this money, $75,000 in cash, in a Las Vegas hotel safe. After a good night at the tables, he would have his profits paid to him through checks made out to fictitious persons, which he then cashed himself. A comparably active imagination stirred the Davenport, Iowa, contractor who charged $500 worth of bridal bouquets for a family wedding as "office supplies" and wrote off a new $78,000 house as "repair work" at his plant. At that, he was less daring than the Cleveland contractor who charged *his* company for a house worth $170,000.

In 1959 a large Southern city was rocked by the trial of the executives of a prominent construction firm on charges of evading more than half a million dollars in corporate income taxes. Those involved were socially prominent and the offenses charged against them were on a grand scale: vicuña coat and a deep-freeze (an interesting bipartisan combination) charged off to business-promotion expenses; the cost of converting a private plane carried on the books as payment for a construction job; a huge labor charge on construction of a house for the firm's president, written off as part of construction costs on a city project.

These people did not overcharge their customers for these added luxuries. The personal expenses were used purely as a tax expedient. They added nothing to their projects' costs, except on the company's tax returns, confirming the considered comment of an Internal Revenue Service lawyer in Washington: "A lot of people wouldn't think of ever cheating their neighbor. In their personal dealings with you and me, they're absolutely trustworthy. With the government, it's different."

The *Wall Street Journal* offered its own confirmation of this view with a survey taken around income-tax time in 1959. In a quote typical of others in the article, the *Journal* has a Boston securities salesman saying: "I think you should beat the government out of every nickel you can. I'm convinced one-fourth of all tax money is swindled, wasted or unnecessary."

The *Journal* went on to extrapolate from his and other opinions of taxpayers in 15 major American cities: "The findings indicate not only that the number of tax chiselers is growing but that evaders make up a sizable proportion of the population—considerably bigger than the one per cent estimate offered by the Internal Revenue Service. Among the ordinary taxpayers, two of each five, after first carefully getting assurance of anonymity, admitted they cheat on their taxes." The article added, quoting H. Allen Long, Chicago District Director of the IRS, "There seems to be no end to the way taxpayers seek to defraud."

One response to this climate of fraud on the tax front is the increased severity of some judges in handing out jail sentences for evasion. After giving a two-year jail sentence to a New York physician, Judge Edward Dimock said: "This is a very serious crime, a despicable one. Every dollar this man did not pay on his income tax had to be paid by others more honest than he. Income tax fraud sentences are effective in preventing the commission of such crimes by others. It is one of the few cases to benefit society by imposing jail sentences." Barely a year later, Judge Ernest A. Tobin in Los Angeles handed down a sentence of 28 years in a multiple-return case, the highest in the history of the income-tax statutes.* "Such fraudulent returns,"

* The multiple-returns artist is the person who sets out, often with striking temporary success, to make money from the income tax by submitting false returns under a number of names, all claiming refunds. The man Judge Tobin sentenced, an itinerant chef, had devised his multiple-return scheme while lodged in the Arizona State Penitentiary for a previous crime.

he said, "are increasing in our community to an alarming extent."

The person who makes a crooked business out of income-tax returns has long since passed the stage of moral confusion about what is right or wrong. He is likely to be an incorrigible offender. One Mary M. Ossendott of Columbus, Ohio, originally prepared 21 false 1954 income-tax returns, which she submitted for refund under various names and addresses. While her case was being reviewed for possible prosecution by the IRS, she filed 31 phony returns for 1955. She was found guilty and sentenced to three years in prison in May 1956. After her release in September 1958, she could hardly wait to get back to the old drawing board. She was arrested again in December of that year on complaint of the District Director in Omaha and given a stiff 10-year sentence in January of 1959. Another such multiple-return veteran managed to cheat the government of several hundred dollars in income-tax refunds while incarcerated in state prison in Tennessee.

Stiff jail sentences, however, do not begin to answer this problem. Nor are trials for evasion anything but the tiny visible part of a huge subsurface problem with the most serious implications for our national morality. Justice Holmes once epitomized that "taxes are what we pay for civilized society." It is fair to ask whether the income tax, as now constituted, is not making us pay through the nose (especially considering the kind of civilization the country has lately come to favor). Or, more specifically, how does the income tax by its very structure encourage chiseling? Is the man who "evades" taxes any worse, except in degree, than the man who makes a profitable business of "avoiding" them?

It was back in 1906, during an otherwise peaceful cornerstone-laying ceremony in Washington, that President Theodore

Roosevelt shocked his Republican Party backers to the marrow by announcing himself in favor of a graduated income tax. Just three years later, in a letter to his friend Henry Cabot Lodge, Sr., Roosevelt added a prophetic postscript. "An income tax," he wrote, "must always have within it elements of gross inequality and must always be to a certain extent a tax on honesty."

Until World War II, at least, the elements of gross inequality did not make themselves very troublesome, or even manifest. The first "radical" income-tax plan, excluding a temporary 10-year measure adopted in 1862,* was a simple 2 per cent tax on incomes over $4,000. This William Jennings Bryan pushed through Congress in 1894. The Supreme Court of that day declared it unconstitutional, after a great hue and cry. The 16th Amendment to the Constitution was ratified in 1913 to take care of this objection.

In early days the tax rates were modest for all except the very rich and the income tax was widely recognized as a way of levying government toll on large fortunes. (As late as 1929, two thirds of the total tax was paid by citizens with an annual income in excess of $100,000.) Only rarely was the tax burdensome to others. In 1927 a bachelor earning a salary of $25,000 a year had to pay only $600 to the federal government. As late as 1939, a married man with a wife and two children, earning $4,500 a year, needed to cough up no more than $59.

World War II changed this picture. Heavy taxes were introduced as the need arose for increased government spending. The whole American philosophy of taxation underwent a change which can be seen most dramatically by looking at what hap-

---

* This tax was the result of Civil War financing needs. In its biggest year, 1865, it netted the government the helpful sum of $61 million. The Commissioner of Internal Revenue who thought the tax up was Joseph Jackson Lewis. His picture now hangs in the offices of IRS headquarters in Washington, in case any taxpayer would like to pay his respects.

pened to our happy, rich hypothetical bachelor of 1927 and the modest but contented family of 1939. By 1959 the hypothetical bachelor could be paying almost $15,000 on his federal income tax alone. If he had had the sense to marry—"for tax purposes," at least—the tax would still exceed $7,000. The family, presuming that it used standard deductions and the "short" tax form, would now have to pay $319.

The comparison could be expressed in different terms. According to figures worked out by the National Industrial Conference Board—which religiously take into account the decreasing purchasing power of the dollar—the family which had a nice $4,441 of disposable income in 1939 would have to earn $12,113 in 1959 to do as well.

The withholding tax, introduced in 1943, saw to it that wage earners would automatically render all or a portion of their tax, month by month, to the government. This system at the same time provides a handy source of record, in case the Internal Revenue Service decides, on the basis of a return submitted, that the 18 per cent withholding deduction falls short of discharging a man's full obligation.

So far so good—as far as the tax collector is concerned. Unfortunately, side by side with this clear-cut policy on withholding the tax of wage earners, Congress was busy making a crazy quilt of exemptions, loopholes, counterexemptions and plugs for loopholes to take care of taxes paid on nonsalaried income. The tangle was further confused by the efforts of the Internal Revenue Service, the courts and Congress itself to clarify it. In the process, the grossest sort of inequality became a commonplace.

Professor Walter W. Heller of the University of Minnesota, writing in *Fortune,* once estimated that the individual income tax is 50 per cent effective for farmers, 60 per cent effective for recipients of rent, 70 per cent effective for small businessmen,

80 per cent for recipients of dividend income and 90 per cent or better for wage earners. It takes no great discernment, viewing these or similar figures, to realize that the tax originally thought of by men like Bryan and Roosevelt as a brake on overlarge fortunes now falls heaviest on the middle levels of American society. In 1959 the major part of the income tax was paid by persons earning $10,000 a year or less. The weight of the tax falls heaviest on salaried people in the $10,000-$25,000 bracket.

For the man who gets nonsalaried income, opportunity to escape tax burdens is almost without limit. (To grasp this opportunity is almost essential to those in the highest brackets, for their taxes would otherwise be so heavy few could pay them for more than several years running.) The concrete symbol of this opportunity to escape taxation is the 1,200-page bulk of the Internal Revenue Code, buttressed by volume upon volume of clarification, interpretation and judicial rulings by the Tax Court, Federal District Courts, and Circuit Courts of Appeals. It was originally a simple code of taxation, on the whole easy to enforce because its regulations were general in nature. Then the amendments started to roll.

The notorious depletion allowance, which has made million-aires out of more Texans than one would care to contemplate, started out as a simple, straightforward clause in the tax law. It was founded on the principle that a man should at least get back his investment in an oil property. As the depletion allowance for oil became well known, pressures from other interests made themselves felt. Oil still draws a 27 ½ per cent depletion, fortified by the massed congressional votes of Texas, Oklahoma and other oil-producing states. But the producers of other minerals have through the years won their own depletion allowances, which range from 5 to 15 per cent deducted from their gross income. Depletion allowances are now claimed on water, as well as on manufactured products in which depletion-allowance minerals appear. (Even if the taxpayer does not directly own the mineral, the current argument goes, he should get a depletion allowance if he has an economic interest in it.) The most obvious result of this widespread system is to lose the government upward of $700 million yearly.

A similar thing has happened with the laws governing the tax on corporate reorganization. Where once one statute regulated all such reorganization, hundreds now obtain. In almost every area of nonsalary income—charitable donations, capital gains, etc.—the law has tried to set forth an infinitude of explanation, like a tailor who keeps patching a suit until the original material, to say nothing of the cut, is beyond recognition. Instead of a few general statutes which it was once risky to flout, the law now includes thousands of fine-print "don't's." If a "don't" is not contained in the fine print, the taxpayer is thereby offered the chance to try and get away with it. Ultimately an amended statute will be written, plugging up his particular tax loophole, but giving rise to an even more profitable form of avoidance by someone else.

As the inequalities and counterinequalities in the Tax Code multiply, the gap widens between justice and legal rule or application. In no other area can an Operator so justify his corner-cutting.

At the root of this problem is the distinction between evasion and avoidance. Tax evasion is a criminal offense against society punishable by large fines and jail terms. Tax *avoidance* is merely the case of a citizen taking advantage of his right to pay as little tax as is legally required of him. ("Minimizing" one's tax is the euphemism currently used.) The federal courts have consistently guaranteed this right of the taxpayer to do as much dodging as possible within the limits of the law. "There is nothing sinister," Judge Learned Hand once said, "in so arranging one's affairs as to keep taxes as low as possible. Everybody does so, rich or poor: and all do right, for nobody owes any public duty to pay more than the law demands."

This is meet and just. There would be no problem in tax avoidance if everyone saw the law with Judge Hand's measure of conscience and clarity. Yet, where the law itself is a Swiss-cheese complex and the taxes high enough in many cases to make loophole-seeking almost inescapable, it is not hard to understand why so many take advantage of it. In practice, as a veteran Internal Revenue Service lawyer defined it, "avoidance is nonfraudulent evasion."

If this sounds like double talk, it is talk which may well mean the difference between a mere adverse legal decision and a jail sentence—or at the least heavy 50 per cent fraud penalties—to a great many American taxpayers. The function of the chief counsel of the Internal Revenue Service and his officers hinges on their daily interpretation of the distinction in thousands of cases. And the interpretation, it must be admitted, balances less on the question of a taxpayer's moral intent than the amount of proof necessary to stick him with an evasion charge.

There are several norms which the government's tax experts can use in trampling out the distinction between evasion and avoidance. If a taxpayer's business is not legitimate, he is auto-matically suspect of outright evasion. A racketeer whose liveli-hood involves dishonesty can be suspected of dishonesty in trying to account for its proceeds. Then there is the question of concealment. However bad the shape of a taxpayer's records, it is highly unlikely that the Justice Department will prosecute him if he has officially listed all the elements of his income, or makes no bones about the fact that he did not regard a certain increment as income, giving his reasons. The businessman who charges off a $40,000 swimming pool as a medical expense may be way off in deep water with the examiners and the courts, if he brings his case to trial; but he is in no danger of criminal prosecution. He has openly listed his deduction. Deciding on its validity is a civil matter. But suppose he had concealed the swimming-pool construction by charging it off to his contracting firm. That is another matter. Here he is concealing something, and the U.S. Attorney who can show concealment is well on his way to proving a willful intent to defraud.

Even when a man has suspiciously little documentation to support his tax return, the IRS cannot hope to make a fraud charge stick—unless perchance a visiting agent finds him burning his account books in his back yard. And the courts, which tend to give taxpayers the benefit of the doubt, have ruled conclusively that the IRS cannot throw a taxpayer's claim out the window solely because of inadequate documentation.

All of which merely clears the field for what might be called "the open dodge." It is far from a crime to take advantage of a tax loophole. Yet it is often hard to see the moral distinction between the petty fraudster who keeps a deceased relative on his tax return for a few hundred dollars' deduction and the financial type whose business success is posited on the tax loophole. It is surely one of the "gross inequities" which T. Roosevelt had in mind that the former may receive a two-year jail sentence, the latter experience at the worst a court decision disallowing his latest money-making plan.

The tax maneuver or gimmick has in fact become a staple of American business life. In essence, it is a "preconceived tax-saving plan," as one court recently put it, a business maneuver performed for the sole purpose of making money out of the Internal Revenue Code. Broken down to essentials, most successful tax gimmicks are founded on the principle of subtracting *expenses* from ordinary income—which is taxed at the usual rates—leaving *profits* to be taxed at long-term capital-gain rates. (As almost every American schoolboy now knows, the capital-gains tax rates are half the normal rates up to a maximum of 25 per cent.)

The expediency of one often-used tax maneuver was clarified by the U.S. Circuit Court of Appeals in Boston in early 1959, in the course of settling a strong difference of opinion between the Internal Revenue Service and a taxpayer named Eli D. Goodstein. Goodstein had put up $15,000 cash for the purchase of $10,000,000 of U.S. short-term Treasury notes selling at a discount. While the notes were being delivered to his broker, Goodstein gave his personal interest-bearing note to a finance company to underwrite the deal—payable when the Treasury notes matured. The finance company received the Treasury notes themselves as collateral, with the right of sale. They were promptly sold, through the same broker, back to the same bond house. All of these transactions took place on the same day.

When the Treasury notes rose about a point, nearing maturity, Goodstein sold out through his brokers—in a complicated process which virtually reversed the steps of the original buying operation. He made a long-term capital gains profit of $147,000. His losses were some $161,000 in interest paid. This would vastly reduce his annual income tax, since interest is always tax deductible.

To show the type of reduction Goodstein might expect, the *New York Times'* financial expert Burton Crane posited a hypothetical case of a married couple with a combined taxable net income of $180,000 a year. Their tax might be expected to reach $117,240 (far less, of course, than if it had been paid at the *really* hypothetical individual rate of 90 per cent). But suppose from the ordinary income one subtracted the $161,000 which went for the "business expense" of a Treasury note deal like Goodstein's. The net ordinary income would be down to $19,000. Then add $36,750, the long-term capital-gains tax which Goodstein had to pay on his profit of $147,000 from the note sale, and stir gently. The original tax of $117,240 would be reduced by $75,550.

Unfortunately for Goodstein, and hundreds of others with similar cases, the Circuit Court pronounced his operation "a preconceived plan which lacked substance." The Court was quick to point out, however, that "the good faith of the taxpayer in attempting to reduce his taxes by this method is unassailable." (It should be noted that the Court's judgment was not necessarily a moral one.)

So complex has the tax situation grown, but so inviting, that the tax lawyer and the tax accountant are now vital consultants on almost any business move; their imprimatur must be given before a single paper is signed. Taxes are now the *motivating* factors in thousands of business maneuvers. The very words "tax considerations" have acquired a magic ring. Walking corpses of corporations, heavy with debts and stumbling into bankruptcy, have become esteemed objects in corporate mergers. By absorbing a "loss corporation" and writing off its liabilities against taxes, any solvent company can save staggering amounts on its own tax bill.

Corporations may set up outposts or indeed headquarters abroad, in areas with a salubrious taxation climate. (The Bahamas have become a recent favorite.) In this way they can escape paying corporate income taxes for years. And when the corporation officers bring back their profits from abroad they are taxed merely for—you guessed it—capital gains.

Hollywood shows signs of the times by successive stampedes toward various forms of tax relief. First, there was the memorable rush through the loophole offered by Congress to U.S. residents of foreign countries (no personal income tax if a person has lived overseas for 17 out of 18 consecutive months). Originally passed to encourage American technical experts to work on foreign-aid projects, the loophole was revised as soon as Congress discovered that a sizable cluster of Hollywood's galaxy had taken up "permanent" residence at the George V in Paris, or *intime* villas in Switzerland and on the Côte d'Azur.

When this escape hatch disappeared, the actors discovered the value of incorporating themselves. As of this moment, there are few stars worth their salt in Hollywood who have not formed their own producing companies. Instead of receiving salaries from the movie companies, some stars have persuaded the movie companies to accept percentages of the take, handled by the star's own production company.

Here are two samples of the latest Hollywood fad, as noted in *Time* (January 19, 1959): "According to Hollywood scuttlebutt, Cary Grant has turned the tables on Universal-International. Instead of taking a percentage from the studio for his current film *Operation Petticoat*, Grant is said to have persuaded his studio to take a percentage from him (10% of the gross) while he produces the picture.

"For appearing in *Bridge on the River Kwai*, William Holden agreed to 10% of the gross, but for tax reasons wanted it paid to him at the rate of only $50,000 a year. The picture has already made so much money that Holden's share now stands at between $2,000,000 and $3,000,000. Not only will it take 40-year-old Holden at least 40 years to get his money, but Columbia can in the meantime invest it and make well over $50,000 a year, thus in effect having got Holden's services for nothing."

Few departments of our national life have escaped the tax operator's notice. Charitable donations in large sums have frequently become an outlet for tax relief rather than philanthropic impulse, in the case of the people to whom such gifts can mean sizable deductions.* The boom in the purchase of expensive paintings and *objets d'art* is not unrelated. Since the price tags of paintings, especially, are open to discussion, some ama-

---

* Occasionally, deductions are prominently listed to charities designed to touch the heart of the local IRS inspector; e.g., noting an increase of Negro personnel in the New York IRS offices, some alert students of taxmanship quickly sent and listed contributions to the Urban League, NAACP, etc. Such patent dodges rarely work.

teur art fanciers specialize in acquiring moderately valuable paintings, then taking huge deductions for them; e.g., a manufacturer buys a painting for $2,000, then calls in an obliging art appraiser who readily, for a fee, discovers that it is actually worth $10,000. His ensuing $10,000 gift to the local art gallery can be of material help the next April 15. This practice has spawned a whole genus of slippery art "authenticators" (whose sharp practices distress no one so much as legitimate evaluators and art experts).

One of the worst cases of loophole-seeking broke surface in May 1958 in Miami, when an officer of the Civil Air Patrol was startled to find CAP stickers on some sleek yachts tied up in the harbor. On investigation, he found the boats proved to belong to the New York branch of the CAP. They were the "gifts" of wealthy New Yorkers who found an extremely useful tax dodge in the donation of well-depreciated yachts to such a worthy cause. It was never clearly established who collected the majority of the Miami rental and charter fees.

This climate of avoidance-evasion is not alone the fault of Congress and individual taxpayers. The federal government in its own levies has seldom displayed the rapacity for taxes shown by some hard-pressed states and communities. The inequities of New York State's income tax on nonresidents (higher than that foisted on New Yorkers) are well known. Probably the all-time high in tax-reaching was attained, however, by the Commonwealth of Massachusetts, which has for some time collected a nonresident state income tax from airline pilots who have the good fortune to fly over Massachusetts soil.

Agitation has been growing for sweeping tax reform on both the federal and state level—but most especially in the matter of the federal income tax. Congressional tax experts like Representative Wilbur Mills have been talking it up for some years. Enough of an outcry has lately been generated on the subject of tax inequities to sweep at least some reform legislation through. The country may emerge, if we are lucky, with a simplified tax rate and really Draconian reductions in the special deductions which have spawned most of the loopholes. The tax rates could then be lowered, with no loss in revenue, to end a ridiculous system where a person's industry is in effect penalized and the incentives to chicanery and crookedness vastly multiplied.

As things now stand, if the taxpayer can cut corners on his tax returns in imagined safety, he will do so. When he feels or imagines the breath of the IRS down his neck, he will act accordingly. A man of orderly instincts, this pillar of the Genial Society would probably no longer be capable of putting on Indian war paint and joining his ancestors in so flagrant a breach of public order as the Boston Tea Party. But he has read history books and the example of the Tea Party is not forgotten. Just as soon as he acquires enough power and pelf to hire a few Indians of his own, disguised as lawyers and tax accountants, he will stage his own version of the Party, at the government's expense.

IX
GRAFT AND GOVERNMENT

"Clean as a hound's tooth . . ."
—Recently revived political saying

In 1876, during the course of a visit to the United States, the Polish novelist Henry Sienkiewicz sent this comment back to a newspaper in Warsaw: "I have already mentioned in previous letters the large amount of graft in government. I have explained this by the fact that a politician remains in office only so long as his party is in the majority; whenever the party changes, the public officials likewise change. Thus, when an official leaves his business, that is, his means of livelihood, to assume the duties of public office, he knows that within a few years he will lose this office. Consequently, the politician has but one recourse: to steal—and he steals as zealously as he knows how. This is the fault of the machinery of government. For this very reason, these abuses must not be taken as an indication of the morality of the entire nation . . . I can say that I know of no people who are more law-abiding than the Americans."

In the 19th century, Sienkiewicz' observation had great relevance. Grafters like Boss Tweed scarcely bothered to draw the curtains when they were rifling the public till; even the

225

Presidential election of 1876 was scarred with open fraud and manipulation.* His distinction between the immoral politician and the law-abiding citizenry was almost equally relevant. The high-minded Virginia and New England gentlemen who built the Republic had disappeared after a generation or two. Their descendants, along with the "respectable" element in most American communities, had long since gone into other lines of work than politics, and glad of it. As the flagrant scandals of the Grant administration gave way to newer excesses, there was sealed in the public's mind the image of the conscienceless ward heeler whose very profession of "politician" amounted to an admission of moral ill-health. When Max Weber, the great German sociologist, came to the United States in the early 1900's, he was enough impressed by the truth of this image to stick his hypothetical yardstick of national ethical behavior down the back of the businessman, not the public official. This was in sharp contrast, he noted, to the standard of official conduct to which Europeans had been accustomed.

The stereotyped difference between the politician and the "law-abiding" citizen has been asserted far into our own time. "Graft and corruption" still make a humdinger of a battle cry for a temporarily aroused electorate. Retailers who shortchange their customers, advertising men who misrepresent their products, income-tax cheats, expense-account wizards and stock-market sharpers—all go to the polls with the indignation of innocents betrayed.

Yet it has been clear for some time that such a polar contrast between the politician and the citizen is no longer valid. The flagrantly stealing politician is becoming an anachronism in a

* Although Samuel Tilden, the Democratic candidate, won a popular majority and seemed to have gained the election, the Republicans, screened by federal troops dispatched for the purpose, performed prodigies of last-minute ballot-stuffing in three of the former Confederate states, enough to swing them decisively behind the Republican candidate, Rutherford B. Hayes.

complex government where most of the actual governing is done by a Civil Service bureaucracy. The bureaucracy may be tolerant of waste, but its very organization militates against most striking dishonesties. At the same time, as the preceding chapters have suggested, Sienkiewicz' description of the American people as singularly "law-abiding" is equally outdated, unless by "law-abiding" we mean merely a population which displays an impressive obedience to traffic lights.

The peculiar corruption of American politics, as it stands on the threshold of the sixties, results from watering down both these extremes. As ward heelers disappear and politicians grow more respectable; as government impinges, generally with necessity, on ever-more areas of the national life; as the public morality of so many private citizens—once comparatively sound—gives way to an atmosphere of looseness, the flagrant individual graft of yesteryear is transformed into a general slippage. The slippage is not so spectacular, but its wide spread compensates for the lack of numerous glaring examples. The big graft disappears. In its place we see (when we are lucky enough to see them) the thousands of little "fixes."

There is no better illustration of changing patterns in political corruption than the record of the Truman and the Eisenhower administrations. In neither administration, it can safely be said, was there any outright attempt at plunder like the scandals of the Harding administration. Setting aside the personal integrity of Presidents Truman and Eisenhower, which made its example felt in certain areas, the mass of intersticing checks and balances within the government bureaucracy would have rendered impossible such a clearly dishonest grab as Albert Fall's sale of the Navy oil reserves in the Harding era.

Yet in the Truman administration there were damaging exposures of chiseling inside the Reconstruction Finance Corporation and the Bureau of Internal Revenue—the latter not too surprising a location in view of the strain and temptation posed by the heavy personal income tax. Two high officials of the executive branch, the President's Appointments Secretary Matthew Connally and Assistant Attorney General T. Lamar Caudle, were ultimately sentenced to jail terms for what amounted to high-level "fixing."

The Eisenhower administration roared into office on the President-elect's thundering promise to "clean up the mess in Washington." But this President, too, suffered the humiliation of influence-peddling by members of his official family: notably the late Harold Talbott, who solicited private business for his firm under the letterhead of his office as Secretary of the Air Force; and Sherman Adams, whose interventions on behalf of friends dealing with the U.S. government deserved a stronger description than his admitted "imprudence." Once again, federal regulatory agencies were involved in scandal or impropriety— the Federal Housing Administration early in Eisenhower's presidency and, in his second term, the Federal Communications Commission, whose chairman, John C. Doerfer, resigned under fire in March 1960.

The abuses were unquestioned and more widespread than the extent of the public investigations. Far from ward-heeling graft, they often represented collusion between government officials and various groups—corporations or, often, unions—to frustrate the regulation of private affairs which the law now deems necessary. They proliferated in the weakest area in the modern American system: the flabby giants of regulatory power like the FCC which contain within themselves a hodgepodge of ill-marked executive, legislative and judicial function—although, as we have seen earlier, in the case of the FTC and others, they are charged with increasingly important duties.

Before going on to the modern political Operator, we must acknowledge the survival of a few figures directly descended from the dinosaur age of political bossism.

Few of them are in very good repair, and for excellent reasons. The feudal loyalties the old-fashioned boss once inspired and exploited can be more readily seen in some corporations or labor unions. The handouts he could give are not so necessary in our modified welfare state and the political plums he disposed of, at least on the lower branches, have lost their savor to the prosperous citizen of the Genial Society. Book readers and movie audiences may have chuckled or shed a random tear over the antics of the archetypal boss in Edwin O'Connor's *The Last Hurrah*. Few of them would have voted for him any more, as the book itself pointed out and the declining fortunes of the book's apparently real-life model seemed to prove.

Probably the last boss to operate strictly on the old-fashioned model was a Texan, George B. Parr, whose career finally ended with both federal and state jail sentences handed down in 1957. Parr's old realm, Duval County, is a square of ranchland in southern Texas, between Corpus Christi and the Rio Grande. It is not heavily populated, nor are the neighboring counties, where Parr also enjoyed considerable influence. But Parr's quiet hammer lock on the local electorate there gave him a formidable balance of power in his state. For thirty years he elected governors, U.S. senators and lesser officials on the strength of the votes in Duval and the neighboring counties. Traditionally, the Duval vote always came in last, after preliminary totals from the rest of the state had been registered.

Parr was known for years as the "Duke of Duval." He inherited the title. His father, Archie Parr, began his reign in 1911, when he took the side of the Mexicans, who formed the bulk of the county's population against the "Anglo" minority. Hoisted into power on the shoulders of the aroused Mexican vote, Archie Parr stayed there and got rich. He followed the same principle by which the old big-city bosses of the North had prospered: find a downtrodden immigrant population, help it, nurture it, scare it (occasionally)—and trust it, consequently, for obedience of the most unswerving type. As the years went by, Mexican names began to appear on Duval's roster of public officers and finally they dominated it. The office-holders were of course hand-picked by one of the Parrs.

George Parr started taking over from his father not long after he left college in the mid-twenties. As second duke, he produced many improvements in the fiefdom, not least of which was his own 50,000-acre ranch and a town house which boasted a swimming pool and a private race track. He continued the pattern of benevolent despotism, and citizens who did not question his rule did reasonably well. For his favors and patronage he asked only a straight-ticket vote on election day, or more particularly primary day. The votes were always given. Parr went into oil, took over a bank and a lucrative beer concession.

In 1948 Parr stood at the height of his power. In the runoff primary election for Democratic candidates—in Texas still tantamount to formal election—he swung the county solidly against a former friend named Coke Stevenson and in favor of a rising congressman named Lyndon B. Johnson. After the other county returns were in, the election was still close. Whereupon Duval racked up a vote of 4,622 to 40 in Johnson's favor. This won Johnson the election, as well as the local nickname of "Landslide Lyndon." But it also called attention to Duval County's voting record.

In 1949 Parr's faction was beaten in neighboring Jim Wells County, and a radio commentator, who was against Parr, was killed by one of Parr's sheriffs. Another accidental killing occurred in 1952. Although Parr was not implicated in the killings, the law, as well as some newspapers, was by this time enough aroused to look closely at the Duke's domain. Parr had already served some time for income-tax evasion in 1936. Other than that he had been unscathed (interestingly, President Truman formally pardoned him for the income-tax crime in 1948).

In the end Parr was treed by the Post Office Department, whose investigators worked up an impressive bill of particulars against him, based on the fact that he had used the mails extensively in managing the affairs of the duchy. He was sentenced to 10 years in prison on the charge of using the mails to defraud in connection with the theft of sizable portions of the Benavides District school funds.

Parr's case is now before the Supreme Court, after a series of appeals. (His lawyers are attacking the verdict on procedural grounds, as well as on the theory that no federal crime was committed.) Since his conviction his political machine has kept running, but at a slackening pace. Too many voters are awake— and angry.

While the law was engaged in making a commoner out of the Duke of Duval, other modern political operators were busy at influence-peddling, group grafting and cases—individual or collective—of outright nonpartisan embezzlement. A classic scandal broke out in Parr's own state capital at Austin.

The Lone Star lobbyists had been long notorious for aggressive and unfettered behavior. But the latest scandal was enough to outrun the bounds even of Texas' traditionally broad tolerance. It was climaxed in October 1958, when former Representative James Cox was convicted of taking a $5,000 bribe from a lobbyist for his assistance in killing a piece of legislation. The lobbyist in question represented the state's naturopaths, a flourishing paramedical community, who would have had to shut down all their activities if a bill that Cox sponsored had passed the legislature.

This very specific bit of crookedness came at the end of what amounted to a decade of open bribery among various Texan lawmen. It followed the exposure of one BenJack Cage, an extremely persuasive promoter, who had taken over the insurance business of some 241 AFL locals in the state, and formed his own ICT Insurance Co. in 1951. He then proceeded on a career of violently illegal personal investment, equipped with the union's money and abetted by some official connivance.*

In the course of the two investigations, before Governor Price Daniel finally put through a bill regulating lobbyists' activities, there was uncovered an amazingly comprehensive network of planned entertainment, benefits and outright cash payments to legislators who would vote the right way on specific bills. For years, individual companies or industry lobbies treated the Austin senators and representatives to well-organized bread and circuses, from free products, continuous buffets for lawmen and their families to gambling excursions, brothel tours along the border and occasional junkets to Kentucky for the races.†

One lobbyist, who happened to find his way into a local district attorney's office, spoke of the *modus operandi* with frankness. He had occasion to offer an Austin senator an undisclosed amount for "handling the expenses of a bill." "I told him," the lobbyist added, "that if there were any additional expenses, why, we would take care of them."

As the boom was finally lowered, the legislators grew belatedly reflective, if not repentant. "It's a much tighter situation," one lawyer-senator admitted. "It's gonna have to be in retainer fees, that's all." A colleague, mindful of smaller favors, seconded him. "Last session," he said, "we had all kinds of little gifts—lemon juice, beer glasses, fly swatters, books. . . . This time all we've had is a six-ounce jar of honey and a bag of rice. It's been slim pickin's."

---

* Cage proved also to have been associated with the wayward corporation juggler Lowell Birrell and his friends. As of this writing, Cage is rusticating in São Paulo, the familiar shade of Brazil's nonextradition policy.

† The fullest picture of these activities was given by the able Austin newspaperman, Ronnie Dugger, in a *Harper's* article in March 1957.

At about the same time the Texas legislators were pondering the injustice of justice, the General Assembly up north in Illinois was attempting to put a few extra locks on its own barn door, after the former State Auditor, Orville Hodge, had galloped away with $2,500,000 of the public funds. Hodge was exposed and resigned from office in July of 1956. (Governor William G. Stratton's narrow victory in the election just four months later remains a tribute to the fidelity of the Illinois Republican voter.) Hodge received a 12-to-15-year jail sentence. His trial laid bare a three-year record of bogus checks, faked endorsements and juggled accounts, all of them dedicated to the State Auditor's love for fancy apartments, horse racing, parties and generally luxurious living. Like many of the new-model political operators, he preferred perquisites to power.

Hodge was exposed by chance, after a Chicago *Daily News* reporter began to get suspicious of some state checks he had seen.* Thanks to his position, he might have continued his graft for years before anyone was the wiser. Few members raised their voices in opposition when the Illinois General Assembly rushed through a 1957 bill setting up a powerful Auditor General, with the right to subpoena, who could order out the records of any officer in the state. There were those who said the Hodge scandal was a good thing. Coming so recently after the interesting repercussions of Governor Dwight Green's administration (separated from it only by the brief reform era of Adlai Stevenson), it made responsible folk in the state wonder whether it was not time to maintain a continuing interest in their government.

Not to be outdone by this downstate Republican embezzlement, Chicago Democrats pulled off a series of scandals of their own barely three years later. They began in 1959 with a $250,-

* A not-uncommon occurrence in American life. A majority of the Pulitzer Prize winners in journalism have earned their awards with exposés of some form of political corruption.

000 bail-bond scandal in the Chicago courts. Shortly after this, the lid was pried off a widespread system of ticket-fixing and fine-stealing in the city's traffic courts. This graft had apparently been costing Chicago $500,000 a year. After its disclosure some 65 persons either resigned or were fired from their jobs in the traffic-court system. A third scandal broke over Chicago after an investigation of the city pay rolls, which showed a considerable number of minor functionaries feeding from the public trough without even perfunctory gestures at performing their jobs. One man collected wages as a city timekeeper for the six months he spent in a Fort Lauderdale, Fla., jail on a bookmaking charge.

All this was only a prelude to the police corruption exposed by the chance confession of a burglar in January 1960. On January 4, Richard Morrison, a convicted thief at 23, unfolded a story of how Chicago police had not only assisted in but planned a program of burglaries, taking the loot home with them in their squad cars. The resulting investigation turned up instances of police corruption so extreme as to be barely credible: one cop selling heroin while in uniform, another tearing up a traffic ticket for a bribe of 60 cents, a third getting extra money acting as night watchman for a store he subsequently looted. The gravity of the scandal—too bad even for Chicago to ignore—lay in the extent to which the most flagrant kind of dishonesty had apparently penetrated the local law. The causes were lack of interest in good government by Chicago citizens and lack of anything like a moral standard or tradition in the department of city government that needed it worst.

In many cases corruption does not have to strike a state or municipality. It is virtually built into its governing system, thanks to outmoded codes or organizational structures. Although the American mind displays its mania for organization and reorganization in government at the Washington level, often uselessly, there is notable reluctance to tamper with the governing system closer to where the voters live.

It is beyond the scope of this book to suggest the sweeping changes that might be made—the growth of sprawling, connected metropolitan areas, for example, has made both state and city boundaries incapable of doing the job they were drawn for. The obstinate preservation of ancient voting representation, based on virtually colonial population patterns, not only deprives city people of the vote their numbers deserve, but holds out a blank check to crooked local politicians.

The state of Georgia offers prime evidence. There the Democratic nomination (in this one-party state synonymous with election) is not won by popular vote, but by vote of Georgia's counties, in the so-called "unit system." From the earliest times, *i.e.*, since the first Georgia farmer became suspicious of city folks, unit voting has been controlled by the rural counties. There are 159 counties in the state, each with at least two unit votes and—by law—no more than six. The city of Atlanta (Fulton County) has only six votes in the legislature. Atlanta's population, however, is equal to that of the state's 72 smallest counties, which control a total of 144 votes.

A study of campaign financing in Georgia was done recently on a Social Science Research Council Fellowship by Joseph L. Bernd. Wrote Mr. Bernd (as quoted in the *Wall Street Journal*): "A prominent editor, himself a veteran of the political wars, has reported that 60 counties . . . are for sale to the highest bidder. Some political leaders in reminiscent moods have given apparent validity to the reports. A former gubernatorial candidate has related with obvious relish how his campaign manager obtained $50,000 to buy counties. . . . What is for sale, in more precise phraseology, is not the county but the support of some local bosses and courthouse crowds who can control the outcome in a number of bailiwicks."

The first part of Governor Ernest Vandiver's administration in 1959 was given over almost exclusively to an emergency repair job on the corruption left over by "courthouse politics." By June of 1959, 25 persons connected with the preceding administration had been indicted by the Fulton County grand jury. So flagrant had graft become that firms who wanted to do business with the state were likely as not sent on to various persons—campaign contributors, big vote getters, local politicians—to whom the administration owed favors. A firm would then have to work through such an informal agent if it wished to get any business from the state. Naturally the agent received a normal 10 per cent fee.

The Vandiver administration was able to put some of the worst practitioners of this system out of office and behind bars. But such relief was only temporary. The tragedy of a situation like Georgia's is that the local system of electing officials invites corruption by its very makeup.

As vested and politically anachronistic as Georgia's system of voting representation is the office of Borough President in each of New York City's five boroughs. Although they were originally intended to help distribute the mayor's burden, the functions of the borough presidents have gradually atrophied, as city administration grew necessarily centralized. Now they are known principally as roosts for deserving politicians. At present the borough presidents and their 5,869 employees cost the city $27,000,000 a year. Of this sum only a portion is paid back to the city in the public-works services rendered by the borough presidents' employees. An understandably indeterminate amount is lost either by political hacks holding useless jobs or by unqualified appointees doing the engineering work and important contracting supervision which are now the Borough Presidencies' principal legitimate function.

It is a wide-open secret in New York City that many employees of the Borough Presidents' offices—members of important political clubs, district leaders, etc.—hold down their jobs as pure political perquisites, seldom bothering even to appear at their offices. Through the years Borough Presidents have been removed in significant number for corruption in office; the latest to come into suspicion, under charges of having accepted lavish gifts from a real-estate promoter, was Manhattan's Hulan Jack, who first suspended himself in January 1960, awaiting the actions against him.

In testimony before a Senate subcommittee investigating the subject of public morals, Judge Learned Hand once summed up the problem of public lethargy which allows such worn-out political satrapies to continue. "Take the government of the city of New York," he said. "There have been periodic arousals when the lid was opened and the people saw what had been happening, and then you have reform movements. You are too young, but I remember Travers Jerome.* He did a great deal of good, and we were all keen about him. His efforts quickened into some good administration, but then things slumped back as people got indifferent."

Senator Paul Douglas then asked the judge: "Do you think the situation ever goes back to quite where it was before?"

"Yes," said the judge, "I'm afraid it does, Senator."

Without doubt the most expensive form of civic corruption now barnacled on the Genial Society is the man with political favors to sell, who knows a lot of people in Washington or City Hall or at the State Capitol. This man is a crook. Equally dangerous at times is the open lobbyist who shuns crude vote buying, but sells his particular point of view to legislators or executives of the government with zeal, professional skill and a full wallet. This man is definitely not a crook. More often

* A noted and highly effective reformer, Jerome served as New York district attorney from 1901 to 1909.

than not he is reputable. Yet, particularly in matters of complex technical legislation, he may influence government far more than he ought.

The influence-peddler has walked across the Washington stage with aggravating frequency in recent times, his numbers swelled by the same simple taste relationship that draws flies to sugar. If the government is going to spend so much money on so many projects, the influence-peddler reasons, why not help certain preferred parties get it?

These fixers and five-percenters were staple fare in the closing days of the Truman administration. Few newspaper readers will soon forget Harry "the Hat" Lev, Henry "the Dutchman" Grunewald (since gone to his reward) and similar luminaries. Behind the gaudy testimony of these and others, however, lay not only the disturbing truth that "graft and corruption" had penetrated two such sensitive agencies of the government as the Reconstruction Finance Corporation and the Internal Revenue Service. There was a wider realization that the spread of influence-peddling could in the long run ruin the country as utterly as military defeat or economic collapse. Federal Judge Dawson said, in sentencing Grunewald and his partners: "This great republic can be undermined by these defendants in the same way as by termites gnawing at its foundations."*

All the fixers and five-percenters operate on the same principle. They know somebody, or knew somebody who knows somebody, who might be in a position to say a word about an important loan or government contract, or help out with a bad tax muddle. All the "client" need provide is money—or, alternatively, a favor in return, like giving the fixer a chance

* Ironically, but by no means atypically, the "termites" in question succeeded in dragging out their trial so successfully and introduced so many legal technicalities that the Supreme Court ultimately disallowed their conviction on an intricate question of law. By the time the Justice Department was again in a position to try the case, the statute of limitations had run out on the most serious of the charges against them.

to buy valuable stock or presenting him with an interest in a business.

Appallingly large sums of money or property have changed hands in this way and, as usual, some of the most reputable businessmen were found participating—like the fabled deacon found enjoying himself in the red-light district. It is no easy matter to find out which favors were innocent, which were "imprudent" and which were done with criminal intent.

The good influence-peddler, or influence-seeker, gets his start socially as well as in a business way. One device is to intrude himself among the board members of certain important charities, through heavy contributions. United in this eleemosynary bond, he can then "firm up" a contact with his target by inviting him to lunch, perhaps progressing to entertaining him at dinner. Business is discussed from time to time.* But the skillful operator will take pains to present himself primarily as an interesting conversationalist, a witty time-killer, a helpful asset in getting to hit shows. When the time comes, the Operator will make his wants known. Or, if he is in the business of influence-peddling per se, he will make some friend's wants known.

The Eisenhower administration made it plain to the country when it took office that "corruption" and "graft" were to be

---

* In the same testimony quoted above, before a 1951 subcommittee of the Senate Committee on Labor and Public Welfare, Judge Hand elaborated also on this theme:

Senator Douglas: For instance, if anyone were to try to talk to you in chambers or at dinner about a case which you had under consideration, in the first place I do not believe he would dare to talk to you, but if he did, we all know you would walk away.

Judge Hand: That happens more than you think.

Senator Douglas: Oh, does it really? That is very interesting.

Judge Hand: I do not mean personally. I have got so old that they do not do it.

Senator Douglas: You mean that lawyers actually do sidle up to judges at dinner parties?

Judge Hand: Sidling up is not perhaps the best word, but they communicate, yes, they do.

things of the past. Rarely has a more millenarian approach been made to American politics. "Clean as a hound's tooth" was the way the President expressed his insistence on personal probity in the government, and he meant it sincerely.

Politics, however, have a way of running into corners of darkness uncontemplated by an orderly General Staff mind. It was not long before the hound's tooth began to show a little tartar. Early in the President's first term there were forced replacements in the Federal Housing Administration. The Dixon-Yates controversy broke in 1955, starting a partisan uproar that took a long time dying. Stripped to essentials, it was an effort of the Eisenhower administration to foster the private-enterprise power industry—an honest if debatable aim —by most indirect methods. It involved substituting private power for some of the Tennessee Valley Authority power used to service, among other things, the city of Memphis; TVA was then to divert some of its own power to the increased needs of the Atomic Energy Commission. It was disturbing enough that this roundabout way was used to hamstring the further growth of TVA. Worse yet was the fact that in this "bold" strike for "free enterprise" there was no competitive bidding allowed.

In 1958 a House of Representatives committee investigating activities of the Federal Communications Commission came to suspect improprieties in allocating TV frequencies. It was a serious charge, since the authority of the FCC in this field is virtually beyond appeal. Although the House investigators and their counsel turned themselves into a caterwauling sideshow, they stumbled on some real evidence of improper influence. A recently resigned member of the Federal Communications Commission, Richard Mack, was hastily indicted in July 1958* on charges that illegal pressure had secured the award of TV Channel 10 in Miami. The indictment came, as luck would have

* Mack's trial was delayed while he received medical treatment.

it, just after the Republican National Committee's new speaker's handbook had declared that "there has not been one indictment, conviction or prison sentence of an Eisenhower appointee."

Contemporaneous with the Mack case was the sudden rise to prominence of Bernard Goldfine, a Boston businessman whose friendship with the President's executive assistant, Sherman Adams, put rugs and vicuña coats into the same limbo for the Eisenhower administration which deep-freezes and minks had occupied during the tenure of Harry S. Truman.

Goldfine's business activities were a study in corporate tightrope walking. His career has been studded with stockholders' suits, conspiracy charges and other court actions in which he was accused of defrauding corporations, local governments and individuals. He was cited for contempt of Congress in August 1958 for refusing to answer certain questions about his business activities. He received a suspended sentence a year later, when the contempt issue was brought to trial in a federal court, on condition that he answer the questions at issue. As of this writing actions remain pending against him, notably a massive audit of his income-tax returns by the Internal Revenue Service. Goldfine's legal problems were almost as varied as his business interests. While one company, for example, Northfield Mills, was running afoul of the FTC because of mislabeling, another holding company, the East Boston Company, was chronically avoiding the annual financial reports which the SEC requires. (In December 1958, after the furor had begun, Goldfine agreed to a $662,000 settlement of a minority stockholders' suit against East Boston and an allied corporation for what the stockholders charged was "continuous looting" of the companies' assets.) What made his persistent indifference to state, local and federal laws so serious was his close gift-bearing relationships with so many influential government officials.

The story of Goldfine's gifts to Sherman Adams of the coat and the rug became household conversation throughout the country. ("With the coat," said a staunch Republican journalist, "he's got to go.") Adams had allowed Goldfine to pay his and his wife's hotel bills. By way of worsening matters Goldfine had to admit that he had charged off such gifts on his income-tax returns as business expenses, e.g., $3,000 worth of hotel bills he had footed for Adams and three fellow Republicans, Senators Payne (Me.), Bridges (N.H.) and Cotton (N.H.). Far worse than the gifts was evidence that Adams had made telephone calls from the White House on two occasions to ask about progress of cases pending against Goldfine with the SEC and the FTC.

Adams defended the telephone calls. "Is there any member of this committee," he said, "who has not made a phone call for a constituent? Is there any member of the committee or of the Congress . . . who has not made an appointment . . . ?" President Eisenhower told his news conference that Adams might have been "imprudent," but that "I respect him because of his personal and official integrity. I need him."

In September, on the eve of the November 1958 election, Adams resigned. In a final statement he denounced "a campaign of vilification" against him. He repeated that "I had never influenced nor attempted to influence any agency or any officer or employee of any agency in any case, decision or matter whatsoever."

This may have been true in Adams' mind. But this mind, by general acknowledgment a keen instrument, showed a strange blindness to political facts. It was of course not true, as Adams suggested to the congressmen, that his telephone calls were no different from the ordinary service rendered by senators or congressmen to their constituents. To intercede for a constituent, the while keeping the intercession open and within the law, is a congressman's bounden duty; he is that constituent's representative in Washington. Members of the executive branch have been schooled to deal with such inquiries. But when a federal commission receives a phone call from the White House asking about a matter, the implications are not very cloudy, especially in a Washington bureaucracy so constantly sensitive to the slightest weather changes of its betters.

In the circumstances, President Eisenhower's tortured admission that he may have been "imprudent," but "I need him," sounds as convincing as Bacon's famous statement that he took the bribe, but did not let it influence his judgment. I dwell on the statement and the incident because of the peculiarly damaging effect it had on the national morality. Adams himself had been the sternest upholder of a rigid code of public morality, and he and President Eisenhower had hitherto acted by it. The Adams disclosures and the slow action taken on them by the President only served to buttress the "everybody's doing it" philosophy. Again, *quis custodiet ipsos custodes?*

Walter Lippmann said well, in his column of July 8, 1958: "The argument that money may be accepted provided nothing is given in return is an attempt to befuddle the real issue. It conceals the main point that what is customary and perhaps tolerable elsewhere may be intolerable in the close official family of the President. Of those who are at the top, the country has a right to demand a self-imposed standard of conduct which is much higher than the laws against bribery and graft. That was in essence the principle on which General Eisenhower ran for President in 1952.

"The ultimate power of the state cannot be entrusted to men whose conception of public virtue is that their integrity is adequate if they cannot be convicted of crime."

There is one sure way to handle problems like Sherman Adams' gifts and it has a distinguished historical precedent. Just after his inauguration, a Philadelphia saddle maker sent

Thomas Jefferson a specially padded "elastic" saddle. Jefferson was intrigued and gladly accepted it. But he added the condition that the manufacturer accept payment from him. "I have ever laid it down as an unalterable law to myself to accept no present while in a public office. I am sure that your own reflections on the tendency of the contrary practice will justify in your eye my adherence to this principle."

The problem for Jefferson admittedly was relatively simple. The modern officeholder is beset in ways that Jefferson's tidy 18th-century conscience never dreamed of. When Federal Judge Charles Wyzanski, Jr., was presiding over a trial where Bernard Goldfine was a defendant, Goldfine ostentatiously donated $1,000 to one of Wyzanski's wife's favorite charities. The donation, he said, was "in honor of" Mrs. Wyzanski. (Needless to say, Judge Wyzanski was not impressed.)

Yet as the number of federal government employees nears the 2,500,000 mark—not to mention the hordes of officeholders on the state and local level—the diversity of function and situation among them makes any formal rules of official ethics well-nigh impossible. What standards we have were most of them made in the era of little government, when men could hardly foresee interlocking relationships among public, private and business life. Now standards vary. When a State Department official accepted a car as a gift from the King of Saudi Arabia, for whom he had performed official services, the late John Foster Dulles had him transferred from his post. But there was no thought of transfer for the high-ranking military officers, including the Chairman of the Joint Chiefs of Staff, who flew south for an easeful Bahama week end in 1959, as guest of a leading military contractor. "Imprudent," perhaps.

There is another type of dishonesty in government, harder to define because it is not so often thought of. Members of the

Genial Society, so prone to shout "graft and corruption" at the wave of an expense account (and often so right), think of public morality mainly in economic terms. Yet this is barely half the story. A public trust can be betrayed by cowardice, inaction or verbal misrepresentation as surely as it can be betrayed by graft. Generally the cost in these instances is greater.

The man who grafts $200,000 from a corrupt city machine may be far less dangerous to the nation than the impeccably mannered gentleman who takes nothing tangible himself, but makes a few phone calls, or suppresses a few facts.

Few abuses are less studied than the matter of political misrepresentation. If a company is guilty of misusing its advertising, how much more culpable is a government which develops a systematic pattern of misrepresentation? Is the technique of the controlled Washington press leak ultimately as destructive of public morality as the depredations of a Goldfine? It is very possible. One man's "misrepresentation" may be another man's courageous effort to "shield the public" from wrongs or hazards which it apparently only dimly comprehends.

It is shielding the public, in fact, which has prompted most of the political sleight of hand during the last decade of American history. In the main this sleight of hand was performed by exceedingly public-spirited men, confident that they were acting in the public interest.

A memorable accusation of political misrepresentation was that leveled at Lewis L. Strauss in 1959. Strauss at the time was acting as Secretary of Commerce on an interim presidential appointment, after years of service on the Atomic Energy Commission, notably as its chairman. He was by any standards a dedicated public servant, respected by enemies as well as friends. His zeal and intelligence were beyond question. In a money way he was absolutely incorruptible. Why, then, did the United States Senate fail to confirm Strauss as Secretary of

Commerce, rebuffing a presidential cabinet appointment for the third time in 100 years?

The answer was that a majority of senators felt that Strauss had shown a distressing lack of candor in testifying before them —some would imply that he lied. The points at issue were only tangential to Strauss's qualifications as Secretary of Commerce: they involved his performance and relations with other agencies of government as Chairman of the Atomic Energy Commission, e.g., his withholding from Congress of information that nuclear submarine plans were being sent to the British, his denial that he had ordered a security report from the AEC on a scientist who had opposed him. But in dealing with these and other questions, Strauss displayed an arrogance rarely seen even in Washington and showed himself a man renowned for his reluctance to admit that he may have made a mistake or a slight misjudgment (significantly, speaking of misjudgments, it was Strauss who approved the Dixon-Yates deal without having bothered even to inform his fellow commissioners on the AEC). It was not such incidents themselves that bothered the senators. It was his refusal to make known to representatives of the American people anything but his own professedly omniscient version of them.

In refusing Strauss confirmation the senators deprived President Eisenhower of the services of an able Secretary of Commerce. But they belatedly showed their recognition of a principle which has been increasingly violated of late: the duty of American public officials to be candid with the country. Strauss's own administration of the Atomic Energy Commission, however competently performed, had been characterized by an arrogance and refusal to divulge information to the public which went far beyond mere security considerations. Influenced by its chairman, the AEC grew into the habit of treating newspapermen virtually as potential spies. Strauss had strong personal feelings about various scientists. Though the incorruptible chairman's friends went unrewarded, his enemies often claimed to have been victimized in circumstances unrelated to their capacity or their use to the country.

The Strauss affair was only one case of political misrepresentation breaking surface. Enough light has been thrown by this time on the announced policy of the Eisenhower administration to "liberate" the East European Communist satellites or to "unleash" Chiang Kai-shek on the Chinese mainland; each of these once-popular catchwords proved to have been at direct variance with what American foreign policy really intended, and actually did, in the period when the slogans were enunciated. The inspired press-agentry of the White House Press Secretary, James Hagerty, should have drawn technical praise from anyone in the news business. But it is questionable whether the duty of the White House Secretary does not encompass acquainting the American public with all the facts in a given presidential action, as well as putting the boss in the most favorable light possible.*

A crowning instance of political misrepresentation occurred through the years following the lofting of the first Soviet Sputnik, when the administration set out determinedly to minimize the magnitude of the Soviet achievement and the consequent national peril to the United States by inflating American resources and prospects in the space and missile field.

A look at the record is instructive. In the period between 1955 and 1960 the United States, at the highest levels of gov-

---

* In an article written in *Esquire,* Joseph Kraft, one of the few writers with courage to discuss Hagerty in public, noted a typical example of the best-foot-forward technique. In 1955, when Secretary of the Air Force Talbott resigned under fire for his business activities while in office, Hagerty delayed the announcement of the resignation until he could fish up an announcement of a *projected* U.S. space satellite—thus nicely crowding Talbott out of the headlines. Perhaps all is fair in love, war and press-agentry.

ernment, refused to admit either the awesome importance of the new scientific and military frontiers in space and rocketry or the fact—an increasingly obvious one—that this country was committed to a race for mastery of these new media with the demonstrably hostile Soviet Union. Two years before the first 1957 Sputnik, President Eisenhower sent down the first of a series of orders forbidding the U.S. Army to put a satellite into space—which it could have done in 1955-1956. Throughout the 1955-1960 period, every bold plan, every attempted reorganization, every imaginative scientist or military man in the space and missile field was rendered to a greater or less degree ineffective by two things: 1) President Eisenhower's apparent conviction that a balanced budget was the primary goal of a nation, and 2) the President's insistence, in the face of all the facts, that somehow an arbitrary distinction could be made between "military" and "scientific" applications of space and rocketry.*

The struggle between President Eisenhower and the counsels of efficiency went on for the most part behind the scenes of government, not really breaking out in the open until the defense debate of 1960. A similar struggle went on in the conventional military sphere between the Eisenhower reliance on "massive retaliation" as the one prop of the nation's defenses and the repeated conviction of Army leaders that lack of conventional striking power was fatally crippling the U.S. for the kind of "small" wars which it had fought before in the postwar period and would doubtless have to fight again. As a result of both disagreements—on space and ground-warfare—and the White House's refusal to permit any conflicting interpretations,

---

* This problem was discussed in detail in an article by the writer, "The Missile Mess," in the January 1960 *Harper's*. The massed testimony of almost every authority in the field confuting the Eisenhower view can be found in the testimony before both the Senate and House committees on Space and Astronautics, 1958-1960.

two Army chiefs of staff, Generals Matthew Ridgway and Maxwell Taylor, resigned in frustrated anger. So did the Army's two most able military space and missile experts: Lieutenant General James Gavin and Major General John Medaris.

During the same period the accomplishments of the Soviet Union were all too plain to see, in a scientific-military race which almost everyone in the world except the President of the United States regarded as a supreme demonstration of rival world power systems—with military, political and psychological factors rolled into one. On October 4, 1957, the U.S.S.R. lofted the first satellite. On September 13, 1959, a Soviet rocket was first to reach the moon. On January 20, 1960, a Soviet missile was sent 7,800 miles to a prearranged target site in the Pacific. The extent to which the United States was "behind" the Russians in this regard was estimated as from three to five years.

Yet this is what the President of the United States was saying about the space and missile race with the Soviet Union during this period.*

1. "Let's take the earth satellite, as opposed to the missile, because they are related only indirectly in the physical sense, and in our case not at all. Never has it been considered as a race.—Oct. 9, 1957.
"It is my conviction, supported by trusted scientific and military advisers, that, although the Soviets are quite likely ahead in some missiles, and special areas, and are obviously ahead of us in satellite development, as of today the over-all military strength of the free world is distinctly greater than that of Communist countries.—Nov. 7, 1957.
"There has been no place that I can see where there has been any possibility of gaps occurring.—Aug. 27, 1958.
"Today the so-called missile gap is being rapidly filled.—Oct. 20, 1958.

* As quoted in a Washington *Post* editorial (February 16, 1960).

"Today America—and all the world—knows that in less than four years we are rapidly closing the missile gap that we inherited. And Sputniks have been matched by Explorers, Vanguards and Pioneers.—Oct. 31, 1958.

"It is absolutely fatuous and futile to try to balance, item by item, the progress of two great nations in their technology of defense. To disturb ourselves too much that we have not yet caught up with another great power and people with technical skill in a particular item, it seems to me to show a loss or a lack of a sense of balance.—Jan. 14, 1959.

2. "I am always a little bit amazed about this business of catching up. What you want is enough, a thing that is adequate.—Feb. 3, 1960.

"There are too many of these generals with all sorts of ideas. I cannot be particularly disturbed because everybody with a parochial viewpoint all over the place comes along and says that the bosses know nothing about it.—Feb. 3, 1960.

"The biggest problem there is in the United States today is to make sure that her own people . . . understand the basic issues that face us and form their own judgment."—Feb. 11, 1960.

One would hesitate to accuse President Eisenhower of the same conscious misrepresentation used by some members of his administration. (A high official of the executive branch, explaining to congressional committee aides the rationale behind the Space Act of 1958, said: "The people in this country were getting hysterical about this Sputnik business. We thought we'd better give them something to salve their mood.") But it is hard to hold back the word "misrepresentation" from excuses like the foregoing, made about a matter of the most vital national security. Suppose an official of a manufacturing company had made similar public statements about the value of a product, over a period of years. The verdict of the market place, I fear, would have been unmistakable.

Political misrepresentation is of course hardly a monopoly

of the Eisenhower administration (although a self-styled "crusade" with tarnish on its armor is likely to attract more than normal attention.) But it is becoming more of a danger every day simply because of the enormity of government, the growing complexity of its decisions—and the apparent reluctance of most Americans even to try to participate in them. The tolerance of such misrepresentation reflects the moral negligence of the Genial Society as fully as the tolerance of ancient public till-robbers like Mayor Hague in Jersey City or Tom Pendergast in Kansas City. While allowing, indeed urging government to stick nose and finger into most compartments of the national life, the citizen stoutly pretends that he is still back in the horse-and-buggy days when all the graft was visible and localized in City Hall and all that it did was to enlarge slightly the tax rate.

There is something wrong with a civilization where millions are lavished without a murmur on the better white lipstick or the nicer portable TV set, and such essentials as road building, education and medical services are begrudged because they are "public" enterprise, where contrariwise a citizenry can lavish a good bit of its waking hours debating whether TV performers like Jack Paar and Arthur Godfrey are sympathetic characters, while uncritically shrinking from any close look at the public officials who hold their country's destiny.

X

THE PUBLIC MORALITY

I see the better course and I approve of it, I follow the worse one.
—Ovid: Metamorphoses

It is the thesis of this book that our national future is being misshaped, far more than we realize, by the witless optimist gulled into phony stock purchases, by the two-bit chiseler padding his outsize expense account, by the corporate dodger who writes off his Florida yacht as a business expense, the influence-peddler who tampers with legislation. The old motto "republics live by virtue" is no idle saying. It is true of the United States —a society of free men which moves efficiently, sometimes grandly, thanks to the honest acceptance and mutual fulfillment of thousands of contract relationships between its citizens and each other, between citizens and governing authorities, between the levels of government and, very importantly, between citizens, governments and those corporate labor and management entities which must carry a heavy burden of responsibility in a free capitalist state.

A climate of fraud eats at these free relationships. In this concluding chapter I should like to examine some of the factors underlying this climate. I am aware that anyone who criticizes deeply will sooner or later be called an "alarmist," or a "prophet of doom," the terms in which the Genial Society most often defines critics. Many judicious commentators have been telling us that the excesses of the white-collar criminals and their associates have been roughly canceled out by the growth of the regulatory apparatus, on all levels of government. This is admittedly, as Professor Crane Brinton phrased it, in his *History of Western Morals,* "a whiggish conclusion: the total situation is not so bad as the professional complainers make it out to be, nor as good as the professional happiness boys make it out to be. In a culture as competitive and as multanimous as ours there is bound to be a good deal of cheating, a good deal of pretense. But the growth of public regulation and even, in part, the very competition that spurs on the evil help correct it. . . . The era of the Robber Barons is well over. Political and economic competition, if it heightens the nervous tension of our lives, also makes it difficult to continue for long any major fraud save what to a few Westerners must seem the fraud of all life on this earth. The voice of a modern Cicero against a modern Verres gets magnified and broadcast by all the means technology gives us. The whole apparatus of publicity, the sales apparatus, that terrifies or disgusts an Ortega, an Orwell, a Koestler, can be, and sometimes is, used on the side of the angels . . ."

This view has the advantage of echoing the calm "on-the-other-hand" mentality which has so long passed for wisdom in American academic circles. But it hardly holds true for this moment of American history. Its validity was sorely tested— and I would say found wanting—with the symptomatic appearance of TV "fix" and "payola," in the summer of 1959. The reverberations, which continue, have led us from apparently little bits of trickery to a much-needed basement tour of our moral foundations.

The celebrated TV quiz scandal began unobtrusively in August 1958, when a second-rate quiz program called "Dotto" was dropped by the Columbia Broadcasting System. For the preceding year and a half quiz programs had been about the most popular item on the national entertainment circuit. For the magic hours of prime network time each week, the nation watched enraptured while prodigious 10-year-old boys, popular band leaders, obscure file clerks with unnatural memories and attractive girls who seemed to have recondite interests (like boxing statistics) stammered, grimaced and twitched before giving their profitable answers in the "isolation booths." When the first hint of foul play darkened this entertainment *genre*, there was almost no American to whom quiz program was not a household word.*

By the early fall of 1958 accusations that the quiz programs had been "fixed" were flying around New York, substantial enough to warrant investigation by the district attorney's office and a grand jury. Principally because there was no law on the books directed against rigged quiz shows and similar excesses, the district attorney and the grand jury had difficulty making a legal case against the quiz-show producers. The public case against them was made—such is the wonder of our system —by a subcommittee of the House Commerce Committee whose original job was to investigate "legislative oversight."

Its climax came on November 2, 1959, when Charles Van Doren, the scholarly Columbia English instructor who had won $129,000 on N.B.C.'s "Twenty-One," appeared before the subcommittee and admitted that he had been in on the fix himself,

---

* The programs spread also to Europe, notably in Italy, whose imported quiz show was a good bit livelier than the American originals. There was even a Soviet imitation, which did not last.

that he had accepted "coaching" for his answers, and had, as other contestants had previously testified they had done, gone through a prescribed Stanislavsky ritual of affected perplexity, confusion and concern when answering the questions—to help make it, as one of the quiz producers put it, "a good show."

Van Doren had been a virtual idol to the viewing public, a scholar from a scholarly family, the sort of clean-cut intellectual who showed that an I.Q. did pay off to the extent of nationwide fame, big winnings, and a $50,000 job on a network show, won after his quiz-contest popularity had been established. It was a depressing morning when Americans found out that the reputation was based on a faked game.

The networks, the sponsors, the advertising agencies stampeded into the public confessional, bursting to assure the American public that they may have been imprudent but they had done nothing wrong. In fact, the networks protested, had they known anything about the fact of this quiz-show rigging, the shows would have been immediately banned from the air waves. N.B.C. President Robert E. Kintner admitted that "by hindsight we should have dug a little deeper." Such admissions were hardly calculated to reassure the country.

When the full effect of the TV scandals finally penetrated, late in 1959—along with attendant disclosures of disk jockeys living off under-the-counter "payola" from the record companies, of manufacturers paying journalists and entertainers for "plugs" for their products—society felt a brief moment of truth. The first reaction of many had been merely to applaud the confessions (by now a hallmark of Washington investigations) and shake a warning finger. But continuing revelations could not so easily be dismissed. Out of 150 witnesses summoned by New York's District Attorney Hogan, for example, in connection with *his* quiz-show investigation, he estimated that two thirds had perjured themselves! The cries of "everybody's doing it" and "what's the difference?" for once were too loud to pass unnoticed.

In the furor that followed, there have been rising shouts for more laws, more regulations. Our first impulse in a moral dilemma is to demand explicit laws to solve it. (Regarding government regulation of his programs, N.B.C.'s Kintner, a real phrasemaker, said: "We feel that, if any legislation is to be considered, it should be legislation aimed directly at the wrong-doer.") Yet a government of laws cannot cure a moral dilemma without some strong self-governing help from the men who live under those laws.

The futility of mere legal correctives can be gathered from a look at the types of fraud exposures which were crowding into the newspapers in a chain reaction of publicity dating from the TV and payola scandals. In February 1960 the FBI announced the arrest of a multimillion-dollar loan racket, which extracted FHA-backed loans from banks for nonexistent household improvements. The disturbing thing about the racket, run by a few crooked contractors, was the readiness with which some 400 homeowners participated in an obviously crooked scheme. The New York *World-Telegram,* later the same month, brought the authorities' attention to the work of private agencies which did a lucrative business faking academic themes and dissertations, not merely for college-exam crammers, but in some cases for graduate students who used the fake theses as credits for doctors' and masters' degrees. Commenting on this disclosure—and doubtless aware of some recent and discouraging academic surveys on the subject of student cheating—the president of Columbia University's Teachers College, Dr. Hollis Caswell, said: "The general moral tone in our country tends to encourage this sort of thing. It is a little like our attitude toward the income tax—if you can get by with it, it's all right."

St. Thomas Aquinas, who talked about a great many more

things than theology in his famous *Summa,* made the effective point that the more law there is, the less it will be respected. "Therefore, economy should be practiced."* Almost every study of the federal or state regulatory agencies notes with regret the profusion of laws and regulations but concludes that most of the fine print is made necessary by ever-more refined violations. This is especially true in the areas of securities trading and taxes. It is no accident that the *Wall Street Journal's* column on new tax decisions is one of its most popular features. Learned Hand once remarked, "The result of statutes and regulations is a wilderness of words, although indeed that is inevitable, since it is the only protection of the individual against the unlimited discretion of small officials. But it is a hideous thing to find one's way through, and people cannot possibly get on without expert help, *i.e.,* without lawyers."

As the laws proliferate and grow more technical, injustices paradoxically seem more apparent.

The law moves slowly, in any case. Fleet-footed criminals, like the proprietors of medical frauds, can make their killing in a few months' time. When, after the fullness of investigation, the Post Office Department or the Federal Trade Commission catches up with them, they are only too happy to bow out of the picture and meekly accept a cease-and-desist order.

The classic criminal law of fraud, also, is of little protection against crooked or sometimes wicked advertising. As Professor Ernest Sutherland said in his *White Collar Crime,* it developed long before mass advertising was ever heard of. It is very difficult to bring to court a case against the author of widespread misrepresentation because: 1) the misrepresentation is so provably small per capita that few of those injured will bother to prosecute, and 2) the fraud laws are almost hopelessly

---

* I have used the translation of one of St. Thomas' best modern interpreters, the English Dominican Thomas Gilby, in *Principality and Polity.*

hedged with precedents regarding the strict proof of intent and the actual damage caused. There are, finally, so many third parties intervening between the injuring advertiser or producers and the injured consumer that cases are apt to bog down in confusing legal parallelograms.

To these legal difficulties we must add two important states of mind. The first I have already mentioned: the age-old reluctance of the sucker to admit that he has been taken. The second is the compartmented mentality of so many American businessmen. As we have seen, very often the pillar of the community turns out to be the real operator, and one without any sense of moral guilt at what he has done. Likely as not, he has been operating on the principle of selective obedience to the law, now dangerously prevalent in the United States. This view developed among many businessmen during the New Deal days of Franklin D. Roosevelt, if not indeed during the first Square Deal trust busting of his Republican cousin, Theodore. "These fellows in Washington," the train of thought ran, "are ruining the country with socialistic philosophy. What they're doing is immoral, and a really good American has every right to pay no attention to it." And, of course, the prohibition era had already seen millions flouting an unpopular law.

The unfolding story of businessmen flouting the law rivals, in scope at least, the extent of the thuggery and monopoly practiced today by James Hoffa and others in the name of organized labor—as disclosed by the McClellan Committee. Sutherland's study, published in 1948, dealt with 70 large corporations—all but two of which were listed among the 200 largest nonfinancial business firms in the United States (at that time). Over a period of years, these corporations had piled up a total of 980 unfavorable decisions for violation of government regulations. (The average was 14 apiece.) The violations included restraint of trade, patent infringement, unfair labor practices, advertising misrepresentation and rebates. Only 159 of these cases were dealt with by the criminal courts alone. But since 583 involved both civil and criminal jurisdiction, Sutherland is correct in his statement that 742 out of the 980 cases represented what are legally considered crimes.

Anyone would have to concede that the climate of enforcement during the late thirties and early forties, included in the Sutherland survey, was largely stormy weather for businessmen. Yet the fact remains that the companies indicted and convicted displayed no hesitation about returning to the scene of their crime, albeit with slightly changed ground rules and perhaps a different set of lawyers.

In the postwar decades, this attitude has not changed. Antitrust violation is the most venerable and prestigious crime in American business and a good barometer of big business's attitude toward government. As cited previously, it has multiplied in recent years—if we are to judge anything by the flurry of prosecutions initiated by the Republican Attorney General's office. Whether the law is here efficient or blundering, the important thing is that companies repeatedly flout it.

Such conduct would be bad enough if it were done solely in the interest of the companies served by these lawbreaking directors, managers and chief executive officers. If it were, they could at least take refuge in a chamber-of-commerce edition of Count Cavour's notable nineteenth-century aphorism, "If we did for ourselves what we did for our country, what rascals we would be." But the rise of profit sharing, the corporate expense account, the complicated tax structure and the manager-stockholder have tended to identify the interests of company and manager, or even company and employee, as they never have been identified before.

Before going further, we had better say that this climate of fraud is hardly an American phenomenon. Temple-fund scandals in India, baby-powder adulterations in France, Japanese shipping rebates, expense-account scandals in Moscow—the art of the Operator has been advancing everywhere in the world. The London *Economist* editorialized several years ago: "It is clear that graft—bribery and extortion, squeeze or protection, wire-pulling and nepotism—has persisted and found its place in the most complex twentieth-century political organizations. Not only have the corrupt foreign regimes which the long arm of Victorian imperial reform failed to reach continued to flourish, but power has been given back to dependent peoples long before they have abandoned what is conveniently known as the custom of the country."

There was a time when the British could claim to have eliminated a great deal of Operating from certain areas. There doubtless were real-life civil-service officials of the Victorian era who habitually kept two inkwells on their desks, one using government ink for official correspondence, the other—for personal letters—filled at their own expense. But these incorruptibles had the advantage of membership in a privileged class unhampered by the temptations of economic or social want. In this generation the British "establishment" is going the way of all such oligarchies—the inevitable result of war, periods of national indigence and semisocialism. Currently London businessmen, released equally from their forefathers' traditions and security, are burning up the expense-account trail as fast as their American counterparts.

In foreign societies not endowed with the curious insulations of the Anglo-Saxon moral code, a certain amount of fraud has been more or less openly licensed, out of a feeling that human frailty is in the long run best contained by allowing it a little maneuvering room. Note, for example, the following Neapolitan version of *caveat emptor*. Not long ago a foreign visitor in southern Italy was half-shocked, half-awed at the behavior of a well-born Naples housewife on her morning round about the fish markets. After a friendly but rigorous bout of haggling with the proprietress, Donna X made her purchase and went home. Before taking her coat off, she marched into the kitchen and tossed the fish on her own scale. The weight was found wanting. "Just as I thought," she snapped. "That woman cheated me again." Whereupon she pulled a long fish out of her shopping bag, where it had been illicitly concealed, and flipped it on the scale. This, added to the rest, came to exactly the poundage for which she had paid the fish woman.

On a more official level, it is interesting to compare the French and Italian attitudes toward taxation with our own. They popularly regard taxation as a supreme effrontery on the part of the government. Collecting taxes in these countries has become a hare-and-hounds game, with both parties convinced of the other's base motives. A prominent Paris executive of my acquaintance walked to work for years rather than invest even in a modest Citroën. His reasons were excellent. In France the tax collector's only standard of assessment is what in American circles is the last resort of tax investigation, the net worth of the taxpayer. (All declarations and formal sworn statements of a man's earnings are presumed to be false.) So the addition of a car, this tangible evidence of wealth, would be enough to tip the scales for moving the man's tax to a higher bracket— the last straw in a painfully collected cumulus of information about trips to Deauville, new girl friends, expensive furniture and superior cooks and valets.

In Japan, at least until recently, no businessman in his right mind would think of recording his fortunes in only one set of books. Invariably there is one set for the use of the Tax Office. This is a regrettable tale of misfortune and missed opportunities, written in red. The other set of books, hidden somewhere in the chief bookkeeper's domain, is by contrast a story of rising dividends, lowered costs, plant expansion and progressive money-saving innovations. Really enterprising Japanese companies have been known to sport *three* or *four* separate sets of books, the more somber collections organized for the benefit of less-favored partners, the brighter put at the disposal, say, of a larger company investigating merger prospects. Even tax officials have on occasion been found with several sets of books to *their* credit. One of the principal public and private grievances against Hayato Ikeda, a postwar Finance Minister, was his sudden insistence that taxes should be paid on the actual value of properties, and that the multiple-book system was not only illegal but immoral.

Eastern civilizations like the Japanese or Latin civilizations like the French have come to make a sharp distinction between personal honesty and, if you will, the public honesty. In the modern Anglo-Saxon scheme of things, however, the state is still seen as a compound of individual moralities, a righteous closed corporation which in principle resembles the structure of a 17th-century Calvinist congregation. He who sins against the common body sins against the several individual members. Paying taxes is a *civic* duty, in the sense that it was in Rome of the Senate before the Emperors inaugurated statism, bread and circuses.

This is not necessarily a better position morally than the other ones, although we like to say it is every Fourth of July and Thanksgiving Day. People have argued that the moral zeal we invest in civic duty is balanced by a profound moral laxity in matters like family solidarity, the education of children or dealings between individuals. Various statistics on juvenile delinquency, for example, could be marshaled to support this position. But relative moral superiority is not at issue. What *is* pertinent is the fact that so much of the Anglo-Saxon ethic is invested in public morality. Accordingly, a slippage in public morality is far more dangerous to the whole society.

Which suggests why the moral fabric of France can survive heavy amounts of tax fraud and why the moral fabric of the United States cannot. Most foreign societies have some form of less abstract legitimacy to cling to: the Crown among the English, simple nationalism among the Germans or the Russians, the inbred superiority complexes of peoples like the Chinese or the French. Even a Communist society has its own self-announced form of legitimacy in Marxist scripture. Legitimacy in the United States, if we rule out the particular protection of Divine Providence or deified Progress, depends solely on the probity and the united will of the citizens.

The origins of public morality in the United States are far-flung and oddly assorted. Viewed superficially, their totality looks like the product of some metaphysical hot-rodder's home-made assembly line: frame by Calvin, chassis by the firm of Jefferson, Rousseau and Locke, motor British common-law traditional with Cavalier styling and a frontier battery, imported brakes and supercharges from the Vatican, radiator by Emerson, dashboard instruments by John Dewey and William James, headlights by Wesley and Lucretius, tires by Goodyear. Ethical elements have been added by each wave of immigrants. But two leading influences predominate: the deterministic, yet workaday piety of the Puritans; and the progress religion of Jefferson's much-loved Enlightenment. Neither can be overlooked in any discussion of the American morality.

The Progress Religion: Here is the strongest ancestor of the Genial Society's philosophy. Jefferson and Madison were products, philosophically, of the Age of Enlightenment whose French standard-bearers took the old statement that "man is a rational animal" and put an unfortunate adverb, "perfectly," in front of the "rational." When they and the other Founding Fathers hammered out the Declaration of Independence, they incorporated a phrase, "the pursuit of happiness," which had actually been borrowed from another Virginia gentleman named George Mason. The Pursuit of Happiness went into a multitude of state constitutions (although not into the federal). It became an accepted part of American folklore and legal tradition. The Pursuit was often interpreted by the courts as a safeguard for the acquisition and retention of private property.* But where Jefferson and Co. held it as a philosophical concept, succeeding generations began to interpret it more literally, divorcing it from its moral connotations. As wealth grew more abundant, the literal interpretation of the Pursuit intensified. This trend, unbraked by some feeling of civic responsibility, would have unfortunate moral results anywhere.

The premise of the Pursuit, the Jeffersonian belief in Progress, was more substantial. As confirmed time and time again by the nation's growing wealth and power, it gave rise to the American optimism about which foreigners constantly marvel. In Volume II of his brilliant war memoirs, General de Gaulle said: "I observed with admiration the flood of confidence that sustained the American elite and discovered how becoming optimism is to those who can afford it."

At its best this optimism of the Progress religion has shown itself in American industry and invention, in the spectacularly broad dams and high skyscrapers. For a long time, it seemed to know no bounds, to have no ceiling. Unfortunately, near the mid-point of the 20th century, the Progress religion finally ran into evil. The evil was twofold: evil in the form of a scientific capacity for destruction beyond man's capacity to repair; evil in the form of hostile ideologies which after centuries of steady modern education and enlightenment had come closer to enslaving all of human kind than any tyrannies known to history.

This discovery of the world's imperfectibility came as a fear-

---

* Howard Mumford Jones' *The Pursuit of Happiness* is a most interesting examination of the concept's birth and evolution in U.S. thought.

ful shock. The shock has not yet been fully appreciated in this country nor have its implications been examined. It is enough to note a most important symptom. Checked in their zeal to improve the world to the nth power, Americans have fallen back on the literal pursuit of happiness and concentrated on improving *that*. Where the cry used to be "How can we produce more?" as it still is in the Soviet state, the American slogan is "How can we consume more?" Production is no longer the problem—as any student of the steel industry, for instance, could attest. In the July 1959 issue of *Fortune,* the J. Walter Thompson Co. ran a full-page ad celebrating the joyful potential in "America's newest marketing phenomenon—The Two-House Family." The ad continues: "With the Two-House Family, American has clearly entered a new age of consumption . . ."

Half-consciously, members of the Genial Society are grabbing all they can for the present, dimly aware that a few well-placed ICBM salvos could make all The Two-House Families, and the artificial philosophy that created them, a collection of burnt vegetation. This universal grab has already become uncomfortable socially. Its full moral effects are yet to be felt, but what we have seen of them thus far is hardly encouraging. Selfishness breeds crime as surely as bad environment.

The Workaday Piety: The Puritan contribution is a more complex factor than the Progress religion, in its workings on the American morality, but it is equally important. We know how the Puritan, or Calvinist, mentality quickly established its primacy in the intellectual and moral life of the United States. Puritanism was a religion of work and certainty. Calvin's awesome doctrine of predestination gave to his "godly" ones not only a sense of spiritual responsibility and dedication to their daily tasks, but a dawning conviction that such dedication by the "communion of saints" to its earthly work was bound to receive material rewards.

Within their communion the Puritans practiced the democracy attainable among full members of a well-regulated club. They tended to look down on outsiders as doomed and they treated them as such.* But they developed an acute sense of a shared public morality, and in this lay their great strength. In the literal sense of the word, they were probably the most God-awfully responsible people who ever existed.

Thanks to those two non-American observers, Max Weber and R. H. Tawney,† we are by now familiar with the theory that Puritanism played a central role in the development of the American business society, and business society in general. The new middle-class Protestants put into their everyday work the religious fervor that the Catholic Middle Ages had most generally reserved for the monastery. Business became an active act of worship, in which the godly expected their privileged spiritual position to be reflected on the profit side of the ledger.

As generations became less pious and business more profitable, it was a logical step from worship *in* business to the worship *of* business. It would be most unfair to lay the blame for this condition at John Calvin's door. Long ago in Geneva Calvin had warned his followers against that "carnal confidence that creeps upon the saints in prosperity." But unfortunately he had hardly imagined a country where resources were so seemingly boundless and the rewards of industry so obvious.

The Puritan religion of work became a license to plunder. Men to whom horse racing was sinful had no qualms of conscience about crooked horse trading. It was no accident that

---

* Samuel Butler wrote of the English Presbyterians:
　　　　　"They prove their doctrine orthodox
　　　　　By apostolic blows and knocks."
† In *The Protestant Ethic and the Spirit of Capitalism* and *Religion and the Rise of Capitalism*, respectively.

business rascals like Uncle Daniel Drew remained pillars of their local churches. Religion shrank into the narrow dimensions of the Sunday sermon and the collection basket.

Too late American Protestantism devised the social gospel of the late 19th and early 20th centuries. The social gospel met with some success, but in the process of setting up soup kitchens and building Y.M.C.A. gymnasiums, Christian revelation was often temporarily forgotten.

The coming of Roman Catholics, in strength, injected another and potentially invigorating element in the American ethos. The Catholic view of life, which seemed conservatively to reject the new business ethic in the 17th, 18th and 19th centuries, proved for all its foibles more long-lived than the Puritan, for it had far less trouble melding with the combinations of corporate identities and individual privacies to which the 20th century gave rise. The differences between the traditional Catholic world-view and the Protestant, or more exactly the Puritan, are easier to sense than they are to define. To name a few: the Catholic worries more about the honesty of his general spiritual and intellectual premises, the Protestant about the honesty of his individual actions; the Catholic worries about the birth control or family planning that to his mind kills life, the Protestant worries about political corruption that kills integrity. The Catholic Operator's conscience is least bothered when he is rifling the public till; the Protestant Operator's conscience is least bothered when he is fleecing private investors.

The Catholic horse-player and the Puritan stock-market manipulator theoretically view each other with an abhorrence born of differing basic premises. Each in the other's eyes is a crook—the horse-player a hopeless wastrel, the market manipulator a dangerous bloodsucker.

The philosophical clash between these two classic religious points of view might yet have a quickening effect on the American religious consciousness. But thus far, or at least until recently, its stimulus has been blunted by American Catholicism's peculiar evolution. American Catholicism has tended to concentrate on the practical issues of getting churches and schools into physical commission, and creating its own pressure groups, which often use their power in retaliation for the slings, arrows and snubs of yesteryear. (This process has been observed at work more recently in American Jewish circles.) Differences in the national ethical approach have not interested most American Catholics. The general feeling of Irish Catholics, who still constitute the major force in American Catholicism, has been to confirm a form of Puritanism, rather than to oppose it. So the influence of Catholicism has been diluted. Only in some areas, like aspects of the Negro segregation problem, has Catholicism tranfused the vigor of its moral resources into the national blood stream. In a negative sense, it has at least helped by its presence to cast ridicule on the type of Protestant clergyman who equates innocent gambling or drinking with some form of Satanism. But all too often the nobility of Catholic thought, evident in other areas of the world's surface, has been concealed behind the threatening boycott letters of local pastors to the theater featuring Brigitte Bardot, or pulpit denunciations of the lack of support for the new parochial school.

There is no reason why religion must be officially installed at the core of a national society in order to keep the society morally healthy. Separation of Church and State is a workable and sound principle for a democracy. There will always be some with us who find their own kind of evil abroad if a public-school teacher admits that God exists, but they are not numerous. By and large the Church-State separation principle has kept the

United States from the inconveniences of clerical parties and anticlericals. Religion has thrived under it.

Yet a tendency remains strong among Americans—deriving from their religious past—to try to legislate morality on everybody—and the morality, at that, of only a certain group of people. Tradition dating from the impossibly strict moral code of three centuries ago bids the spiritual descendants of Calvin's saints to clothe their public acts and utterances in the garments of righteousness, while privately or not so privately each saint is pondering the old mercantile question: "What's in it for me?"

An abiding example of this moral-legal unrealism is modern prohibition legislation. Decades after the repeal of the Volstead Act, hundreds of American towns and counties, and even some states, try to perpetuate it in one form or another. The public reasons given are always on the surface practical as well as moral ones. What happens in fact is far from the expressed plans of the prohibition sponsors; and most of them know it.

Take the familiar case of the absolute ban on liquor sales in so many college towns. The city fathers decide to remove temptation altogether—not content with setting limits to the amount a student may drink and the hours at which he may drink it. The result is seldom to deprive students of alcoholic nourishment. On the contrary, the local ban merely ensures that the students drive long distances to the next county to get their liquor, causing no end of grief to the local highway patrol and themselves on the way back. Really unsavory roadhouses and state- or county-line spas develop as social centers, far beyond the reach of either college or local authorities. The city fathers sleep in the knowledge that whatever ill befalls the college youth, they won't have to observe it at first hand.

The convolutions of partial or local prohibition are particularly well known in the western and southern United States. The bottle clubs, the wine-only social centers, the restricted sales, the blue-law hours, etc., are surpassed in their intricacy and foolishness only by the legislation of Sweden and Australia.* They have become part of American folklore and are undeniably relished for the ingenuity lavished in circumventing them. Few college students in Alabama, for example, have failed to participate in the sport of loading a car with liquor across the state line, sending decoys back ahead of them to confuse the troopers and bringing the balm back to the fraternity house in a blaze of esteem.

A prominent matron in Oklahoma City, until recently the great Mecca of the American dries, told me: "I know they go out to get liquor from bootleggers," she said. "Everybody in town does it—and people say it would be a lot healthier if we let them buy it here in town, but we like it this way. Look at the streets at night—you don't see anybody out drinking or carousing. We want to keep them that way." This was uttered in a town where the first thing a visitor used to hear was a barrage of offers to sell him some bootleg merchandise.

Prohibition reigned in Oklahoma from 1908 to 1959, and successfully resisted the assaults of civic reformers, people who wanted a legal drink of liquor and legislators who wanted to give the state a profitable source of tax revenue in legal liquor sales. It was maintained by an odd group of allies. Out in front were the obvious dries—some Protestant church groups and a powerful local chapter of the Women's Christian Temperance Union. Mrs. Elizabeth House, Oklahoma's W.C.T.U. president, explained it: "We are our brother's keeper, and we are failing our duty if we let him destroy himself by providing him with liquor." The state's bootleggers, most of them highly respected citizens, lined up solidly with the W.C.T.U. against repeal. A

---

* Few Americans, however, could quarrel with the Draconian laws about drunken driving in Norway, where a man found driving with only one aquavit under his belt courts immediate loss of his license and a jail sentence.

really big-time bootlegger could earn as much as $50,000 a year at his craft. Law enforcement was sporadic, eliminating major risks in the multi-million-dollar bootlegging industry.

Bringing up the rear was a large group of Oklahoma citizens who had no trouble getting a drink at the state's 200-odd bottle clubs, unless they preferred regular deliveries (Sundays, holidays and Election Day included) by their local bootlegger. Prices were low, even when the bootlegger's commission was figured in, since there was no liquor tax to be paid. Will Rogers used to say, "The people of Oklahoma will vote dry as long as they can stagger to the polls to do it."

The well-organized hypocrisy was finally ended in 1959 by a young and vigorous governor, J. Howard Edmundson, through the simple expedient of enforcing the law to the teeth. Bootleggers were arrested, stocks impounded, private clubs closed down, and road-blocks set up at the state borders. Tulsa newspapers were forced to announce that the year's annual press-club party, renowned for its liquid liberality, would serve nothing but 3.2 per cent beer.

The governor's efficiency was rewarded. As soon as the voters found they could no longer stagger to the polls, they voted out prohibition, in favor of a system of well-supervised liquor stores. The state's revenues soared accordingly. And no crime wave appeared as a result.

If the long series of American prohibition laws tells its own story about national hypocrisy, it cannot hold a candle to a far more notorious chapter: the black market of World War II. It is easy to understand why the black market days have been allowed to fall into a quick obscurity. For they marked one of the most wholesale abandonments of public morality in American history. Yet the modern Operator learned much of his craft in this period. And the black market excesses, along

with the grotesqueries of prohibition, have a signal importance
to the theme of this book. The black marketeer and the blue-
law prohibitionist are the classic illustrations of the principle
that makes the present-day Operator so dangerous: *selective*
obedience to the law.

Rationing of essential commodities began on February 11,
1942, at the darkest moment of the war, when the Office of
Price Administration was established. The job of the OPA,
which became one of the most controversial sets of initials in
Washington history, was to work out and enforce a system of
rationing and rent control and, in addition, a system of ceiling
prices. There was constant questioning of the OPA's effectiveness—by 1945 the howls of indignation and protest had stabil-
ized at a roaring whine. But there can be no doubt that a system
of controls was necessary. World War II was the first, and,
one presumes, the last great struggle where the issue was
decided by the relative power of factory assembly lines.

During the period of controls and rationing, the country
was amply informed about the critical nature of World War II.
Compliance with the OPA directives was rightly seen as a
matter of patriotism, if not self-preservation. Repeated polls
and samplings of public opinion supported the fact that wartime rationing and controls were approved by the majority of
the American public. At least that is what the public said.

Now for the actual record. From the beginning of controls
to their end on May 31, 1947, the OPA had to issue 259,966
formal sanctions against business violators. There were 13,999
federal criminal prosecutions for OPA violations and 5,127
local prosecutions. These formal sanctions represented only part
of the story. Marshall Clinard recorded in his book, *The Black
Market*: "Between 1943 and 1945, for example, volunteer citizen price panels held 623,503 conferences with retail violators.
These conferences were the outgrowths of 1,375,380 reported

violations. . . . There were tens of thousands of actions under local anti-black-market ordinances in the five states [!] and seventy-five municipalities which had them. In New York City alone there were 18,875 prosecutions of retailers and 4,000 wholesale prosecutions in 1944. . . . *Approximately one in every 15 of the three million business concerns in the country were punished by some serious sanction.*" (Italics added.)

Clinard went on to cite the FBI estimate of a total of 900,000 OPA violations of all types brought before various government agencies for the year 1944 alone. This was roughly the same number as the total of "ordinary crimes" recorded by police statistics in the same year. Since the OPA investigative staff was never large, many firms escaped with no investigation into their activities. "If our comparison is restricted to large concerns," Clinard wrote, "namely manufacturing and wholesale, approximately 70 per cent of those concerns, or two out of three concerns, investigated during 1944 were found to be in violation."

The operators involved were in the great majority ordinary, "respectable" citizens. Few had a sense of guilt or wrongdoing about their violations. They shared the feeling that "it's all right, if you can get away with it."

Take the Navy training center which was set up during the war at Norman, Okla. The influx of officers and enlisted personnel resulted in the inevitable harried wartime search for housing. The prewar population of Norman, a quiet university town, was 11,429. In a town of this population the OPA found fully 1,500 violations of rent-control laws. The gougers, who followed the nationwide practice of making prospective tenants buy useless furniture, etc., before they were rented an apartment, included all the respectable elements of the community—college professors, doctors, lawyers. In a time of national emergency, like other Americans from Maine to California, they were all ready for a little effortless thievery.

No amount of mitigating circumstance can obscure the black fact that a good part of the country went crooked during this period. It went crooked not impelled by dire want, as in European countries where the theft of a loaf of bread might mean the difference between living and starving. All through the war Americans enjoyed what would pass among other peoples as a sufficiency of material things. There was nothing resembling the rigid rationing of essentials like bread, eggs and clothing, as practiced in the United Kingdom and elsewhere. To all this many black-market operators replied, "I don't believe in government regulations," and many business associations, e.g., the National Association of Manufacturers, lobbied in favor of the abolition of the OPA.

From the mass crime of the black market a dirty thread runs straight into the excesses of the Genial Society today. Most of these violations, as we have seen, are still judged leniently. But they are nonetheless acts of a criminal nature, whether viewed from the standpoint of sheer lawbreaking or of a morally sinful bearing of false witness. The selective obedience to the law which they symptomize has its roots in the American past and in the national view of ethics and morality, of which it is a dangerous perversion. It has become so widespread now in testimony to the strains of mechanized living on our democratic governing and social processes. It is, in any case, a dangerous storm warning for our democracy.

Older powers than ours have been fatally undermined when the gap grew too great between the citizen's private sense of wrong and the public morality to which he and his fellows were pledged; when the righteous word, instead of accompanying the right deed, began to replace it. Republics, we can only repeat, do and must live by virtue. If this republic continues to live by shirking, pleasure-seeking or outright fraud, we must be prepared one day to pick up a fearful check for it—without any expense account left to put it on.

INDEX

279